THE ROCK THAT IS HIGHER

MADELEINE L'ENGLE

Story as Truth

THE ROCK THAT IS HIGHER

Harold Shaw Publishers
Wheaton, Illinois

The Wheaton Literary Series

Unless otherwise noted, Scripture quotations are from the *Holy Bible, New International Version.* Copyright © 1973, 1978, 1984 International Bible Society. Used by permission of Zondervan Publishing House. All rights reserved.

ISBN 0-87788-726-8

Cover photo © 1993 by Ron Thomas, FPG International Corp.
Photo of Madeleine L'Engle © 1993 by Maria Rooney

Library of Congress Cataloging-in-Publication Data

L'Engle, Madeleine.
   The rock that is higher / Madeleine L'Engle.
     p. cm.
   ISBN 0-87788-726-8
    1. Storytelling—Religious aspects—Christianity.
  2. L'Engle, Madeleine. I. Title.
   BT83.78.L46   92-24204
   242-dc20   CIP

---

99 98 97 96 95 94 93

10 9 8 7 6 5 4 3 2

To Frances and David Somerville

From the ends of the earth I call to you,
I call as my heart grows faint;
O set me upon the rock that is higher than I.
Psalm 61:2, *Coverdale*

CONTENTS

Story as Homecoming

1

ON THE 28TH OF JULY, 1991, I was being driven from San Diego to Escondido, California, to a lecture job to which I was looking forward. It was a bright, sunny Sunday afternoon, and Sally, my driver, had just pointed out the sign to Escondido, when there was a sudden crash, a spider-webbing of the windshield, a crumpling of the engine, a tearing of pain across my body.

A truck had run through a red light and broadsided us.

Sally moaned, "Oh, Madeleine, Madeleine."

"Sally—" I breathed. I knew I had been badly hurt. I said, not out loud, *Lord, is this it? Is this the end of my story, God?*

The ancient words of the Jesus Prayer, *Lord Jesus Christ have mercy on me,* surfaced in my mind. They have been with me for many years, like a deep, inner fountain.

When I wake up in the night they are there—those strong, affirming words. They were with me as I sat in the crumpled car.

"Are you all right?" I asked Sally.

"I think so. My ribs hurt. I did have a green light, didn't I?"

She did.

A man thrust his hand and a piece of paper through the window into the car. "Here's my name and phone number. I'm your witness," he said. Another man took pictures. Someone called the police and the ambulance. Help came quickly. We did not see the truck driver who hit us.

We answered a few questions. Both of us were completely conscious. Sally was put in the ambulance on the gurney, as it seemed to the paramedics that she was the more severely injured of the two of us. I was put on a board and slid in beside her, and the ambulance took off. After a few moments I heard a little voice ask, "I suppose there's nobody to hold my hand?" And almost immediately someone took our hands and put them together, and I held Sally's hand firmly until we were taken into the hospital. What loving sensitivity on the part of an unknown paramedic!

The University of California San Diego Hospital is an enormous teaching hospital with a fine trauma center. After a doctor examined me and asked a few questions, he said, "I think you're all right. I think we'll be able to let you—" and then he stopped. "Your upper lip is wet with sweat."

I said, "I feel very strange."

The next thing I knew I was being rolled along the hospital corridors with an oxygen mask over my face. I wasn't all right at all.

But the Jesus Prayer stayed with me. I was still completely conscious, and able to answer questions and to tell the doctors that I'm allergic to iodine—important, as they were going to do a CAT scan and needed to use an alternate dye. The doctors treated me as though I was an intelligent human being, capable of answering their questions, capable of asking questions. They told me, after the CAT scan, that all my vital organs had been lacerated and were bleeding—the spleen, kidneys, liver, pancreas, intestines. They would probably have to remove the spleen. They might have to remove one kidney.

It's an odd and unexpected way to die, I thought, *but I am seventy-two years old and I've had a wonderful life.*

My clothes were cut off me, and a hospital gown was slid on. A gastric tube was put down my nose. I was told what some of the surgical procedures would be. "We're going to remove your spleen."

"When?"

"Now."

I was wheeled to the operating room. I asked a question about what kind of anesthesia was being used. I was answered, and then told to breathe deeply. I knew that once I went under the anesthetic I might not come out of it, not in this life. I was not afraid. The Jesus Prayer was still with me, a strong rope to which I held like a sailor fallen from a ship. If God was ready for the curtain to come down on this final act of my life's drama, I was as ready as I was ever going to be.

I am grateful for that feeling of readiness, for the lack of fear, for the assurance that whatever happened all would be well.

♦ ♦ ♦

I woke up from the anesthesia. God still had work for me to do.

♦ ♦ ♦

So was this experience all faith in Jesus and assurance of God's love for me?

No.

The next two weeks were as dark as any I have known.

My body had taken a terrible battering. The truck had hit the driver's side of the car, and Sally had two broken ribs—miserable, but not life threatening. Why and how I sustained the injuries that nearly killed me we don't know because it all happened so quickly that we aren't sure what happened—except that the truck driver ran a red light and hit us.

I lay in the Intensive Care Unit wrapped in pain and thought, *Lord, if I'm going to die, that's all right. But please let me die. If I'm going to live, help me.*

Deborah, who was to have been my boss for the week of lectures I was missing, came to see me in I.C.U. and reported later that I was so plugged into all kinds of tubes that I was barely visible. I said to her, "I've been lying here asking what the meaning of all this can be."

Deborah said, "When you're well enough to leave the hospital, of course you'll come to me." And with that great kindness she left me.

I had one other visitor in I.C.U., a clergyman who was a friend of a friend of mine in New York. He came in, big and rather loud, wearing a clerical collar. He beamed at me and said, "Now, if there's anything I can do for you, anything at all, just call me." And left. No prayer. No assurance that he was with me, or that God was with me. "Just call me." How on earth was I going to be able to call anybody?

I was far from home, far from friends. At that point I was so ill that all I could do when I was awake was to keep on breathing. And breathing hurt badly, because my sternum had been bashed and bruised. Later the doctors said that my ribs had also taken a beating, and some were probably broken. Both legs were black and blue. Because of the internal bleeding my entire left side was black with bruises.

My only prayer was the Jesus Prayer and that was there for me because it has been part of my inner rhythm for many years, the prayer that fulfills Paul's exhortation to pray constantly, at all times and in all places.

Time, instead of racing at its usual incomprehensible pace, crawled interminably slowly. There were no windows in I.C.U., so I had no way of knowing whether it was day or night. There was a large clock on the wall, but when the hands pointed to ten o'clock I had no idea whether it was ten at night or ten in the morning.

I was moved from I.C.U. to Intermediate Care, and eventually to a four-bed room where two television sets were blasting. There was no way for me to control volume or program. Visitors for the other patients came in and out. There was a phone by my bed and when it rang I answered it, and it was Deborah.

"Aren't you glad to be out of I.C.U.?"

"No," I replied. "It was much quieter there."

"Where are you?"

I told her, and she said, "I'll do something about that."

Deborah had been on the board of this hospital. Within an hour I was moved to a private room. It wasn't much quieter than the four-bed room because they were rebuilding the hospital to make it earthquake proof, and outside my windows was scaffolding on which workmen were walking back and forth with hammers, wrenches, blow torches, and loud voices. But I did not have to watch other people's television shows.

Once I was in the private room I learned that a network of prayers had been set up as soon as people learned of the accident. My telephone had to be unplugged because it was not where I could reach it without great effort, and I was too exhausted and in too much pain to talk. One temporary effect of the accident was that my voice was a froglike croak, not good for telephone conversations. But flowers and get-well cards poured in to tell me that people cared, and that if I could not use the phone, they could. One friend wrote, "We're supporting AT&T, but we're really getting to know each other. And we're all praying." So I knew that although I was still too ill to pray for myself, I was being prayed for, upheld in a wonderful web of prayer from all over the country.

Time was a slow blur of pain. My son and daughter-in-law flew from Connecticut to San Diego to talk to the doctors and see what was going on. My elder daughter was somewhere in France with her husband, celebrating their twenty-fifth wedding anniversary; there was no way to reach them. My younger daughter and her husband were in Connecticut with their two little boys.

When my son walked into my room, I said, "Oh, Bion, the last time I was this glad to see you was the night you were born." My daughter-in-law, Laurie, is a physician. She and Bion were able to talk with the doctors and satisfy themselves that everything was being done for me that needed to be done, and that Deborah's offer of taking me in when I was well enough to leave the hospital was a firm and good one. But delighted as I was to see these two wonderful young people, I was still too injured to enjoy visiting, and sent them off in their brief time in California to see something of San Diego. And of course they could not stay, but had to get back to Connecticut.

So I was alone again, and as I gained a little strength I felt a terrible sense of isolation. The trauma my body had suffered wakened all my primordial fears, fear of isolation, fear of being enclosed, fear of dark. I knew that these fears were a result of the accident and that ultimately they would leave, but there was no denying the fact that they were very much with me. One of the nurses suggested that I draw the curtains across the windows to shut out the scaffolding and the workmen. But to do that would have made my small room feel like a tomb. I didn't care about the workmen; I didn't want to be shut in. At night I wanted the door to my room open, not only to keep from feeling enclosed, but for the light.

Because I was no longer in critical condition I saw very little of the overworked nurses; hospitals at this late end of the century are woefully understaffed. I felt lonely, isolated, in pain. Not back into life, yet not out of it. Still too wounded to pray for myself, I was aware enough to be grateful for the prayers that supported me, for the flowers that made my sterile room a bower. I had my small travel radio-alarm clock with me, and San Diego has a good classical music station, so I could listen to music, though I was careful not to keep the radio on constantly and run down the batteries; listening time was precious.

After a few more days I remembered the red box in the closet in my room that had in it nearly six hundred manuscript pages of the new novel on which I had been working for over two years. The draft I had with me was the seventh. *Certain Women* was ready to go to the publishers. I had lived with this story and with the story of King David of Jerusalem for all this time. King David, I knew, had been through periods of isolation far more terrible than mine. During wakeful periods in the night I would think that in the morning I might be strong enough to ask for my manuscript, but I was not. It seemed, in fact, that I did my best thinking about it during the long nights. I was now off morphine, so my mind was clear. It, like the rest of my body, suffered from the trauma of the accident, but it was still capable of thinking of my novel and its characters. As so often happens with my stories, the book changed radically as I worked on it. The truth of a story is what the novelist strives for, and quite often the writer is taken down strange and unexpected paths on this search.

I had started out to write a novel about King David's eight wives, and I realized fairly quickly that I could not put myself completely into the bodies and minds of women who lived approximately three thousand years ago in a culture completely different from ours. I needed a twentieth-century point of view. What happened was that my twentieth-century cast took over, and the story of King David and his wives became a play that Nik Green, one of the twentieth-century characters, was writing. It didn't mean that I had to live any less with King David and his wives—and his friends and enemies and his battles and his joy in the Lord—but that this story and its marvelous truth was being approached from a different perspective. King David brought his people from the bronze age into the iron age; what age are we living in?

The electronic age? It's different. We think differently. We certainly live differently.

Much of the research that went into the writing of the first draft ultimately was put into the enormous pile of discarded manuscript pages on which I write telephone messages for my college-going granddaughters. But I wouldn't have missed what I learned from it. I read 1 and 2 Samuel and the beginning of 1 Kings over and over, coming to the end of David's story, and starting again at the beginning. But where is the beginning? It starts long before David's entry into the tale, perhaps not as far back as the birth of Samuel, but certainly as far back as Samuel's anointing of Saul as the first king of the Jews.

Now the problem was that the Jews had never before had a king. They had the Lord, and they had the prophets and patriarchs. They did not need a king. The Lord did not want them to have a king. When the elders of Israel came to Samuel and said, *Now appoint a king to lead us, such as all the other nations have,* the Lord told Samuel, *they have rejected me as their king. As they have done from the day I brought them up out of Egypt until this day, forsaking me and serving other gods.* The Lord was not pleased at the people's clamoring for a king, and el warned them, through Samuel, what would happen when they got this human king, of their own making. This king would take their sons to be soldiers and their daughters to be cooks. The king and his men would take the fields and the vineyards, and everybody would cry out because of the king they had chosen,

and the Lord will not answer you in that day. But the people refused to listen to Samuel. "No!" they said. "We want a king over us. Then we will be like all the other nations, with a king to lead us and to go out before us and fight our battles."

And the Lord said to Samuel, *"Listen to them and give them a king."*

The story of the people of God wanting a human king is told in the seventeenth chapter of Deuteronomy, in verse fourteen through the end of the chapter:

When you enter the land the LORD your God is giving you and have taken possession of it and settled in it, and you say, "Let us set a king over us like all the nations around us," be sure to appoint over you the king the LORD your God chooses. He must be from among your own brothers. Do not place a foreigner over you, one who is not a brother Israelite. The king, moreover, must not acquire great numbers of horses for himself. . . . He must not take many wives, or his heart will be led astray. He must not accumulate large amounts of silver and gold. When he takes the throne of his kingdom, he is to write for himself on a scroll a copy of this law, taken from that of the priests, who are Levites. It is to be with him, and he is to read it all the days of his life so that he may learn to revere the LORD his God and follow carefully all the words of this law and these decrees. . . .

What? What? Saul did not have multiple wives, but David and Solomon certainly did. And Solomon is known for his silver and gold. And if Saul, David, or Solomon wrote out a copy of the law and read it daily, we are not told about it.

Why did they need a king when they had the Lord? They were God's chosen. The Lord was with them wherever they went. El had traveled with them in a cloud during the day and with fire by night. El spoke directly with Moses on Mount Sinai and gave them the commandments by which they were to live. They had a heavenly king; they did not need an earthly one.

But they wanted a king. They did not learn.

Have we learned?

◆ ◆ ◆

When the people wanted a king like other peoples, when they turned away from God, they were also turning from home, their real home, the kingdom of God. David himself had a vision of this kingdom, but he also suffered many times of painful homesickness, homesickness for the quiet hills where he tended his sheep, homesickness when his son Absalom turned against him, homesickness for his holy city of Jerusalem, homesickness for the Lord who had, through Samuel, anointed him king after Saul.

In my hospital bed I was homesick. Here it was August, but I found myself thinking of Holy Week. Lonely week. The most painful part of the story. Jesus, at the end of his earthly mission, facing failure, abandonment, death.

What kept him going? What keeps us going when we're in the middle of the worst of it? The knowledge that we are loved by our Creator. Everybody else left Jesus. The disciples, those he had counted on to be with him to the end, all left him in the Garden. No one understood who he was, what he was about, what he had come for. How many times in our lives have we faced that utter and absolute abandonment? He knew that his mission had been high, and it was in ruins about his feet.

He stood in front of Pontius Pilate and he held to his mission and his position because of love, God's love, which did not fail, not even when he questioned it on the cross.

What has happened during the centuries to that God of sustaining, enduring, total love? How can we survive without it?

I cannot. I know I live and die by the assurance that *God so loved the world that he gave his one and only Son,* and in that Word's hour of need what pain must God have felt! Jesus was able to endure the agony of Holy Week and of the Cross only because he was never separate from the Source, and never doubted that he was loved or, at least, only for a fragment of a minute.

"My God, my God, why have you forsaken me?" For our sakes Jesus went through all the suffering we may ever have to endure, and because he cried out those words we may cry them out, too. The night I knew my husband was dying I turned, as usual at bedtime, to Evening Prayer. It was the fourth of the month, and the first psalm for the evening of the fourth day is Psalm 22, and I read, *"My God, my God, why have you forsaken me?"*

Don't confuse me by saying that Jesus was merely quoting David in the Psalms. Allow me to know that Jesus was willing to go through the same kind of anguish that sooner or later comes to us all.

This is the story that gives meaning to my life, that gave meaning to those draggingly difficult days in the hospital, and if it isn't story it doesn't work. The life-giving, life-saving story is true story that transcends facts.

There's been considerable interest lately in checking the Gospels and trying to decide what Jesus really said, what he might have said, what he surely didn't say, and too often the result of such academic research is not illumination, but loss of story. For such academics, miracles have to go. The Resurrection has to go. The story gets edited until there's no life left in it and there's nothing worth believing in.

I read a refutation of this in a magazine that went to the opposite extreme and insisted that every word in the New Testament came out of Jesus's mouth in exactly those words (in English), which were written down after many years of oral repetition. So we're still stuck with a literal interpretation of facts, going from one extreme to the other.

In the hospital in San Diego I didn't get much comfort from facts. First of all, it's easy to believe in facts. We certainly don't need faith, not for facts. Faith is for the part of the story that superficially isn't believable. Virgin births? Miracles? Resurrections? Unrealistic. Childish.

Or is it maybe not so much childish as child-hearted? Children are better believers than grown-ups, and better theologians than many academicians. One child whose sister told her that there is no Santa Claus answered calmly, "That's your problem."

In a world where we're brainwashed by the media into thinking that life should be easy and painless and reasonable, it is not easy or painless or reasonable to be a Christian—that is, to be one who actually dares to believe that the power that created all the galaxies, all the stars in their courses, limited that power to the powerlessness of an ordinary human baby. That's not reasonable.

It is equally unreasonable to believe that this ordinary baby grew into a man who was totally human and simultaneously totally divine. Who was, as the Athanasian Creed affirms, totally incomprehensible.

But who wants a comprehensible God in the aftermath of an incomprehensible accident?

I remembered a conference during which a man announced, "I am a devout literalist. If I cannot believe that the stories in Scripture are literally and factually true, then I have to accept that there can be more than one interpretation of a story."

"Yes," I said. "That's right."

"Then how can I know which is the right one?"

Aye, there's the rub. We can't. But one thing I'm learning is that I do not always have to be right. Or maybe we can look at two different interpretations of a story and understand that they are *both* right. If I have to take every story in the Bible as literal, and capable of only one interpretation, I will lose the story.

What a story it is! It begins with conception, with Creation, and moves on through life and death to Resurrection, and most of it is impossible in ordinary terms of provable fact. If I have to keep in the Bible only what can be proved, I'll be left with a book of very few pages.

As July turned into August, and the August days drooped slowly by, I was grateful in the hospital for the prayer of Jesus that stayed with me, a continuing, strengthening rhythm that was as strong as my heartbeat. I was grateful that Jesus left all the good sheep and went out into the storm after the lost and strayed one. I was even grateful that he paid the workers in the vineyard the same amount of money, no matter how long they had or hadn't worked. I was grateful for his promises to us that were either true or insane. I looked at the bruised and battered matter of my body and I was grateful that I believe that *matter matters*, matters to me, matters to the God who made it, and who took it on when all Love came to us as Jesus of Nazareth. I was grateful that my faith is more a matter of joy than of security. I was grateful that I still have a lot of questions that I do not expect to have answered, at least not by facts.

There's nothing anyone can tell me about death that's in the realm of laboratory proof or literalism. To think about death is an act of faith, a courage that the unknown is not empty, a belief that God is love, and Love does not create and then abandon or annihilate. I can't prove it. Sometimes I don't even believe it. And then hope, the deep, innate faith, surfaces.

I had been gone from home since the fifteenth of June. Those last two weeks of June were spent teaching a writers' workshop at Mundelein College in Chicago, where I am very much at home. The first two weeks of July were at the C.S. Lewis Summer Institute in Oxford, at Keble College. Then I met my eldest daughter and her husband in London for four nights of theatre and enjoying friends, after which we had six marvelously stress-free days on a barge in Burgundy. Our one great excitement was going up in a hot air balloon at eight-thirty in the evening, floating through sunset and moonrise over fields of golden sunflowers.

After the barge we had two nights together in Paris, and then Josephine and Alan took off to continue celebrating their twenty-fifth wedding anniversary, and I flew to San Diego. I had been away from home, I felt, too long, and I had a vague sense of foreboding, a wondering if I would ever be home again.

We are all strangers in a strange land, longing for home, but not quite knowing what or where home is. We glimpse it sometimes in our dreams, or as we turn a corner, and suddenly there is a strange, sweet familiarity that vanishes almost as soon as it comes.

In literature the longing for home is found in the many stories of paradise, of the forgotten place where we once belonged. In the Judeo-Christian tradition we have the story of the Garden, the beautiful place of love and spontaneity where we were in touch with our Source. But there are stories of an almost-forgotten beautiful place in the myths of all cultures—and of course I am using *myth* in its ancient meaning—that which was true, that which is true, that which will be true, that strange truth which is as elusive as home.

We know in our hearts that the Garden was there, the place of beauty and home where we were all what human beings are truly meant to be. And somehow we blew it. We messed it up. We lost it. And we have been homesick ever since.

It happens over and over again, the move from the beloved home place. It must have been hard on Sarah, when God told her and Abraham to leave home. On Jacob, fleeing, after he had cheated his father and his brother. On Rachel, after Jacob had incurred her father's wrath. On Joseph, ruthlessly sold into Egypt. On Moses, leaving the land of Goshen which was no longer home because the Jews had been made into slaves. On David, fleeing his holy city of Jerusalem because his son was fighting him for the throne. On Mary and Joseph and the baby escaping to Egypt. Leaving home—it is a theme all through Scripture.

When my mother was growing up in the south it was the norm for people to be born into one village or town, grow up there, marry there, have children, grand-children, and ultimately die there—sometimes all in the same house. That is no longer the case. We are scattered, almost as radically as the Jews were under the Babylo-nians. Is it that different when an enormous con-glomerate sends its employees all over the country, from one city to another, as the work demands?

C.S. Lewis points out that our roots are really else-where. True. But we do not get to that elsewhere except through our journey in this life on this planet. While we are here we must put down roots so that we will not be uprooted by a passing storm. The roots may reach down through earthly life to "elsewhere," but they have to go through the earth and our life on earth before getting to "elsewhere." What else does the Incarnation affirm? Jesus came not to deny life, but to offer life, and life more abundant. We are not to retreat from life, pinning our hopes on "elsewhere," but to know that we will come to that final destination best by living fully here and now, be it through joy, or pain, or a mix of both.

In my book *Meet the Austins*, the family—which is very close to my own family—has been away, and they are coming home. Vicky Austin says,

> We sang and sang on the way home, and suddenly we were in Clovenford. There was the road up the hill to the hospital, and there was the street that led to Daddy's office. We passed the school and the church and the store, and then we were driving up our road, and we saw our house, our own beautiful rambly white house, and Daddy was pulling up to the garage, and we were home.

Home!

Our tongues and our muscles were suddenly freed and we piled out of the car and in through the garage and into the house, into the kitchen.

It was home and I remembered it with every bit of me, and yet in a funny way it was completely different. I can't quite explain. Sizes weren't the same. When I first looked at things they seemed smaller, and yet when I came back to them and looked at them again they seemed the same size they ought to be, and it would be as though we'd never been away at all. . . .

And then we were dashing all over the house to our special places. . . . We ran all the way around the house, looking at it from all four points of the compass, and then back into the house again, and Mother had a record on the phonograph, and the phone kept ringing, all the kids to ask us about our vacation, and the office phone, because Daddy's patients knew he was home again.

Mother called us to help, and she was getting dinner and we realized that it was dinner time and we were all starved, so we set the table and I mashed the potatoes and Suzy cut up the tomatoes for salad and Rob went around the table giving everybody three napkins. Then we were all around the table holding hands to say grace, and we said the kind of grace we always do on special occasions, each of us in turn saying our own, and when it came to Rob he said, "Thank you God that we are home, and thank you for my good dinner, for the meat and mashed potatoes and gravy and 'sparagus, oh, no, God, I forgot I don't like 'sparagus, and thank you for the milk and rolls and butter. Amen."

I don't think any writer could make up that particular grace, and indeed it is a homecoming grace said by my son when he was seven.

Home. And Vicky was right. Things look smaller. They aren't quite the same. And then we readjust to them as they are. Why do things look smaller? What does our memory of home do to us?

There is a theory that angelic events in the heavens are re-enacted in a smaller way on earth. Angels, of course, are larger than we are, and the biblical angels are not pretty little females with feathered wings. Angels are always home. They have never left—except for the fallen angels, of course, and their homesickness must be devastating.

In the beginning of the Book of Job, the sons of God are gathered, and Satan is one of them, and God asks him what he is doing, and Satan replies, *"Oh, walking to and fro on the earth seeing what I can do"* (1:7, adapted). Satan has left heaven, has fought with the archangel Michael, has fallen, plummeting, to the earth (Jesus says, in the tenth chapter of Luke, *"I saw Satan fall like lightning from heaven."* What does that do to ordinary chronological time?) and yet when the sons of God are gathered together, Satan is still one of them. And that must make his homesickness even more terrible.

Despite our clumsy efforts at inclusive language, Scripture was written in a masculine world, which is a sign of things skewed and out of order. Where were the *daughters* of God? But we can't rewrite Scripture, though there have been some forlorn attempts to do so. The God of Scripture is seen through male eyes (Jacob, Moses, David), so what we are given is only a partial vision of God.

Jesus gave us the full vision. In his lifetime he astoundingly reconciled male and female, harmonizing all aspects of the human being. This terrified the religious leaders of his day, and still seems to terrify many people. Will we be ready for home before we human beings, male and female, know each other as our Creator intended when, in verse 24ff. of the first chapter of Genesis,

> God said, "Let the land produce living creatures according to their kinds: livestock, creatures that move along the ground, and wild animals, each according to its kind." . . .
> So God created man in his own image, in the image of God he created him; male and female he created them.

Male and female, made to love each other. That's the first story of the creation of us human beings, male and female created simultaneously to be the image of God. Eve coming from Adam's rib is a completely different story and perhaps more pleasing to male vanity and the desire to dominate. I prefer the first version.

My bishop told me that when the wise men gave their gifts to the Christ child, they were giving him their magic; they were magi; magicians; alchemists; and they gave up their power to the one they recognized as Lord. At the same time that I heard this, I was reading a novel in which alchemy played an important part, and which postulated that for the true alchemist what was far more important than turning base metal into gold was reconciling male and female, what was called "the chymical wedding."

So that, too, was part of the gift of the magi, and Jesus accepted it and, in turn, gave it to us. His treatment of women was extraordinary for his day, when women were defined entirely by the male. If two people were caught in adultery, it was the woman who was punished by being stoned to death. It takes two to commit adultery, but the man was not considered the wrongdoer. Women had no rights; their husbands could—until Jesus changed it—write them a letter and divorce them and keep all their property. Jesus broke all the patriarchal rules of his society. Not only that, his close friends were women, Mary of Magdala and Mary of Bethany. Martha of Bethany, like the woman at the well, like Peter, also recognized Jesus as the Promised One. As we view Mary and Martha in Scripture we might have expected it to be Mary who recognized the Messiah, but it was Martha (see John 11).

The world of Jesus' time, as the world now, could not believe in the reconciliation of male and female, and we still are struggling to learn the lessons Jesus taught, recognizing the male and female in each of us, and in all the people we meet. Marriage should be, and seldom is, an icon of reconciliation. So should friendship. And when we are reconciled we are close to being home. But most of the time we are homesick.

Our homesickness is alleviated only by love, that love that transcends our self-centeredness, our pettiness. And love, of course, is a word that has been dwindled and diminished so that to many people it means nothing more than sex. Sex is, of course, a part of it, but only a part. Another of our confusions about love is that it is a feeling. Sometimes it is. It is very nice when it is a pleasant feeling. But it isn't always pleasant. Love is not so much what you feel as what you do, as I have learned in my own life, and often to my rue. When I am enabled to act with love, God will take care of my feelings.

When we are truly *in love*, not in the sense of romantic, erotic love, but in the sense of God's love for all that the Power of Love created, then our homesickness is alleviated. When we are *in love* we are no longer homesick, for Love is home.

And where is this home that we long for? I lay in my hospital bed and wondered. Surely I was alive because of the skill and immediate care of fine doctors. But ultimately my life was beyond their skill. God calls on us to collaborate with the divine purpose. I believe that the Spirit can guide the doctors' minds and hands. I believe that I was called on to be willing to die, and then, to be willing to live, and that willingness included work, moving my bladder and my bowels on my own once the tubes were out, walking down the corridor, pushing my I.V. stand and, later, pushing a wheelchair to keep my balance. God urges us to collaborate. But we cannot do it ourselves. We need the everlasting love pushing, nudging, if not outright shoving.

So my question was: What, dear Lord, is your purpose for my life? Where, during the rest of my mortal years, is home? Ultimately it is with you, Lord, but meanwhile I believe that I am to make a home in the strange island of Manhattan for my granddaughters, who have been so good for me as they have been in college in New York, teaching me, pushing me, not allowing me to get into any kind of rut. I believe, too, that our home is to be an open one, so that friends who are called to be briefly in the city have a welcoming place to stay.

But where, ultimately, is that home that we long for? It is not the Garden, for we cannot go back to the Garden. When the human beings left the Garden, it was forever.

So where is the home for which we are so homesick? It is something that is still to come; it is that towards which all Creation is groaning in travail. It is the kingdom of God that will be ready when Christ comes again, not only to us on our little planet, but to all of Creation. We are homesick not so much for something that was, and was lost, as for something that will be, and is to be found.

We get foretastes of the kingdom, of the City of God, in myth and dream and fairy tale, and occasionally in our own lives. My granddaughters and I live on the upper west side of New York, one of the most polyglot neighborhoods in that great city. I was born in Manhattan, and it is still home for me, despite all the changes. But it is far from being the City of God. It is sometimes referred to as Sodom and Gomorrah, and perhaps some of it is. There are several million more people living in the same amount of space than there were when I was born. There is drug addiction among young business executives as well as among the poor and destitute. There is prostitution and perversion of all kinds.

But there are also people trying to live quiet, decent lives. I go to church with a lot of them. An island cannot expand outwards, spatially; it can only expand *up*. So my city is crowded, and the split between the very rich and the very poor gets larger every year. It is a dirty city, and this realization hits me anew whenever I am in a European city full of flowers and trees and clean streets. My husband's theory about the filth of Manhattan was that most people who live there have not been born there. It is not home to them, and so they take no pride in it.

As the city gets more crowded, people get more angry; consequently, there is more crime. As the city gets more difficult to live in, people search frantically for some way to ease their pain, with the resulting abuse of alcohol and drugs. My neighborhood is one of the dumping grounds for mentally disturbed people who have been tossed out of the mental institutions. It makes the statistics look good, but most of the people wandering the streets screaming out curses, or singing, or dancing are incapable of caring for themselves. In the past couple of years the number of homeless and panhandlers has increased radically. In this affluent nation, people starve, and sometimes die of cold on the streets of New York. This is not the only city or town with such problems.

Some of the difficulties are desperately real, but there are also scams, and some of them are so odd they almost make me laugh. A friend of mine was approached by a man begging for food. He happened to have a bagel with him, so he gave it to the man, who took it, looked at it, and said, "What! No cream cheese?"

The homeless, the hungry, the lost—the city is full of them. How, with this image for city constantly in front of me can I envision the City of God, that city where no one is hungry, everyone is home, and all our homesickness is over?

I find it difficult, but the City of God has been a metaphor for many centuries.

Perhaps the City of God is not so much a place in space, as a place in the heart.

Sometimes, even in the middle of Manhattan, I get glimpses of this as I walk home with my dog and someone calls out, "That's a beautiful dog!" (He is.) At home, I set the table, and sometimes two tables, for a group of friends of all ages—my friends, my granddaughters' friends, and people of all ages in between. As we hold hands for grace I am grateful for this tiny foretaste of the heavenly banquet.

Last winter my granddaughter Lena decided that on Sunday afternoons we would "do culture." For one of our culture afternoons we went to the Frick Museum, a marvelous small museum in an old mansion on Fifth Avenue, intimate enough so that it can be comfortably seen in a couple of hours. It happened that there was an all Bach concert that afternoon, to be played on period instruments. We were too late to buy tickets, but we were told that we could sit in the garden and listen. While we were waiting in the lovely, glass-covered room full of green plants and the smell of growing things, Lena pulled out of her capacious handbag an old copy of *Idylls of the King* that had been mine as a child, and we took turns reading aloud to each other. When the music started, Lena put the book away, and this college senior leaned her head against my shoulder with the affectionate trust of a small child. And it was indeed a foretaste of heaven.

One of my favorite books is *The Book of Daniel*, and one of my favorite parts of *Daniel* is the story of the three young men in the fiery furnace. The song of the three young men, or the *Benedicite Omnia Opera*, is a great paean of praise of all Creation singing its joy to the Creator and being exactly what it was created to be. When what is, is totally fulfilled, totally itself, then there is joy, no matter what the outer circumstances, and where there is true joy, there is home. (Were Lena and I being fully what we were created to be when we sat together in the museum garden, listening to the great music of Bach?)

The three young men in the fiery furnace, Shadrach, Meshach, and Abednego (or, in Greek, Ananias, Azarias, and Misael) sang for all of Creation.

O all ye works of the Lord, bless ye the Lord, praise him and magnify him forever. O ye angels of the Lord, bless ye the Lord, praise him and magnify him forever. O ye Heavens, O ye waters, O all ye powers of the Lord, O ye Sun and Moon, O ye stars of Heaven, O ye showers and Dew, O ye whales . . . *The Book of Common Prayer, 1928*

And so it goes, all of Creation singing its praise of the Lord from the place of joy, which is home.

And where were the three young men singing this paean of praise? In the fiery furnace, in the heart of the flames. They sang with joy within the fire, for the fire was being fully fire, and they, the three young men, were being fully human; there was no conflict between them.

♦ ♦ ♦

Joy is often at its deepest when it comes in time of trial and pain. At the time of the story of Daniel and the three young men, Nebuchadnezzer had taken Jerusalem; the Jews were once again in captivity; the society surrounding them was as secular as is society today and, as always in such times, the rich were very rich and the poor were very poor; the wicked flourished and the innocent suffered.

It was not an easy world for the young man, Daniel, and his three friends, Shadrach, Meshach, and Abednego.

Nevertheless, they refused to eat meat sacrificed to idols (a practise the Babylonians followed), and they continued to live according to the commandments of their God, who was One, who was All in All.

Because Daniel and his friends lived as God created them to live, because they were at home even in captivity, they became the object of suspicion and the cause of bitter jealousy. Things would have gone far worse for them had not Daniel been able to tell dreams—not just to interpret dreams, like Joseph, but to tell Nebuchadnezzar what his dream had been and then to interpret it. This was a feat that impressed the king, and so he had Daniel and his friends treated kindly.

But then Nebuchadnezzar built a golden image, a man-made god, not an icon created to the glory of the One True God, but an idol to the glory of the king. All the people of Babylon at the sound of the trumpet were to bow down and worship it, but Daniel and the three young men refused to bow down to this idol.

Obviously, someone found great satisfaction in reporting their disobedience to the king, and Nebuchadnezzar was so furious that he ordered Shadrach, Meshach, and Abednego to be thrown into a fiery furnace.

Shadrach, Meshach, and Abednego, their faith in the Maker of the Universe unshaken, stood there in the midst of the flames, and from their lips came the song of praise for all of Creation, fire and ice and beasts and trees and stars and birds and whales and all that is, singing the joy of their being and their praise of the Lord of all. Out of the depths, out of the fire, all being cried joy:

O ye Mountains and Hills, bless ye the Lord, praise him and magnify him forever, O all ye Green Things upon the earth, O ye Wells, O ye Seas and Floods, O ye

Whales, and all that move in the water, O all ye Fowls of the air, O all ye Beasts and Cattle, bless ye the Lord, praise him and magnify him forever. *The Book of Common Prayer, 1928*

King Nebuchadnezzar was astounded, astounded that the young men were alive and singing, and he asked his courtiers,

"Did not we cast three men bound into the midst of the fire?" They answered and said unto the king, "True, O king." He answered and said, "Lo, I see four men loose, walking in the midst of the fire, and they have no hurt; and the form of the fourth is like the Son of God." (King James Version)

And that is the most astounding part of the whole story. Who was the fourth man in the fiery furnace? Christ! God did not take the three young men out of the flames; God was in the fire with them, the fire that is so hot that it scorched and killed the men who lit it.

Christ in the Old Testament? Indeed, yes! Paul talks about the Rock that went before his people on their journey to the Promised Land, and affirms, *"That rock was Christ."* Only one small country and only a few people therein knew Jesus, but Christ always was, is, and will be, and no one, at any time, or in any place, is denied the love of the Word. Christ, if we look, is all through the Old Testament.

And Christ was with me in my sheet of flame in the hospital in San Diego, even when I was too ill to be aware of the loving Presence.

If we cannot sing for ourselves, the song is there for us:

O ye people of God, men and women everywhere, bless ye the Lord, praise him and magnify him forever. O ye priests and servants of the Lord, praise him and magnify him forever. O ye spirits and Souls of the Righteous, O ye who are holy and humble of heart, bless ye the Lord, praise him and magnify him forever. O let us bless the Father and the Son and the Holy Spirit, praise him and magnify him forever. In the firmament of his power glorify the Lord, praise him and magnify him forever. *The Book of Common Prayer, adapted*

It is a marvelous story, and a potent reminder to us of the love of the Creator, a love so great that it is beyond our imagining.

In the beginning was the Word, says John in his Gospel,

and the Word was with God, and the Word was God. . . . Through him all things were made; without him nothing was made that has been made. In him was life, and that life was the light of men. The light shines in the darkness, but the darkness has not understood it.

Wonderful words about the Word! The three young men sang their words about the Word in the fiery furnace, and they were not alone. And they were at home.

How multileveled stories are! With the story of Daniel and three young men we can dig and dig and never come to the bottom.

Nebuchadnezzar was so impressed that he called the three young men forth, and they came out of the fiery furnace. And all were amazed when *they saw that the fire had not harmed their bodies, nor was a hair of their heads singed; their robes were not scorched, and there was no smell of fire on them.*

Daniel, too, was hated for his single-minded love of God and for his obedience to God's laws, and in his turn was cast into a den of lions, but the lions, in their full being, lay down beside Daniel like the animals in Eden when all Creation was still what it was meant to be.

Isaiah foretells the life in the kingdom when he writes, *The wolf will live with the lamb, the leopard will lie down with the goat, the calf and the lion and the yearling together; and a little child will lead them.*

A little child. Jesus said that unless we have the hearts of children we cannot enter the kingdom of heaven. Children love story and understand that story is truth. Tell me a story, I demanded of my mother, and so my children and grandchildren have demanded of me. Tell me a story, and I still love story. When I go to bed at night I want to relax and read—story. It was an added problem for me in the hospital in San Diego that I was not strong enough to hold the physical weight of a book, not even a paperback, for several weeks. Story makes us more human, and until we become fully human we will not be ready for home.

> *"And the cow and the bear shall feed; their young ones shall lie down together: and the lion shall eat straw like the ox. and the suckling child shall play on the hole of the asp, and the weaned child shall put his hand on the cocatrice' den."*

When my mother was a little girl in north Florida, she and her friends used to play amidst the great jungle of trees and Spanish moss and vines, and she and a little group of girl cousins, unbeknownst to their parents, played for weeks with a nest of tarantulas, those terribly poisonous red and furry spiders. Did their innocence save them? The mother spider allowed them to hold and stroke her babies. Of course, when the grownups found out, they were horrified, and the children were forbidden to go near the tarantula nest. But what does this story tell us?

Isaiah continues, *"They shall not hurt nor destroy in all my holy mountain: for the earth shall be full of the knowledge of the Lord, as the waters cover the sea."*

The king did not want to put Daniel into the lions' den, but he had to, or break his word. He said to Daniel, *"May your God, whom you serve continually, rescue you!"* but as we read the story it does not sound as though the king put too much stock in his own words. After Daniel was thrust into the den, and the den was sealed, the king fasted all night and did not sleep. Very early in the morning he went to the lions' den and called to Daniel, *"Daniel, servant of the living God, has your God, whom you serve continually, been able to rescue you from the lions?"*

And Daniel called out and told the king that God had sent an angel to be with him and that the lions had not hurt him.

A den of lions, Daniel, and an angel. "Fear not, Daniel!" the angel must have cried. And the lions lay down beside Daniel and slept quietly all night.

Daniel, fully Daniel; the angel, fully an angel; the lions fully lions; each one wholly what each was meant to be; all of them living together in peace.

What has happened to us? We have not been wholly what we are meant to be for a long time. When I am in the fiery furnace, I burn. My faith is not the pure faith of Daniel, or of Shadrach, Meshach, and Abednego. Can we ever again become wholly what we are meant to be?

Story helps to show me. Sometimes in the darkest of moments we are fully human. There is a story told of the evil time when Adolf Hitler and his armies tried to enslave Europe and destroy the Jews. A village in Poland was taken, and all the Jewish men were rounded up and put into the synagogue. While the women and children watched, the synagogue was set on fire. From within the burning building came the sound of the men singing the Kaddish, the great Jewish prayer for the dead, singing it for themselves as they died, in total affirmation of the Lord of Creation who cares for us creatures—in life, and beyond.

One of the results of the Fall is that we have forgotten who we are, and so have forgotten how to be. Learning to be hurts. We can sing songs of happiness without knowing pain. But we can sing the joy of our creation and honor our Creator only from within the fire.

We walked through fire and water, David the psalmist cried, and affirmed that even in the fire, even in the deep waters, God is there. And Solomon sings in his great love song, *Many waters cannot quench love, rivers cannot wash it away*. Nor can the fire destroy it.

That love which cannot be destroyed has been the central core of stories since stories were first told or chanted around the campfires at night. Sometimes that love is shown by what we human creatures do to hurt it. We learn about love by being shown the abuses of love in *Anna Karenina*, or *The Brothers Karamazov*, or *King Lear*. Often when I am tired at night my bedtime reading is a murder mystery. Most of the writers to whom I turn are committed Christians, because it takes a firm grounding in the love of God for a writer to go into the darkest depths of the human heart. Often in these mysteries that love which will make us more human shines through the ugliness of greed and murder. Love does not triumph

40

easily or without pain, but <u>story gives us the courage to endure the pain.</u>

When did King David go home? As I have lived with his story, it seems to me that he learned what home meant only after the deaths of many of his children, the betrayal of his beloved son, Absalom; only after he had been driven out of his holy city, and everything had been taken away; only when he knew himself completely dependent on God's love.

Wordsworth, in his "Ode on Intimations of Immortality," writes,

The sunshine is a glorious birth:
But yet I know, where'er I go,
That there hath passed a glory from the earth.

The glory of our home, the home to which we journey throughout the story of our lives.

Story as a
Family Affair

2

OFTEN I AM ASKED if the fact that I married and had a family has affected my writing.

Of course it has! We write out of our own experience, and my experience is that which springs from being a wife and a mother and from my struggles to be human under these particular circumstances. Certainly I could not have written about the Murrys or the Austins without my own family experience.

And now I write from the point of view of a single woman, a woman whose husband has died. Why do I dislike the word *widow?* Several other women whose husbands have died agree with me. We are women who no longer have a husband and who must get on with life as well as we can, living, loving, continuing to work, to see friends. I have had the blessing of living, for the first years since Hugh's death, with my granddaughters through their years of college, and now Charlotte is in graduate school in New York. We entertain together, and this is a great joy, but it is very different from entertaining with a husband. Not better or worse, just different. But I know that sooner or later both these young women will be gone from my nest, and life will be different once again. And my writing will reflect my living.

If I hadn't married and had children and grandchildren I would still have written, though undoubtedly I would have written differently, out of different experience.

And my own experience of course goes back to long before I was married, goes back to my solitary childhood. I was an only child, born late in the marriage of my parents. I did not do well in school. I was slightly lame and was not appreciated by either my classmates or my teachers, who thought I was stupid. I went home from the hell of school to my own small room where I wrote, and asked all the big questions—mostly to myself, or to God. My parents were busy, and I didn't want to bother them. I asked why there was war, why people are cruel, why the wicked flourish and the innocent suffer. I asked what life is about and my own small place in it. Does each one of us really make a difference? Does God really count the hairs of our heads? I knew about that because my parents were Scripture readers, and taught me to love the Bible, that great and wonderful storybook.

As I read Scripture I saw that God used strange people to do the work of Love, ordinary people who were just like the rest of us, not perfect, not morally virtuous, but people who listened to God and, often reluctantly, did what was asked of them.

Women did extraordinary things in Scripture. Deborah was one of the first judges. Esther was not only married to a king, she virtually ruled the country, and with an iron hand. Jael was a heroine, if a bloody one, in rescuing the Israelites from defeat in battle by driving a tent peg through the head of Sisera, their enemy. Certainly their stories helped me to hold high the image of women. And my reading of the biblical stories was the start of a life-long habit of Scripture reading.

I don't think I learned anything in school until the last four years, my high school years. We left New York when I was twelve, and I went to a boarding school which was even grimmer than my day school in New York because I could not come home at the end of the day. But I survived it, and we returned to the States in time for me to go to Ashley Hall, in Charleston, South Carolina, for four productive, creative years. Finally I had teachers who believed in me, and I lived in an atmosphere that stimulated and challenged me. Ashley Hall was started by Mary Vardrine McBee, a remarkable Southern gentlewoman who gave us treasures we didn't even begin to appreciate because we simply took them for granted.

Every December we performed three plays from the Chester Cycle. I was tall, so I always got to play one of the major roles, a shepherd or a king. The girls with the best singing voices were the Red Choir, and the rest of the school dressed as medieval peasants, carrying tapers, and going to church on Christmas Eve—which is, of course, where those wonderful plays were first produced—in church. Miss McBee turned out to be a marvelous director. One year the girl playing the youngest shepherd did not react with proper awe when the Christmas Star appeared in the sky, with the angel, as usual, calling out, "Fear not!" Nothing Miss McBee said made Martha react properly. So Miss McBee picked up a chair, leaped up onto the stage and flung it at Martha. Martha reacted.

"That's right," Miss McBee smiled. "That's how I want you to play that scene."

In the spring we performed one of Shakespeare's plays, outdoors in the gardens, with the girls who had been in the Red Choir now singing Elizabethan madrigals. One of my most enjoyable roles was Sir Andrew Aguecheek in *Twelfth Night*. We lived with great language. Every evening during the hour before dinner, Miss McBee read to us—*The Wind in the Willows, Winnie the Pooh,* and, of course, the Bible.

When, my second year at Ashley Hall, we held class elections, it never occurred to me that I would even be considered a candidate. When I was elected president I could hardly believe it. I was still caught up in the picture of myself as the one who was too dumb ever to make it.

Ashley Hall was good for me. And I loved the family I found there, Miss McBee and the teachers and my friends. I not only was allowed to think of myself as a writer, I was encouraged to do so. I left Ashley Hall and went to Smith with hope and courage and there again I found, in my professors and my friends, a wonderful sense of family.

With such a background it is not surprising that when I married I wanted to have a family, to be part of a family, and still do, though patterns change. But as long as we remember that the human creature is a family creature, there are dozens and dozens of ways to be a family—a family of ten, or two, or one. Right now my immediate, in-my-home family consists of Charlotte and me, three cats, and one great golden retriever. But the other two rooms tend to fill up periodically, even if only for a few nights at a time. As I write this, we have staying with us one of the staff members from my church, who needs a bed for a few weeks until he can get into his new apartment. Another friend, from San Antonio, Texas, here in New York for meetings, found that there was no room in the inn, so he, too, is with us. Family tends to happen, I've found. Back when my children were little, one baby sitter came for an evening and stayed for two years. One of our friends used to announce, "I'm Hugh's and Madeleine's first illegitimate child. I was born the year before they were married." Over the years we acquired many such "illegitimate" children, who have brought great joy and who have indeed become family.

During the first few weeks in the hospital after my accident one of the hardest parts for me was isolation, separation from family. I think I missed Hugh more during those dark days in the hospital than at any other time since his death, a deep, longing ache.

But I was also separated from my normal routine of cooking for people I love, from deep and challenging conversations, from my daily reading of Scripture that puts everything together for me. My small travel Bible was in the closet in my hospital room in San Diego. While I was still in pain, unable to turn over, breathing with difficulty, I could hold neither Prayer Book nor Bible, and somehow I felt that God was telling me not to push—*Be patient, Madeleine. When you're ready, you'll know.*

But at least I had in my head the family of the characters in my novel-in-manuscript, *Certain Women,* and these included all the characters in the King David story, as human and flawed and fallible as any of us. The characters of my stories *are* family for me, and that is why so many of them appear in more than one book. I don't want to leave them at the end of a book; I want to find out what happens to them.

But in *Certain Women* all the twentieth-century characters appeared in my imagination for the very first time, with the exception of one of the characters, minor in the novel, Canon Tallis, who makes, chronologically, his first appearance, when he is a very young man. But he is in two small scenes only and while it is almost as comforting for me to have him there as it was for Emma, my protagonist, most of the people of this story were people I had to learn about as I wrote.

The characters in the King David story have been given, with a few strokes, an amazing amount of their personality by the scriptural narrator, but the storyteller, like most great artists, prods the imagination of the reader. In the Bible there is often more than one interpretation to a story.

Heresy? Blasphemy? Not at all. Take, once again, the familiar story of the Good Samaritan who cares for the man set upon by thieves. The priest and the Levite, who were the "good" Jews of Jesus' day, walked by the man lying wounded and nearly dying by the side of the road. They did not want to risk ritual uncleanness. There is a story that the priest was in a hurry to get to Jerusalem to preach his famous sermon on compassion. In any case, the last person one would expect to stop and help was the Samaritan, for the Samaritans were wholly other to the Jews. Their belief in God was different from that of the good Jew. They worshipped in a different holy place. They were socially unacceptable. We have no equivalent. (Well, maybe the New Ager?)

Anyhow, it is this unacceptable man who stops and tends the injured man, puts him on his own beast, takes him to an inn, gives the innkeeper enough money to continue tending him until he is well enough to be on his way. Jesus asks his questioner, *"Which of these three do you think was a neighbor to the man who fell into the hands of robbers?"* And the answer is given reluctantly, *"The one who had mercy on him." "Go and do likewise,"* Jesus says.

In the Western world the Christ figure in this story is the Good Samaritan. But in the Russian Orthodox world, according to my friend the theologian, the late Edward N. West, my beloved Canon Tallis, the Christ figure is the man set upon by thieves. It is exactly the same story, but there are two totally different ways of looking at it. So it is with all stories, including those in Scripture.

This is because Scripture is *true*. Truth is deeper and wider and much more demanding than many people would like, but Jesus promised that it would set us free.

So there is more than one way of looking at the characters surrounding David, and at David himself. Over and over in the Psalms, David prefigures Jesus, so surely the Christian looks at David differently from the observant Jew—but he is the same David.

And Samuel. One year for Christmas a friend of mine gave me a charming small statue of the child Samuel in prayer. I still have it, and I love it, and perhaps this slightly idealized version is true to the child who was called out of his sleep by God. But the Samuel who appears in the story of David is an old man whose sons have not followed in his footsteps, have not listened to God, but to mammon. Surely this was a terrible grief to Samuel

(Where was his wife? We are not told. Perhaps sorrow killed her.) and made him bitter and perhaps suspicious. It is partly because Samuel's erring sons could not possibly take over his mantle as a prophet that the people clamored for a king. Despite the warnings that the Lord gave them through Samuel they did not listen, and they wanted to do it their way, and they wanted a king like other peoples. And so Samuel anointed their new king, and how terrible a mistake this was is shown throughout the rest of the Old Testament.

But there was another mistake, and that was the choice of the first king, King Saul. Saul, who was tall and handsome and a mighty warrior and so strong that *he took a pair of oxen*, and *cut them into pieces* single-handedly. He was, it would seem, a logical choice for the king. Saul was taller than anybody else and comely. He is referred to as a son of Kish, the Ethiopian, so it is likely that Saul was dark of skin and that he glowed in the fierce desert sun. Samuel anointed him and there was great rejoicing, and Saul smote the Amalekites and had a great victory.

Though Saul was told to *"totally destroy everything that belongs to them. Do not spare them,"* Saul spared Agag, the king of the Amalekites, and the best of the animals. Everybody else he slaughtered—women, children, old people, animals. All pretty bloody, isn't it? But we're pretty bloody, too, with our bombings and burnings in Central America, in Korea, in Vietnam—and that's only a small part of the list. But were we told to destroy everybody and spare them not? I don't think so. War is always confusing. A twelve-year-old wrote to me, asking, "We're studying the Crusades in school. Can there be such a thing as a holy war? Is it ever right to kill?"

Is it? What does this do to the family of God's human creatures? I graduated from college into the Second World War, and that was not an ambiguous war; Hitler *had* to be stopped. But what about all those bombs dropped on Germany? On hospitals? On women and children who had nothing to do with the war? Was all that necessary for the winning of the war? That's one of many questions for which I have no answer. Sometimes we are in situations where there is no right choice, and we have to make the choice which we prayerfully believe to be the least wrong, never forgetting that it is wrong.

Should Saul have killed everybody? Was it necessary? Was it really God's command? Because Saul had saved Agag neither Samuel nor the Lord had anything to do with Saul ever again. And here we come to one of these odd scriptural quandaries. All the Amalekites have been slain. Saul slew all of them except Agag, and Samuel slew Agag *(And Samuel put Agag to death before the LORD at Gilgal)*, so therefore there were no more Amalekites. Finis. Kaput. But in the first chapter of the Second Book of Samuel, we read, when *David returned from defeating the Amalekites*, it was an Amalekite who told David of the death of Saul, that he, the Amalekite *stood over him and killed him*. Where did this Amalekite come from? Where did the other Amalekites come from if they were all slain by Saul and Samuel? This is not the first—or the last— time we find differences in Scripture, and this does not mean that Scripture is errant, or untrue, or false. The history in the Old Testament was compiled by more than one scribe, and what we are given is a general picture, and if we put it all together it adds up to a true picture, despite the inaccuracies. God is interested in truth, and that is what this book is about, our human struggle to understand and accept that truth that Jesus promised would make us free.

♦ ♦ ♦

After Saul had

spared Agag and the best of the sheep and cattle, the fat calves and lambs—everything that was good. These they were unwilling to destroy completely, but everything that was despised and weak they totally destroyed. Then the word of the LORD came to Samuel: "I am grieved that I have made Saul king, because he has turned away from me and has not carried out my instructions."

Nik, the playwright in my novel, asks the rough question, "Was it God who made a mistake in choosing Saul to be the first king? Or was it Samuel? Was Samuel blaming his own mistake on God?" As one character, David's sister, Zeruiah, proclaims, "God does not make mistakes. We make mistakes. God does not."

What are we to make of this? Do we agree with Zeruiah that God does not make mistakes? And is it all right for us to ask such questions? Dare we question Scripture? Dare we question God?

Yes! All through Scripture God's great protagonists are full of questions, complaints, even whinings.

Why are you doing this to me? How long, Lord? Keep not silence, O God! Wilt thou be angry with us forever? Wilt thou not revive us again? Lord, why hidest thou thy face from me? I have cried day and night before thee!

Do we dare less than God's people in Scripture? What has happened to us? Don't we trust the Lord enough to tell our Maker how we really feel?

We are finite, and the Lord is infinite. We cannot *comprehend* the Creator any more than the darkness can *comprehend* the light, as the KJV reads in the beginning of John's Gospel. We can complain, and we can also worship and adore. We can fall flat on our faces at the wonder of God's loving revelations to us. We can learn what our merciful Abba is like through Jesus, the Incarnate One. But we cannot know with our minds alone the mind of God. We can try to understand with our hearts, and sometimes that understanding comes when we are brave enough to ask questions.

Did the Lord make a mistake in choosing Saul to be the first king, or was it a human mistake, Samuel's mistake? What does it mean?

What does a truck driver running through a red light on a sunny Sunday in San Diego mean to me? What does God want me to learn from this experience?

Life is full of questions, and we are free to ask them, to understand, occasionally, that we are not going to get an answer, or at least not the answer we expect, and then we are called to move on. But I believe that God encourages us to ask questions.

In the hospital in San Diego I didn't ask questions—not because I didn't have any but because whatever energy I had was spent on getting through each day and night. Trying to breathe without hurting. Trying to move without hurting. Trying to eat.

Once I was off IVs the doctors wanted me to eat in order to regain strength. If I had had a doctor other than the trauma team would this have happened? Trying to force me to eat was where the doctors made a big mistake. I was put on a full, regular diet, and there was no way my lacerated internal organs were ready for that. During my surgery my intestines had been examined inch by inch to see where and if and how they were torn or bleeding, and intestines don't enjoy being pulled out and gone over. My kidney, which had been so badly injured it almost had to be removed, was learning to function normally again. My body was not ready for food, and the more I tried to eat, because I was told I must eat to get back my strength, the less ready it was. So my ileum simply shut down. What I ate I threw up; I could not take a pain pill without heaving painfully.

Part of the insistence by the trauma team that I *must* eat in order to regain strength came from the pressure of the insurance company. Members of the team came to my room to warn me that the insurance company was reluctant for me to stay in the hospital any longer. I looked at them. It was visibly apparent that I was not ready to leave the hospital. But the insurance people were treating me as a simple splenectomy, without any consideration for all the other injuries, the torn vital organs, the grossly black and blue left side, bumpy with hematomas, the black and blue legs, the bruised sternum that made breathing a painful effort.

Eat. You must get strong. Eat.

Around me the hospital was being rebuilt to make it earthquake safe. Not a comfortable thought. Were they going to finish their construction before the next earthquake? The noise was exacerbating. So I let myself be pushed out of the hospital, and Deborah graciously came for me, telling me later that she knew I was being released too soon. She was going to be in her beautiful home only overnight; she had to leave early the next morning for a business trip, leaving me to the ministrations of a maid and a gardener, for whose gentle care I will always be grateful. Darlene tried to fix soft foods for me, hoping I would be able to eat; Victor was simply there, ready. And I continued to throw up whatever I put in my mouth and made myself swallow.

The second morning I got through on the phone to the doctor who had performed the surgery, and who told me to come back to the hospital through the emergency room. After four hours of tests I was re-admitted. But the episode was definitely a setback, and I blame the insurance company far more than I do the doctors. Why should doctors be terrorized by insurance companies who have no medical training or knowledge? What right do insurance executives have to make medical decisions?

Not long after this my physician friend, Pat, read an article in the *Journal of the American Medical Association* about what happens to the body after severe trauma. Doctors have not understood why, for instance, someone who has had a bad case of flu, and recovers, is not well, does not gain weight. They are now learning that the body goes through its own timetable of healing. No matter how much hyper-alimentation is given, a patient will go on losing weight until the body completes its process in its own time. Pushing me to eat was not a good idea, and it slowed down my recuperation. When I was out of the hospital and could eat what my body would tolerate—soup, soft foods—I did better. It was nearly six weeks before the body was ready for real food once more. In fact, until then, food did not taste like food. It was just something I managed to swallow without heaving it right back up, food I normally don't go near—ice cream and Fritos, for instance!

Eating has always been important to me, because the focal point of the day is the dinner table, a foretaste of the heavenly banquet. The dinner hour is a sacramental time for me, a time of gratitude for whoever is gathered around the table, for the food, for our being part of the great story of Creation. We share the day's events, tell stories, look up words in dictionaries, linger long after the meal is over while the candles burn down.

The family dinner table is no longer something to be taken for granted. In some families it doesn't even exist. People eat catch-as-catch-can, with various conflicting schedules, grabbing a bite, watching TV, running off, missing the wonderful time of communication. It is a great loss. Often during my marriage Hugh and I had to work hard to keep the tradition, eating at odd hours just so that we could get everybody together, but the effort is worth it, it is *worth* it. I know one family who eats breakfast together; it is their chief gathering time. For me the shared evening meal is the time for gathering together, the time when meaning is made clear—the value and validity of our lives. There have been times of trouble when the dinner table has been the only affirmation available.

And I like an expandable dinner table. I remember my son asking, "Mother, is it all right if I bring nineteen people home for dinner?" And I said, "Of course, as long as you do the dishes." I'll cook for any number, but I don't do the clean-up. Probably the largest group has been fifty—fifty young Christian artists in New York who came at the time of Hugh's and my thirty-fifth wedding anniversary to listen to us talk about marriage between two artists. My granddaughters often invite twenty or so people, outgrowing the table, but not the living room and dining room, which open into each other. And this is family, all these disparate people gathered together. We are not always of one mind, theologically, politically, artistically, but seldom so far apart that conversation is not possible. Good arguments, with passion but not rancor, are part of a good evening.

Sometimes we are careful to have a group small enough to sit comfortably at the table, and then we may spend the evening reading and talking about poetry, our own poems, or poems which have particular meaning for us. Sometimes we will be all women, and will talk about what being a woman means to each one of us and what we have learned from each other.

For the Christian, the Trinity is the true metaphor for family, but in the churches nowadays we seem to be skipping over the Trinity, or dispensing with it altogether, and this may be because we are also skipping over and dispensing with family, forgetting the joys of unity in diversity.

A metaphor of unity in diversity is the world of the theatre, where I was always a very small part of the making of a play. But, as Stanislavski reminds us, "There are no small parts; there are only small actors," and I rejoiced in being a part of this Oneness. No one was expendable; everyone was needed to make the play work. Another metaphor is the orchestra, where the lowly tuba may be as important as the first violin. All the instruments have to play together to make unity, a symphony, a concerto, or an orchestral suite.

Of course one problem with the Trinity today is language—either the old, paternalistic language, or the newer, supposedly inclusive language. Father, Son, and Holy Spirit does seem to lean heavily to the masculine side, even when one thinks of the Holy Spirit as feminine.

And let's not get too literal about this—that's always a terrible problem. If the Holy Spirit is feminine, and Mary conceives by the Holy Spirit, what does that imply? Literalism, that's all. Some of my clergy friends say God the Redeemer, Creator, and Holy Spirit, and that's not bad; it is at least trying to return to the concept of the Trinity in Unity, in oneness, as the prototype of family. We are all trinitarian, inseparably body, mind, and spirit, and this oneness within ourselves helps us to understand oneness in our relations with our families and friends even when we are scattered across the continent and sometimes across the face of the earth. Usually the phone serves to some extent to keep the lines open between us, but the old geographical closeness has been broken. So the families of our churches, our friends, become even more important.

In *Meet the Austins* the family is shattered and shocked by the violent and sudden death of a beloved uncle, and they did what my family and I often did in times of trouble—they went up to the top of Hawk Mountain to look at the stars and try to get things in perspective.

The story is told from the point of view of Vicky Austin (and Vicky, rather than the mother, is the character I identify with) who says,

> The sky was enormous, and terribly high. It's a funny thing, the colder it gets, the farther away the sky seems and the farther off the stars look. The sky was so thick with them it was almost as though it had been snowing stars, and down below us there was a white fog so it seemed as though we were looking out over a great lake. The Milky Way was a river of light. . . .

Mother said, "I know you're very upset about Uncle Hal and Maggy's father. We all are. I thought maybe if we came and looked at the stars it would help us to talk about it a little."

Just then a shooting star flashed across the sky, and John said, "There's a shooting star and I don't know what to wish. I want to wish it back to before yesterday and that none of this would have happened, but I know it wouldn't work."

I said, "Mother, I don't understand it," and I began to shiver.

Mother said, "Sometimes it's very hard to see the hand of God instead of the blind finger of chance. That's why I wanted to come out where we could see the stars."

"I talked to Aunt Elena [Uncle Hal's wife] for a while," John said. . . . "She said that she and Uncle Hal knew that they were living on borrowed time. They'd always hoped it would be longer than it was, but the way their lives were, they only lived together in snatches, anyhow. And she said she was grateful for every moment she'd ever had with him and, even if it was all over, she wouldn't trade places with anybody in the world."

"She said that to you, John?" Mother asked.

"Yes," John said, and then another star shot across the sky, this time with a shower of sparks. We sat there, close, close, and it was as though we could feel the love we had for one another moving through our bodies as we sat there, moving from me to Mother, from Mother to John, and back again. I could feel the love filling me, love for Mother and John, and for Daddy and Suzy and Rob, too. And I prayed, "Oh, God, keep us together, please keep us together, please keep us safe and well and together."

It was as though our thoughts were traveling to one another, too, because John said, "Oh, Mother, why do things have to change and be different?" He sounded quite violent. "I like us exactly the way we are, our family. Why do people have to die, and people grow up and get married, and everybody grow away from each other? I wish we could just go on being exactly the way we are."

"But we can't," Mother said. "We can't stop the road of time. We have to keep on going. And growing up is all part of it, the exciting and wonderful business of being alive. We can't understand it, any of us, any more than we can understand why Uncle Hal and Maggy's father had to die. But being alive is a gift, the most wonderful and exciting gift in the world. And there'll undoubtedly be many other moments when you'll feel this same way, John, when you're grown up and have children of your own."

Yes, and when you have grandchildren. I am coming to the time when my granddaughters will be finishing their education and will leave and move on, and that is right and fitting, and I have to trust that as God provided family for me after my husband died, so family will continue to be provided.

For that is how it is, a great and moving pattern, a cosmic dance of the whole Created Order, of which each of us is a part. The patterns change, the steps of the dance vary, but it is still the metaphor of Great Family, to which we all belong.

Story as Affirmation of God's Love

3

SAN DIEGO WAS FAR, far from home, and I was lonely. For a while after the accident I was so enclosed in a cocoon of pain I didn't realize how lonely I was. When I could think, I remembered that I had a friend in San Diego, Lura Jane Geiger, whose small publishing house, Lura-Media, does fine books and tapes. But I didn't have Lura's number. When I was finally able to get hold of her, she came right to the hospital, despite the fact that she was carrying a double burden of grief, the death of her husband, and of her son and partner. She brought with her a quiet book of meditations on life in the desert and read to me in her peaceful voice. She told me, firmly, that I should not be alone.

I knew that I should not be alone, knew it deep in my heart and deep in my gut. But my deep-seated Anglican training had told me that I should not ask for help, that I should be brave about being alone. I am eternally grateful to Lura for stating so unequivocally that I should not be alone.

So when Luci Shaw returned from Europe, learned about my accident, called me from San Francisco, and told me that she wanted to come to San Diego and be with me, I didn't do my usual Anglican protestations of, "Oh, I'm all right; don't bother." Instead I said, "Please come."

And I remembered that Jesus did not carry his own cross all the way. He stumbled and fell under the burden of the cross, and Simon of Cyrene carried it for him. It is all right to ask for help. We do not have to do it alone.

It was wonderful having Luci with me to be friend, nurse, encourager, to read the Psalms to me—I was still not strong enough to read for myself. Luci and I have been friends for many years. We have shared the grief of our husbands' illnesses and death; Luci's husband, Harold, died of cancer in January of the same year that my husband died of cancer in the autumn. We have been in the depths and the heights together. But this time in the hospital was extraordinary in the way it deepened an already deep friendship. I was almost completely helpless physically and Luci gave me the tenderest of care, helping me with the almost impossible task of walking a few yards out in the hall, buying ginger ale for me to drink, since it was one thing I could keep down, and all the hospital provided was Sprite (a little surprising, since ginger ale has long been known as helpful for nausea).

Luci was patient with me, understanding that I was not refusing to eat because I was being ornery, but because I truly could not eat. We talked about our childhoods, about our spiritual journeys, about how we were comfortable in very much the same spiritual home, though we have come to it from very different directions, Luci from a classically evangelical background, I from an equally classical Episcopalian one—a spiritual oneness Luci's "new" husband, John, had mentioned only a few weeks earlier when we were all together in Oxford. Luci and I talked about how God was coming into this seemingly irrational accident, how nothing, ultimately, is irrational when God has entered into it.

And I learned yet another lesson. Luci needed to get back to San Francisco for various pressing obligations. When she asked me if I wanted—needed—her to stay another night until our mutual friend Marilyn was able to come, I tried to be Anglican and brave. But finally I said, "Luci, please stay." And she did.

After Luci left, Marilyn came. She, like Luci, is a graduate of Wheaton, and had, in fact, grown up there. We three have known each other for a long time. A year ago Marilyn had been bumped from a plane and was given free transportation to and from any destination in the continental United States. So she used it to fly from Niles, Michigan, to San Diego, California, just to be with me. What I would have done without these two friends I do not know, because Lura was right: I should not be alone.

◆ ◆ ◆

Marilyn and I talked about *Certain Women*, because not only had she read this long manuscript in various versions, she had come up with the title for me. I had started out calling the book *The Company of Women*, from the Coverdale translation of the Psalms, and discovered that this title had already been used. When Marilyn looked through her Bible she found, in Luke's Gospel, *Certain women made us astonished*, and I added, from Nik's play, King David's saying to his beloved wife, Abigail, "You sound so certain." To which Abigail replies, "I am." So *Certain Women* is a title with a double meaning.

We talked about David, only a youngster when his story begins, out in the hills with his sheep and his harp. All through Scripture sheep are important, and when we are referred to as sheep it is not a compliment. Sheep are among the most stupid of animals! Indeed, all we, like sheep, have gone astray.

And the Good Shepherd goes out into the rain to find us and bring us home.

It is no coincidence that David comes into his story as a shepherd. It is difficult for us today to understand all the connotations that the word *shepherd* had for people in David's world—and in Jesus' world. We don't have a contemporary equivalent. One friend suggested the school traffic-crossing guard, the man or woman carefully making sure that the children get across the street safely. It's a good metaphor, but not really adequate.

There's a true story I love about a house party in one of the big English country houses. Often after dinner at these parties people give recitations, sing, and use whatever talent they have to entertain the company. One year a famous actor was among the guests. I've been told he might have been Charles Laughton. When it came his turn to perform, he recited the Twenty-third Psalm, perhaps the most beloved psalm in the Psalter. *The Lord is my shepherd. I shall not want.* His rendition was magnificent, and there was much applause. At the end of the evening someone noticed a little old great aunt dozing in the corner. She was deaf as a post and had missed most of what was going on, but she was urged to get up and recite something. In those days people used to memorize a lot of poetry! So she stood up, and in her quavery old voice she started, *The Lord is my shepherd,* and went on to the end of the psalm. When she had finished there were tears in many eyes. Later one of the guests approached the famous actor. "You recited that psalm absolutely superbly. It was incomparable. So why were we so moved by that funny, little old lady?"

He replied, "I know the psalm. She knows the shepherd."

◆ ◆ ◆

David was a shepherd, the youngest son of Jesse. He *was ruddy, with a fine appearance and handsome features,* but he was alone in the hills with his songs as he cared for his sheep. When a lion came, and a bear, and took lambs from his flock, he went after the marauding beasts and killed them, saving the lambs.

Meanwhile, Samuel was furious with Saul for having spared Agag and some of the animals. Yes, I have trouble with this. So does Emma, the protagonist of *Certain Women,* and so does Nik, the playwright. Even Grandpa Bowman, Emma's beloved preacher grandfather, cannot quite explain the violence of what he calls "the tribal god." Towards the end of Numbers, in chapter 33, God commands Moses,

"Speak to the Israelites and say to them: 'When you cross the Jordan into Canaan, drive out all the inhabitants of the land before you . . . Take possession of the land and settle in it, for I have given you the land to possess. . . . But if you do not drive out the inhabitants of the land, those you allow to remain will become barbs in your eyes and thorns in your sides. They will give you trouble in the land where you live. And then I will do to you what I plan to do to them.'"

Such exhortations to kill all the enemies and take their land—and there are not a few—have been used as excuses (reasons) to take land away from other people, as we, ourselves, did with the land that belonged to the Indians. Hadn't God given the land to us? Didn't the psalmist (was it David?) say in the Forty-fourth psalm,

With your hand you drove out the nations. . . . It was not by their sword that they won the land, nor did their arm bring them victory. . . . Through you we push back our enemies; through your name we trample our foes.

Did the British take this literally when they spread their empire across the world, considering the heathen of the other lands to be "the white man's burden"?

But hasn't this always been the way of the world, the taking of other peoples' land when "we," whoever we are, run out of land, or are driven from our own, or for one reason or other need expansion? Or simply lust for power, like the emperors of the Roman Empire? This is the world's way. Is it God's way?

The slaughtering, tribal god has always bothered me. First of all, it implies that "our" god is only one god among many, perhaps stronger, better, but still one god in a pantheon of gods. Indeed, throughout the Old Testament there is much evidence of polytheism, side by side with a worship of the One True Creator of the Universe. I have been told that when the Jews were slaves in Egypt, when they left they took with them Ikhnaton's vision of One God. But the One God seems to me to go right back to the first verses of Genesis, to be affirmed in the God who took Abraham out at night to count the stars—if he could—and made mighty promises that Abraham's descendants would be a blessing to all nations of the earth. The two visions of God are side by side through much of Scripture, as they often are for us—for when we worship church buildings, or the number of people in the congregation, or our denomination over other denominations, or the conservatives over the liberals, or the other way around, we are losing sight of the God of love, the Abba that Jesus showed us, who knows all the stars by name and counts the very hairs of our head.

The god of war has troubled me all my life because I have lived in a century of war, and I don't think that war is ever *right*. I don't know whether or not Desert Storm was necessary or not; it may have been. But it is not right to glorify it, to make heroes out of those who ordered more killing than was needed. When we kill civilians, women and children and old people, it may be because they were simply victims of bombs that were intended not for them but for the ending of the war, but it must never be glorified. And we have tended to do that, because if we can bask in glory it can obscure the fact that we killed, maimed, destroyed. We do what we have to do, prayerfully, and then we need to repent of the evil that has been done through us, not glorify it.

This is hard thinking. I don't like it. I talked a little about it with both Luci and Marilyn, and we prayed together—and how good it was to have someone to pray with, to lead me back into prayer.

With both Luci and Marilyn I talked of my deliverance from death, and what it meant. For my seventy-two-year-old body to have survived all the trauma it did was enough to make me ask why God had spared me. Certainly my life was not saved so that I could turn away from the hard thoughts and relax into the easy ones. Certainly my life was not saved so that I could armor myself with self-protection and avoid controversial subjects that might antagonize some people if those subjects are ones which I believe God wants me to address. It's often said that Americans want to be loved and are upset when people of other nations resent and even hate us, and I guess I'm American that way, too: I want to be loved. And I am loved, and how marvelous that is! But those who love me trust me to try to seek the truth and speak the truth as much as I am able.

♦ ♦ ♦

The basic truth for me, the freeing truth, is God's love, God's total, unequivocal love. That love is evident throughout Scripture. Psalm 139, one of my favorites, says in verse 14: *I praise you because I am fearfully and wonderfully made; your works are wonderful, I know that full well.*

Paul, in his first epistle to the people of Thessalonica, tells us that he has no need to write to us about how we are to love one another, *for you yourselves have been taught by God to love each other.* God made us in love, and he expects us to reflect that love (and how wondrously I saw that love reflected by Luci and Marilyn). We are to love one another even when we disagree with each other. I did not always agree with my husband, but I always loved him. We are to love one another even when we are angry with each other. I am sometimes angry with my friends, but that doesn't stop me from loving them.

In his letter to the people of Rome Paul tells us that all things work together for good to them that love God, and he concludes this magnificent passage by assuring us that nothing can separate us from the love of God which is in Christ Jesus, our Lord. John says that *God so loved the world that he gave his one and only Son,* Jesus Christ, just to show us how much we are loved.

In chapter five of Romans Paul assures us that *God has poured out his love into our hearts by the Holy Spirit, whom he has given us*—our Trinitarian God, Father, Son, and Holy Spirit, all there since the beginning, all here, all now, loving us.

In John's first epistle he commands us, *Since God so loved us, we also ought to love one another. . . . If we love one another, God lives in us and his love is made complete in us.* And John tells us not just to *say* that we love, but to show our love in all that we do. Yes, because God loves us, we are to love each other, and we can love, as long as we are certain of God's love for each one of us. It is much easier for me to love someone who is being difficult when I remember that God loves me even when I am at my worst, at my most unlovable.

In Paul's letter to the people of Ephesus he asks us to walk in love, just as Christ has loved us. What is it about loving that we find so hard, so that Scripture has to remind us to love over and over again? In his letter to the people of Colosse, Paul tells us that our hearts should be knit together in love and that it is love that helps us attain *the full riches of complete understanding, in order that they may know the mystery of God, namely, Christ, in whom are hidden all the treasures of wisdom and knowledge.*

I could go on and on picking out passages of God's love, God's mercy, God's forgiveness, but all I needed in the hospital in San Diego was to remember some of my favorites. I knew that I was alive because of God's love. I knew that God would show me why my life had been spared and would let me know what I was supposed to do. One thing I never lost was faith in God's love.

A friend of mine was viciously and terribly mugged, and while she was in the hospital one of the nurses said to her, "What horrible thing have you done that God is punishing you this way?"

Neither her accident nor mine were punishments. That is perhaps the human way, but it is not God's way. That attitude causes child abuse and battered women and all kinds of perverse ugliness. It is not how God works. My accident happened because a truck driver went through a red light in his brand-new truck. Because we had a witness who was willing to come forward, the truck driver had to assume responsibility, as far as insurance was concerned, for what he had done. If he feels badly about what he did (which, alas, doesn't seem likely), that is surely his punishment.

Punishment can far too easily be misunderstood, mis-construed, turned into vengeance or retribution. Let me tell the only funny story I know of a New York mugging: mine. All muggings are unpleasant, many are horrible, and most are not at all funny. Mine was. I was on the way from my apartment to teach a writers' workshop at St. Hilda's House, half a mile uptown, when a man came out of the shadows of the November evening and grabbed the small bag that was around my neck. Fortunately the strap broke, and he ran off with it. Like an idiot, I ran after him, shouting, "God will not like this!" He ran down the street, across Riverside Drive, grabbed another woman's bag, and jumped over a stone wall. What he did not know was that on the other side of the wall was a twenty-foot drop. He fell and broke his leg, just as a policeman was walking by. Immediate retribution (if not punishment!). My earnest hope was that he remembered the words I had called after him.

But my San Diego injuries were not a punishment, and God came into them immediately in the overwhelming response of love and prayer. That is what loving each other is like, a wondrous network of love and prayer that is greater than each individual who is part of it. I know that is why my recovery has astonished many people, though it has seemed incredibly slow to me. But then, God has been trying for seventy-two years (now seventy-three) to teach me patience.

I am concerned that the nurse who thought my friend was being punished is not alone in her idea of a punitive, forensic God. That is not the God of Scripture! Certainly there are a few angry passages, and surely we stiff-necked people have given God good cause to be angry with us. But if we read Scripture from the first verse of Genesis through to the last line of John's Revelation with a big pad, and set down the angry passages on one side, and the loving and forgiving passages on the other, the love and forgiveness far outweigh the anger. Over and over God calls us to say, "I'm sorry, Daddy, I want to come home," and then the door is flung open.

I have been asked, and many times, "But can't we choose to exclude ourselves?" Of course. Haven't we, as children, haven't our own children flung out of the room in anger? And haven't we waited for them to come back? We have not slammed the door in their faces. We have welcomed them home. Jesus said, *"If you . . . know how to give good gifts to your children, how much more will your Father in heaven give good gifts to those who ask him!"*

A couple of summers ago I was asked to teach a two-week writers' workshop at a well-known Bible college in Canada. I was given their statement of faith to sign. I read it, found it unscriptural, and pushed it aside. There was no way I could sign it.

They called me. "Where's the statement of faith?"

I spoke to the dean of this Bible college. "It's unscriptural. I'm sorry. I can't sign it."

I read him point three, which was one of the two points out of six that I could not sign. "Because of the fall we are in such a state of sin and depravity that we are justly under God's wrath and condemnation." Point four said that the only way God could forgive us for all this sin and depravity was for Jesus to come and get crucified. "What this is saying," I told the dean, "is that Jesus had to come save us from God the Father. I don't believe that Jesus had to come save us from God the Father. Scripture says, *'God so loved the world that he gave his one and only Son.'* The birth of Jesus showed God's love, not God's anger. This is what the Bible says, and this is what I believe."

I was allowed to come to the college anyhow, and I said to one of my students, "I don't think they've looked at that statement of faith since it was penned in Queen Victoria's day," and he replied sadly, "Oh no, Madeleine, that is what they are taught and that is what they believe."

I, too, am sad. But grateful that I was not taught a God of anger and vengeance, but a God of love. I am grateful that I was not taught that I had to earn lots and lots of merit badges in order to receive God's love. I was taught that God's love is so great that it cannot possibly be earned. It is the infinitely wonderful gift of our Maker. We are loved, just as we are, each one of us unique, unlike anybody else, loved by God, because this is how God made us. We are, as Paul reminds us, the temple of the Holy Spirit, and we must honor this temple in the way we live. We also bear within us God's image, and we are to honor that image.

Now, it is not that I am ignoring sin, or that I think any one of us is sinless. It is only as I know myself a sinner that I can experience God's forgiveness. But God does not dwell on our sins any more than I, as a human parent, dwelt on my children's wrongdoing. When we sin, and we all do, then we turn to our loving Father for forgiveness, and as long as our repentance is sincere, forgiveness is never withheld.

Part of my bedtime routine when I was a child was to say my prayers with my parents and then confess any wrong I had done during the day. Sometimes I made my parents sad, and myself, too, but my confessions were always followed by immediate forgiveness, by assurances of love, the love of my parents, the love of God. I am grateful for the teaching given me by my Episcopalian parents, because it grounded me in an awareness of God's all-embracing love.

The God of wrath and vindictiveness is not a new image. It was one of the early heresies, proposed by Marcion, and known as Marcionism: for these heretics the Maker of the Universe is not a good Maker, but a kind of Saddam Hussein, if you will, and Jesus had to come to save us from this vindictive Maker. The early Christian creeds, the Apostles', the Nicene, the Athanasian, were not written because anybody wanted to write creeds or statements of faith, but to combat the heresies that sprang up early in Christendom; many of the heresies sprang from a fear that because this is a wicked world, perhaps God was not good after all. The other prevalent heresy, and it is still around, came from an inability to comprehend that Jesus was wholly human and wholly God—for that, of course, is the extraordinary marvel of our Lord Jesus Christ, that for love of us he was both human and divine. Probably that statement of faith which I could not sign because it was not scriptural was written a hundred or so years ago to combat some current heresy. We no longer know what that heresy was and are left, instead, with the Marcionite heresy. I am not happy with most creeds or statements of faith. I am more comfortable with The Westminster Confession, which tells us that our duty is to love God and enjoy him forever. Forever. Now, and into eternity.

My friend the theologian said that if we die, and Jesus looks at us with love and we respond to that look with love, then we are in heaven. But if Jesus looks at us with love and we respond with fear or hate or anger, then we are in hell. It is the same look, but it is we who make it heaven or hell. Surely we begin to make our own heaven or hell in our daily lives, with our responses of love or fear or anger.

Now, it is not that we are never to be afraid or never to be angry. Jesus was afraid. In the garden his sweat was like drops of blood as he begged that the cup might be taken from him. And there were a number of times when he was angry. He threw the money lenders out of the temple. He was angry with those who were judgmental and hard of heart. But he did not stay in fear or anger. He always turned to his loving Abba, Papa, Daddy. "Not my will," he said in the garden, "not my will, but yours." When he was called "good" he replied that there was only One who was good, the loving Father in heaven.

When I came home from the hospital in San Diego—my son and daughter-in-law once again flew out from Connecticut, this time to bring me to Crosswicks—I was still very ill and weak. Hospitals are no longer good places for sick people once they're off the machines; a hotel in San Diego was not really an alternative, and I could not abuse Deborah's hospitality by staying over-long in her lovely home. And I was eager to get home, even knowing that I was really not strong enough for the chaos of the airport and the long flight. The only direct flight was at seven in the morning, and of course we had to be at the airport well before that. Marilyn was staunchly with me, and we met Bion and Laurie, and Sally, there.

It was not an easy flight. We had treated ourselves to first-class seats, but when we boarded the American Airlines plane the seats that were euphemistically called first-class were, at best, business size. When I tried to take a nap, I was so strictured by the narrowness of the seats that my arms fell asleep.

When we landed in New York, the wheelchair we had ordered for me did not come, despite the fact that we had reconfirmed it when we boarded the plane. Nearly an hour later, when a wheelchair was found, it had no foot section, and I was pushed along with my legs sticking out in front of me, by someone who got lost in his own airport, so that by the time we got to the car my calves were sore from holding up my legs.

Nevertheless I was overjoyed to get home, and the pesto Bion had made for dinner almost tasted like real food. Getting up the stairs was an exhausting feat. Indeed, I was so tired that I was in that strange place on the other side of fatigue. All the primitive fears were still with me; I was like a small child fearful of the dark at the head of the stairs.

I spent the first day, still exhausted from travel, listening to the radio as Hurricane Bob and the coup in Russia vied for first place on the radio and TV. The hurricane raged up the coast and attacked Connecticut where I was lying in bed, weak, and in pain. I wasn't even in my own bed (a big four-poster which I wasn't strong enough to climb in and out of, so I was in the guest room). Trees were crashing under the lashing of the wind, and power was going out all over the state. And I was afraid of the dark, not a normal fear, but a fear brought about by severe physical trauma. And I prayed, "Oh, God, I know it's selfish, but please don't let the power go out."

Our part of Connecticut, the northwest corner, was hit only by the outer edge of the storm and was the only part of Connecticut where the power stayed on. During the wakeful hours of the night I was comforted by the small, steady glow of the night light. Now that I am regaining my strength those primitive fears are retreating, but they were there.

So, yes, there are times when we are afraid, because we are human beings. So I was afraid. And there have been times when I have been angry, usually when somebody I love does something I know is unworthy, is less than that person should be. But I cannot stay in anger, and that is a God-given grace. I cannot go to bed without trying to reconcile with whoever it is with whom I am out of sorts.

We are not meant to be plaster saints who are never frightened or angry. These are human emotions and few people can avoid them. However we are not meant to be stuck in them, but to turn to God and move on. When I am angry with someone I know, to my rue, that there have been many times when I, too, have been less than I ought to be, when I have not honored God's image within me. This understanding alone should be enough to keep us from hanging onto grudges!

I lay in the guest room bed listening to the wind and rain, and I called on God for mercy, and God was indeed merciful. But I knew then and know now that I am human and finite, and God is divine and infinite. Because God is a God of love, that love is revealed to us in Christ Jesus. And that should be enough for us, but over and over again we make God in our own image, see God anthropomorphically, and that is where some of the images of the angry God have come from, the punitive God who refused to speak to Saul because he had not slaughtered all of the Amalekites. Montaigne said, "O senselesse man, who cannot make a worm, and yet makes gods by dozens."

Luci told me of her great-great-grandfather, a highly respected physician, who had twenty-two children. Every morning for breakfast he had a three-minute boiled egg, and every morning he carefully cut off the top of the egg and handed it to his wife. That was her share, the small cap of eggshell filled with a little albumen. At least she didn't have to worry about cholesterol. But such autocrats often become the image we carry of God. Here is a poem of Luci Shaw's which holds much wisdom:

Eating the egg whole

One of my forbears, a vigorous progenitor,
nameless but real by virtue of family
history's sharp details, went through
three wives. One story is that every day
he breakfasted with the current spouse
on toast and a three-minute egg,
chipping off its white cap in the precise
British way, and in a grand gesture,
spooning to his wife that minor albumen,
watery, pale as her self. That was her meal;
he feasted on yolk, rich and yellow
as a gold sovereign, and crushed the shells,
feeding them by gritty doses to
his offspring, lined up along the table—
a supplement to stave off rickets and
accustom the family to patriarchy.

Nourished thus on remnants and rigor,
his tribe multiplied to twenty-two.
The legend astonishes me still. Those
women . . . ! And I still bear, along with traces
of their genes, a vestigial guilt
whenever I cook myself a breakfast egg
and then devour it, white, yolk,
protein, cholesterol, and all. Like
seeing the sun after generations of moons.
Like being the golden egg and eating it too.

Luci Shaw

In the twenty-third chapter of Numbers when Balak is
trying to persuade Balaam to curse the Jews, Balaam ut-

tered his oracle and said, *"God is not a man."* No, God is not a man like one of us, but the Lord of heaven and earth, of this small planet and of all the galaxies, which we too easily forget, with our human need to decide what God is like, and who God's prophets should be. And we feel intense discomfort, if not fear and anger, when the people God speaks through aren't the ones we expect. Hannah gave Samuel to God to make into a prophet, but when the people wanted a king they did not listen to Samuel or God. And this was nothing new. In the eleventh chapter of Numbers we read,

Two men, whose names were Eldad and Medad, had remained in the camp. . . . The Spirit also rested on them . . . A young man ran and told Moses, "Eldad and Medad are prophesying in the camp." Joshua son of Nun . . . said, "Moses, my lord, stop them!"

They weren't the expected prophets, the right prophets, the correct prophets. But clear-sighted Moses replied, *"I wish that all the LORD's people were prophets and that the LORD would put his Spirit on them!"*

And in Mark's Gospel we read something similar: John said to Jesus,

"Teacher . . . we saw a man driving out demons in your name and we told him to stop, because he was not one of us." "Do not stop him," Jesus said. "No one who does a miracle in my name can the next moment say anything bad about me, for whoever is not against us is for us."

Unless we are very secure in God's love this is not easy, this listening to prophets we don't expect. But all through Scripture prophets have not had a comfortable

79

time of it. They told the truth, and the truth is often hard to hear, because we're afraid of that truth which Jesus promised would make us free. So, for telling the truth, the prophets have been stoned, put in prison, discredited.

And how do we know who are God's prophets and who are fakes? Or, even worse, who are followers of the imitator? the Lord of the Flies? It is not always easy or even possible to tell, because God is no respecter of persons and often chooses people to prophecy who seem not only unqualified, but who tell us so many things we don't want to hear that we tend to close our ears.

◆ ◆ ◆

In a letter I received not long after my return to Crosswicks, I was asked if I had forgiven the truck driver who had caused my accident. This was an unexpected thought for me. My focus was on recovering, returning to life. Come to think of it, I do not feel particularly kindly towards that truck driver who, as far as we know, still has never inquired if he hurt or killed the people in the little car he demolished. But I am happy to leave him to God. If there are lessons he needs to learn from this experience, well, he is God's child, not mine, and it is up to God, not me, to teach him.

Do I forgive him? It hadn't really even entered my thoughts. This man, whom I never saw, has not been in my mind. I don't know his name. I never saw his face. I have not been thinking about him, and that's probably just as well. Over to you, God.

What has been in my mind, once my mind was able to be released from enduring pain, was the wonderful love and concern of family and friends, a beautiful network of prayer which sustained me. The love which came to me from all over the country far outweighed the carelessness and irresponsibility of one truck driver.

Who were the prophets for me during this experience? Those who cared, doctors, nurses, friends, those who prayed. If we sometimes entertain angels unaware, we are sometimes upheld by prophets of whom, at the moment, we are also unaware. My prophets expected me to fight to live, to regain health, to look for meaning in what could easily seem meaningless. There is a horrible irrationality about life suddenly being cut in two on a sunny Sunday afternoon in San Diego and, while we understand with our minds that much of life is irrational, when it hits us we are startled and confused. There's much about this accident I don't understand yet, but little bits of meaning, little bits of God's amazing love are revealed daily.

And ultimately forgiveness is a gift of grace rather than an act of will. I have to be willing to forgive, but I cannot will myself to forgive. I can forgive with my mind, but forgiveness is finally a matter of the heart. And the forgiveness of the heart comes from God, not from me. My part in it is to be willing to accept it. One test which indicates whether or not forgiveness has really taken place is to look at whatever it is that needs to be forgiven and see if it still hurts. If it does, forgiveness has not yet happened. But I have also learned, and I have learned it through pain, that I must be patient with myself. Just as my body is going to need more time to complete its healing from the physical trauma of the accident, so my heart, my spirit, also need time, and I, ever impatient, must be patient with myself.

I have understood as far back as I can remember that the mind has an enormous effect on the body; we human creatures are a whole, and what affects any part of us affects the whole of us. And how our bodies respond to suggestion! If someone looks at me with concern, asking, "Are you all right? You look really terrible. Are you running a fever?" I'll immediately begin to feel miserable. But if that same person says to me instead, "Madeleine, you look wonderful. I've never seen you looking better," I'll feel wonderful. I have understood clearly the effect of the mind on the body, but I've only begun to understand the effect of the body on the mind.

It has long been my practise to read morning and evening prayer from the Episcopal Book of Common Prayer, with both Old and New Testament lessons. As I shared earlier, for a while after the accident I was too weak to hold either my small travel Bible or my prayer book. But even after enough strength had returned so that I could write in my journal and read a little, I did not turn back to the deeply ingrained habit of morning and evening prayer, and something (Someone? the Holy Spirit?) told me to be patient with myself. I knew that the time would come when this sustaining routine would be re-established. And it was. When I could eat again, I could read morning and evening prayer again. God's timing is more realistic than our own, or at least than my own. I am back with the wonderful words of prayer and Scripture, and food tastes good! So I am beginning to understand the effect of the body on the mind and spirit.

When it is time for me to face either anger or forgiveness, then I believe I will be given the courage to do so.

However, when I remember the moment of the accident suddenly shattering a peaceful Sunday afternoon, all I feel, still, is surprise. It's almost harder to be alive now than it would have been to die. After all, I had lived a full and wonderful life. I had passed the biblical three score years and ten. Why am I still alive?

If I still have much to learn, perhaps my efforts at learning will be useful to other people whose lives are also filled with unexpected and often terrifying surprises. And the old question rears its ugly head: if God is good, why is there so much pain? Theologians have been trying to answer this question for hundreds, if not thousands of years, and thus far it remains unanswered. The closest we get to understanding is a kind of subdued gratitude that God created us human beings with a modicum of free will. We are not puppets being manipulated by a master puppeteer. We do have some say in our own story, and often we tell the story in uncomprehending and sometimes evil ways, and innocent people suffer because of the wrongdoing of others. But whatever our experience is, God is there, in it with us, as God was in the fiery furnace with Shadrach, Meshach, and Abednego. That isn't really an answer, but it's all we're going to get, and it's enough. Even when we are too lost in pain, physical or spiritual, to experience knowingly the presence of God, God is still there.

That is what the prophets have told us throughout the ages. God is still with us even when we are not with God, even when we have turned to alien gods, pride, greed, lust, God is still with us in the midst of our troubles.

Some of our prophets at this end of a troubled century have themselves been troubled. We've had televangelists who've been tripped by the lusts which are rampant across our land and who have thereby discredited much of what they've had to say, which is a terrible tragedy, because much of what they had to say is good, and their behavior does not negate the good. We've had denominations spending years to formulate statements about sex, as though suddenly, at the end of the twentieth century, we could unravel what has been a tangle since Adam and Eve. We've had those who think they can make the definitive statement about homosexuality, or abortion, or life after death. But that's not what true prophets do. True prophets point out problems, rather than offering easy solutions. They tell us that actions have consequences, that if we fall into sexual or any other kind of self-indulgence we will find that the price can be intolerably high.

Jesus said, *A prophet is not without honor save in his own country,* and it was his own people who could not accept the message of truth and love and forgiveness he offered all of us. They wanted, instead, to know why he healed on the Sabbath, why he ate with sinners, and he told them that he was looking for compassion, not legalism, and that those who are well do not need a doctor, but those who are ill, and he had come for those who knew they were broken and needed healing.

Perhaps our true prophets today, our unrecognized prophets, are people like us, who do not go on television to speak to millions, and do not make grand statements about controversial subjects. Jesus did not start a lepers' rights organization or a lepers' liberation group or make categorical pronouncements about why some people were afflicted with demons. Instead he touched people, one by one, forgave them, and healed them.

Can we be healed until we are willing to accept forgiveness? My forgiveness of that truck driver, and even

God's, will do him little good unless he is willing to understand that he needs forgiveness and accepts it. But that is between the truck driver and God. If I am to be able to accept forgiveness, I must first accept that I need it.

God's forgiveness is, I believe, always available. Was it truly God who would not forgive Saul? Or was it Samuel?

Saul, it seems, was surprised at being chosen king for a people who had never before had a king. And then Saul was disobedient, and the prophet Samuel roundly blamed God for choosing Saul. Samuel condemned Saul utterly.

Saul said to Samuel, *"I have sinned. . . . Now I beg you, forgive my sin and come back with me, so that I may worship the LORD."*

But Samuel's harsh reply was, *"I will not go back with you. You have rejected the word of the LORD, and the LORD has rejected you as king over Israel!"* And neither Samuel nor the Lord ever spoke to Saul again.

Grandpa Bowman, in *Certain Women*, felt that Saul was full of pride, that he disobeyed the injunction to kill everybody—and all the animals—out of pride, not compassion. Certainly he became a mentally sick man, what we might today call manic depressive. But as the story unrolls he is a pitiable figure.

God then sends the prophet Samuel to Bethlehem to Jesse, and *he consecrated Jesse and his sons and invited them to the sacrifice.* And when Samuel saw Eliab, Jesse's eldest son, he said,

"Surely the LORD's anointed stands here before the LORD."
But the LORD said to Samuel, "Do not consider his appearance or his height, for I have rejected him. The LORD

does not look at the things man looks at. Man looks at the outward appearance, but the LORD looks at the heart."

Surely Saul had been chosen by Samuel because of his outward appearance! *Then Jesse called Abinadab and had him pass in front of Samuel. But Samuel said, "The LORD has not chosen this one either."* And so it went, until seven of Jesse's sons had been rejected and turned away, and Samuel asked Jesse if these were all the sons he had. And Jesse admitted that there was still the youngest son, but he was out, keeping the sheep.

David was sent for, and *Samuel took the horn of oil and anointed him in the presence of his brothers.* Saul was still king, remember, and Samuel anointed David. Two kings at once? No wonder there was trouble ahead.

Whose idea was it to anoint two kings? Samuel would say that it was the Lord's. But what kind of a Maker did Samuel understand? He lived approximately three thousand years ago in a universe that was much smaller than ours. The stars were heavenly lights, as were the sun and the moon, all put there for our benefit. The planet was sparsely inhabited (compared with today's population). And backwards, according to our standards. Bathing was occasional. People probably smelled rank. There was no plumbing. No toilet paper. No electricity. But they had the patriarchs, Abraham, Isaac, and Jacob, and they knew the story of Creation, and at least some of the time they knew that the Creator, their God, was the God of the entire universe. The prophets talked, personally, with the Creator, and if they sometimes imposed their own will on what they assumed to be God's, that's what we still tend to do today. Samuel's God was sometimes a projection of Samuel. And there are people today whose image of God is not unlike an image of the prophet Samuel, with his white robes and flowing beard and fierce expression.

What image of God do we have?

It is usually formed early in our lives, and it is not easy to change. I am daily grateful that the God shown me by my parents was a God of love and a God of story. Both my parents came from devoutly Episcopal families, and in those days (is it still true today?) Episcopalians were Bible readers, daily Bible readers. My mother grew up in a household where there was daily family prayer. On Sundays the only game the children were allowed to play was the Bible game; they really knew the Bible.

And they knew that God loved them, and they told me stories of God's love.

One of the stories they told me, a parable we've heard so often that it tends to get blunted, is the parable of the Prodigal Son and the elder brother. We pay so much attention to the Prodigal Son that we forget that the parable is equally about the elder brother, a brother who is not forgiving or loving and who does not want his father to throw a party for the younger brother, who's gone off and had fun while the elder brother has stayed home and worked. He is dutiful but also judgmental and humorless and hard of heart.

This is a parable that does not end. The father goes out and tries to persuade the elder brother to come in, and the story stops there. Last winter I heard an end to it which moved me profoundly. The elder brother is so angry that he refuses to heed his father. He not only will not join the festivities, he leaves home in anger and goes to the city. Because he is intelligent and diligent he starts a successful business. He makes lots of money and has fine houses and clothes and jewelry and all the creature comforts and luxuries anybody could want. But after a while his riches begin to seem thin. He realizes that he is lonely. So he turns and makes his way home. And there is the father, grown old and tired, but still waiting lovingly for the elder brother just as he had waited for the Prodigal Son.

And that's what it's all about: God's love. God's unmerited, unqualified love, waiting for us. We don't have to deserve that love which is ours, ours whether we want it or not. If we don't want it, that love can be terrible indeed. But if we reach out for God with love, God's love will surround us. God made us, made us in love, and that love will never falter. Wherever we are, whatever we do, God's love for us is there, firm, steadfast, forever, and shown us in the love that came to us in Jesus Christ, in whose resurrection we are all newly born and fully alive.

Story as the Search
for Truth

4

TRUTH IS FRIGHTENING. Pontius Pilate knew that, and washed his hands of truth when he washed his hands of Jesus.

Truth is demanding. It won't let us sit comfortably. It knocks out our cozy smugness and casual condemnation. It makes us move. It? *It?* For truth we can read Jesus. Jesus *is* truth. If we accept that Jesus is truth, we accept an enormous demand: Jesus is wholly God, and Jesus is wholly human. Dare we believe that? If we believe in Jesus, we must. And immediately that takes truth out of the limited realm of literalism.

But a lot of the world, including the Christian world (sometimes I think especially the Christian world), is hung up on literalism, and therefore confuses truth and fact. Perhaps that's why someone caught reading a novel frequently looks embarrassed, and tries to hide the book, pretending that what he's really reading is a book on how to fix his lawn mower or take out his own appendix. Is this rather general fear of story not so much a fear that story is not true, as that it might actually be true? And what about the word *fiction?* For many people it means something that is made up, is not true.

Karl Barth wrote that he took the Bible far too seriously to take it literally. Why is that statement frightening to some people? There is no way that you can read the entire Bible seriously and take every word literally. Contradictions start in the first chapter of Genesis. There are two Creation stories, two stories of the making of Adam and Eve. And that is all right. The Bible is still true.

People have always told stories as they searched for truth. As our ancient ancestors sat around the campfire in front of their caves, they told the stories of their day in order to try to understand what their day had meant, what the truth of the mammoth hunt was, or the roar of the cave lion, or the falling in love of two young people. Bards and troubadours throughout the centuries have sung stories in order to give meaning to the events of human life. We read novels, go to the movies, watch television, in order to find out more about the human endeavor. As a child I read avidly and in stories I found truths which were not available in history or geography or social studies.

There is a prevalent illusion that nonfiction is factual and objective, and that when we read history we can find out what really happened. Not so! My mother was a Southerner and my father was a damnyankee, and I got two totally different versions of "the wa-ah," as my mother called what my father referred to as the Civil War. It's two very different wars, depending on the point of view.

After the "wa-ah" all anybody in my mother's family had was story. They had lost husbands and sons and homes and all worldly goods. They did not have enough to eat. Their houses had been burned. I have some of the family silver because it was buried under a live oak tree, and I have some of the portraits because they were cut out of the frames and buried, too. On one of my walls is an indifferent oil painting on wood of a landscape with a windmill. It is fascinating to me because there is a slash across the top made by a Yankee saber, and on the back is a crude chess or checkers board painted by the invading soldiers.

And I have stories. My great-grandmother, the first Madeleine L'Engle, had been her father's hostess when he was ambassador to Spain. After the war the young widow cut up her velvet and brocade ball gowns to make trousers for her little sons and dresses for her daughter; there was no material to buy, and no money to buy it with had there been. I have her Bible, with her markings, and occasional spots from tears, and they, too, tell the story of her long, full life, going from riches to rags, grieving for the death of her young husband. She is remembered with great affection by all who knew her, as a merry person, full of vitality, but my mother, who adored her, told me that after her husband was killed she never wore anything but black or white for the rest of her long life.

Would I want to do that? I miss my husband daily, but I live in a very different world from that of the first Madeleine L'Engle.

Her mother-in-law, my great-great-grandmother, was a storyteller, too. She wrote her memoirs for her descendants, a delightful treasure. One of my favorite stories is that of her friendship with an African princess. Greatie, as my mother called her great-grandmother, was the princess' only champion and friend. This African woman had been brought to Florida by a slave trader and set up in a house on Fort George Island, off Jacksonville, where she was isolated and desperately homesick. Greatie did what she believed to be right, whether it was considered proper or not. Once a week she had herself rowed down the river to spend the day with the princess, and they became intimate friends. It is from the stories of both Greatie and Madeleine L'Engle that I drew the background for my novel, *The Other Side of the Sun.* Is the novel true? I believe that it is. Much of it is not factual; indeed, there are many facts I would have no way of knowing. It is indeed a work of fiction. But it is, for me, true.

"But what," asked Pilate of Jesus, "is truth?"

William Blake writes, "Self-evident truth is one thing, and Truth the result of reasoning is another thing. Rational truth is not the truth of Christ, but the truth of Pilate."

For much of our lives we do need rational truth, the truth of Pilate. But we don't give our lives for it. History would be very different if Pilate had been willing to give his life for truth. But he was not. It was Jesus who willingly gave his life for truth, the truth of Love, the truth that goes beyond reason, through reason, and out on the other side. Such truth does not deny reason, but reason alone is not enough.

If truth and reason appear to be in conflict, then both must be re-examined, and scientists are as reluctant to do this tough work as are theologians. When the theory of plate tectonics and continental drift was first put forward (and how reasonable it seems now), the scientists got as upset as the theologians did when planet earth was displaced as the center of the universe. And as for those seven days of creation, nothing whatsoever is said in Genesis about God creating in human time. Isn't it rather arrogant of us to think that God had to use our ordinary, daily, wristwatch time? Scripture does make it clear that God's time and our time are not the same. The old hymn "a thousand ages in thy sight are but a moment past" reprises this. So why get so upset about the idea that God might have created in divine time, not human? What kind of a fact is this that people get so upset about? Facts are static, even comfortable, even when they are wrong! Truth pushes us to look at these facts in a new way, and that is not comfortable, so it usually meets with resistance.

◆ ◆ ◆

And how reasonable are we, with all our best efforts, able to be? Read two straightforward histories of any war, and you'll get two different wars, with the protagonists and antagonists reversed. No matter how objective the historian tries to be, personal bias will slip in, willy-nilly.

The Bible is not objective. Its stories are passionate, searching for truth (rather than fact), and searching most deeply in story. The story of David is one of the most complex and fascinating in the Bible, with its many prefigurings of Jesus. In working on *Certain Women* I discovered many more contradictions than I had remembered—two different ways of bringing David himself into the story, two different versions of Saul's death, for instance. But what the biblical narrator is trying to do is tell us the truth about King David, and the truth is more important than facts.

One of the major discoveries of the post-Newtonian sciences is that objectivity is, in fact, impossible. To look at something is to change it and to be changed by it.

Nevertheless there is still the common misconception, the illusion, that fact and truth are the same thing. No! We do not need faith for facts; we do need faith for truth. In his letter to Titus Paul speaks of the mystery of faith, and in Hebrews 11:1 he writes, *Now faith is the substance of things hoped for, the evidence of things not seen* (KJV).

The Bible has always challenged my imagination. But there have been many other stories that have opened doors and windows for me. The Greek and Roman myths I read when I was a child deal with basic truths that help illuminate my own problems. The myth of Sisyphus, for instance: there are many days when I feel like Sisyphus pushing that heavy rock up the mountain-side, panting, sweating, as I heave it up, up, get it almost to the top, only to have it slip out of my grasp and roll all the way back down the mountain so that I have to start over again. Such myths have lasted because they are true to our human condition.

And because when I read I read with my Christian bias, whether I want to or not, the myth of Sisyphus offers me another truth. Sisyphus had to push that rock up the mountain over and over again. Jesus had to carry the cross only once. When it was done, it was done.

Jesus, the storyteller, told of a man who had a plank of wood in his eye and yet criticized another man for having a speck of dust in his eye. *"You hypocrite,"* he said, *"first take the plank out of your own eye, and then you will see clearly to remove the speck from your brother's eye."* This parable, like most of Jesus' stories, is true. Why must it be factual? Are we supposed to think that a man actually had a large plank of wood in his eye? The parable is, instead, a true story about our unwillingness to see our own enormous faults, and our eagerness to point out much smaller faults in other people. However, it's a lot easier to see this story as factual rather than true. If we can make ourselves believe that the man had a beam of wood in his eye, literally, then we don't have to look at our own faults, be challenged by Jesus' story, or maybe even feel that we have to do something about our faults. Literalism is a terrible crippler, but it does tend to let us off the hook. Or do I mean the cross?

A Zen story which makes much the same point as the parable of the plank and the speck concerns two Buddhist monks returning from a pilgrimage. It is spring, and the rains have fallen, and they come to a river which is swollen and running swiftly, so that the stepping stones are covered with water. A young girl stands by the river, afraid to cross, and the senior monk simply picks her up, sloshes across, sets her down on the other side, and continues on his way. About an hour later the younger monk speaks. "Forgive me, I know you are older and wiser than I, and have been longer in the religious life, but do you really think that it was right for you, a celibate monk, to pick up that young girl in your arms and carry her that way?" And the older monk replied, "Oh, my son, are you still carrying her?"

How easy it is for us to project our own weaknesses onto other people.

I was once criticized for telling this story because it is a Buddhist story and therefore had to contradict Christianity. But does it? Should we not learn from each other? Jesus lived in a small world with many nations, and in his stories there are not only Samaritans, but Syro-Phoenicians, Romans—and many others. The stories of all nations I read as a child helped me to understand—intuitively rather than consciously—my own development as a human being, a Christian human being. And perhaps I learned even more from the stories I wrote.

James Carroll, in *The Communion of Saints*, writes, "The very act of story-telling, of arranging memory and invention according to the structure of the narrative, is by definition holy. . . . We tell stories because we can't help it. We tell stories because we love to entertain and hope to edify. We tell stories because they fill the silence death imposes. We tell stories because they save us."

My great-great-grandmother, great-grandmother, grandmother, mother are alive for me because they are part of my story. My children and grandchildren and I tell stories about Hugh, my husband. We laugh and we remember—*re-member*. I tell stories about my friend, the theologian Canon Tallis, who was far more than my spiritual director, with whom I had one of those wonders, a spiritual friendship. I do not believe that these stories are their immortality—that is something quite different. But remembering their stories is the best way I know to have them remain part of my mortal life. And I need them to be part of me, while at the same time I am quite willing for them all to be doing whatever it is that God has in mind for them to do. Can those who are part of that great cloud of witnesses which has gone before us be in two places at once? I believe that they can, just as Jesus could, after the Resurrection.

Let me tell you a story. Early in January of 1990 I was on a small boat with my eldest daughter and her family. This was a wonderful and special treat for us, and we were having a glorious time. One night I went to bed, read for a while, turned out the light, and went to sleep. After a while I slid into wakefulness, and I was aware that Hugh, my husband, was in bed with me, and it seemed perfectly natural for him to be there. I was in that state of consciousness that is neither dream nor waking, and I was grateful for his presence, though I knew that I must move carefully and not touch him, because if I did, he would vanish.

At the time that I was having this sense of Hugh's presence, around midnight or a little later, a radio call for us came through on the loudspeaker, and Josephine and Alan heard it and went to the radio room. There they learned that our beloved Tallis had died. They did not wake me. Early the next morning while I was drinking coffee, Alan came to my cabin and told me.

Later that day I told my daughter of my experience of the night before. She is brilliant and mathematical and eminently reasonable, and I asked her rather tentatively, "Do you think your father was there to tell me about Tallis?"

And she replied, "Well, Mother, that thought had crossed my mind."

Certainly it is outside the realm of reason and provable fact, but for me it touches the hem of truth. And the important thing is that I don't need to know anything more than what, for me, happened. That's all. That's enough.

I wish the church would be brave enough to acknowledge that there are questions to which, during our mortal lives, we have no answers. Too many answers lead to judgmentalism and to human beings (rather than God) deciding who can and who cannot go to heaven. I have a young friend whose father was unable to speak or move for weeks before his death, and his young son was devastated because, as far as he knew, his father had not accepted Jesus Christ as his personal Saviour. "Please don't underestimate the power of Christ's love," I implored.

"You have no way of knowing what Christ was doing with your father during those weeks when he could not speak and tell you what was going on within him. If you believe that God is love . . ."

"I do."

"Then trust that Love with your father."

I trust that love.

Does this mean that I do not believe in heaven—or hell, as punishment for our sins?

No. But I do not believe in the medieval versions of heaven and hell. Heaven, for one thing, sounds unutterably dull, and I do not believe that God is ever dull.

In Ellis Peter's *The Heretic's Apprentice*, the young heretic talks about his feelings over the eternal damnation of infants who have died before they were baptized. "A human father wouldn't throw his baby into the flames," he protests. "Why would God do such a thing?"

His heresy is a heresy of love as, indeed, are many heresies. Why do human beings seem to feel the need to have other human beings suffer the torments of hell fire in order to be happy in heaven? I share the young heretic's heresy, though I do not believe it to be heresy. And I do not believe that God's love will ever fail. I do not know what lessons of love my husband or my friend Tallis are learning right now, but I believe that they are learning, going from strength to strength in understanding the astounding love of God for Creation.

But again we are in the language of mystery, not finite fact.

And yet again, like jesting Pilate, we may continue to ask, "What is truth?" And unless we allow truth to be a widening light, we hamstring ourselves. Love, for instance, is beyond the realm of provable fact. Why did my heart open for this man, rather than another? Why does my instinct tell me to say yes, here, and no, there? Why does this piece of music move me to tears, and that leave me cold? Since Hugh's death there are certain hymns I cannot sing without my eyes filling. We sang "A Mighty Fortress Is Our God" at both my mother's and my husband's funerals, and yet I can sing that strong affirmation without heaving with emotion. But I cannot sing "I Am the Bread of Life" without tear-ing up.

♦ ♦ ♦

When I was in high school and college I looked at some of my mother's friends (all good, Christian, church-going women) and thought, *If this is what it means to be grown-up, I don't want it.*

Not my mother herself: she was a remarkable Southern woman, who, long before I was born, had ridden across the Sahara on a camel, and up the Andes on a donkey. In North Africa, in those days before planes, there were often long waits at desolate railroad stations, and my parents, with a couple of my father's journalist colleagues, would spread a blanket out on the platform and would play Halma. Halma, which is to Chinese Checkers more or less what chess is to checkers, was originally an Arab game, and they would often be ringed by Arabs, betting on them. Predictably, they bet on the men. It was a mistake. My mother, who had a mathematical sharpness I have not inherited, almost always won. No, it was not my mother who made me reluctant to be grown-up, but some of the women around her who had closed in, shut down, lost interest in new ideas, went to church to be safe, not challenged, who had forgotten how to play, forgotten story, forgotten how to laugh.

If we limit ourselves to the possible and provable, as I saw these people doing, we render ourselves incapable of change and growth, and that is something that should never end. If we limit ourselves to the age that we are, and forget all the ages that we have been, we diminish our truth.

Perhaps it is the child within us who is able to recognize the truth of story—the mysterious, the numinous, the unexplainable—and the grown-up within us who accepts these qualities with joy but understands that we also have responsibilities, that a promise is to be kept, homework is to be done, that we owe other people courtesy and consideration, and that we need to help care for our planet because it's the only one we've got.

I never want to lose the story-loving child within me, or the adolescent, or the young woman, or the middle-aged one, because all together they help me to be fully alive on this journey, and show me that I must be willing to go where it takes me, even through the valley of the shadow.

◆ ◆ ◆

For centuries there have been stories that have been part of the vocabulary of even the moderately educated person. The great stories from Scripture, the Greek and Roman myths, the Arthurian legends, for instance. Pat, my physician friend, sent me the following quotation from the *Journal of Occupational Medicine*, taken, in turn, from Allan Bloom's *The Closing of the American Mind:*

When I first noticed the decline in reading during the late sixties, I began asking my large introductory classes and any other group of younger students to which I spoke what books really counted for them? Most were silent, puzzled by the question. The notion of books as companions was foreign to them. Justice Black with his tattered copy of the Constitution in his pocket at all times is not an example that would mean much to them. There was no printed word to which they looked for counsel, inspiration, or for joy.

I hope that that is too radical a response to what has happened to our reading habits. While it is to some extent true, I hope that it is not wholly true, and I think that it is not, because of the large number of readers who write to me recommending and often sending me books they think I would enjoy, or who tell me that they turn to my stories for courage and comfort when they are in need. And I am encouraged, too, by my granddaughters and their college friends, and by their groans of anguish and ecstasy when they tell about the large sums of money they have just spent on books, not all of which are for their college courses.

But there is, alas, no doubt that we are becoming a vocabulary-deprived nation—nay, planet. Words have been dropping off all through this century, but the loss increased radically in the sixties with the immorality of "limited vocabulary." How on earth is a child going to learn words if the vocabulary is limited to what some "average" child is expected to know at the age of five or six or seven? When I was a child and came across a word I did not know in a story, I just went on reading, and by the time I had come across the word in two or three books, I had absorbed what it meant. It was easier for me to read Shakespeare in high school than it is for students today, not because my contemporaries and I were any brighter, but because far more vocabulary was familiar and available to us than to comparable students today.

We can, of course, dump the blame on television, but I don't think it's television alone that stops people from reading. It is, I suspect, fear of story, fear of imagination, fear of the unexplainable. The less vocabulary we have, the more limited our words, the more frightening the imagination becomes.

Allan Bloom continues,

Imagine such a young person walking through the Louvre or the Uffizi and you can immediately grasp the condition of his soul. In his ignorance of the stories of Biblical or Greek or Roman Antiquity, Raphael, Leonardo, Michelangelo, Rembrandt, and all the others, can say nothing to him.

It is ironic that my little grandsons are mad about Mutant Ninja Turtles, and their parents have had to explain to them that Leonardo and Raphael and Michelangelo were real artists who lived and painted and sculpted hundreds of years ago. My grandsons find it difficult to understand that they weren't turtles. At least they are learning about great artists as well as turtles.

Bloom points out that these artists expected their viewers to recognize their subjects, to know the stories, and to have been influenced by them intellectually and spiritually. When such potent recognition no longer exists, Bloom says, "the voice of civilization has been stilled. It is meaning itself that vanishes beyond the dissolving horizon."

Meaning that vanishes?

Truth that vanishes?

And can the two be separated?

And how do we come to meaning and truth except through story?

The story of Abraham and Sarah, of Gideon, of Miriam, of David and Abigail, and finally, the story of Jesus of Nazareth—these affirm and reaffirm meaning for us.

Story helps us with the questions that have no answers. I wish the Church (of all denominations) would be brave enough to acknowledge that there are questions which, during our mortal lives, are not going to be answered. There are no answers to the wonder of Creation, the marvel of the Incarnation, the glory of the Resurrection. Too many answers lead to smug self-righteousness and—even worse—to human beings, rather than God, deciding who is and who is not loved by the Maker. Can't we trust God?

◆ ◆ ◆

The storyteller is a storyteller because the storyteller cares about truth, searching for truth, expressing truth, sharing truth. But that cannot be done unless we know our craft, any more than a violinist can play Sibelius's Violin Concerto unless the techniques are there, learned, until they are deep in the fingertips as well as the mind.

When I teach a writers' workshop, all I can teach are techniques. One cannot teach "creative writing." Such writing is a gift, but the gift cannot be served unless the techniques have been learned thoroughly enough to become instinctive.

The best teachers of writing are the great writers themselves. If we read enough, certain truths become self-evident. There are certain things the great writers always do, and certain things they never do, and a proper study of their works will show us what these are.

Some of their words about their work are also helpful: Maritain says, "Fiction differs from every other art in one respect: it concerns the conduct of life itself." That is, it looks at what human beings do and tries to find the truth of it.

Conrad says, "The novelist's first task is to make us see." To make us see not only the readily visible—the sunset over the Litchfield Hills, the snow falling, slanting in from the east, the tooth marks on the fresh-cut wood of a tree the beavers have felled. But also to see the less readily visible—the anger couched in exquisite courtesy, the self-sacrifice given in such a way as to be hardly noticeable, the carefully hidden anguish in the eyes of someone who has been betrayed. The novelist helps us to see things we might not notice otherwise. With a few strokes the biblical narrator shows the confusion of love and hate in Saul's daughter Michal, the quiet wisdom in Abigail, David's growth in honor and true royalty.

And Henry James: "Our task is to render, not report." Show; do not tell. Thus, in fiction the verbs are active, not passive; "did," not "was." "She lost her balance," not "Her balance was lost." The great writer does not tell us what ought to be done, or what we think. The true writer shows us what *is* done, avoiding author's comment. The storyteller doesn't talk about the story, but shows it, immediately locating the characters in time and space. In *Anna Karenina* we learn at once that

Everything was in confusion in the Oblonskys' house. The wife had discovered that the husband was carrying on an intrigue with a French girl, who had been a governess in their family, and she had anounced to her husband that she could not go on living in the same house with him. . . . Three days after the quarrel, Prince Stepan Arkadyevitch Oblonsky woke up at his usual hour, that is, at eight o'clock in the morning, not in his wife's bedroom, but on the leather-covered sofa in his study.

How much we learn in a few sentences!

Aristotle: "A play is an imitation of an action of a certain magnitude." This holds true for any work of fiction. The novelist writes about drama in people's lives, infidelities, discoveries, unexpected love, tragedy, resolution. The characters, the action, are depicted larger than life in order that we may see them more clearly.

Chekhov: "The aim of fiction is absolute and honest truth." Truth, mind you, not fact, that truth which we find in a man and woman eating an apple out of season; in the horror of brother killing brother; in an ark riding out a terrible flood. That truth which we find most ultimately in the story of the Maker of the Universe coming to us through the womb of a young girl.

It has often been said that the perfect form in art is a circle. That is why, when it was discovered that the planets move around the sun in ellipses, rather than perfect circles, the church establishment was horrified! In fiction, too, the perfect form is a circle—though it may be more of an ellipse. The plot of Oedipus has often been called the perfect plot, and it can be diagrammed, as can any other masterpiece, in the following way:

Draw a circle and put a line down the middle. The left half of the circle is marked *C,* for complication. The right side of the circle is marked *R,* for resolution. Now surround the circle with another circle. The left side of this outside circle is marked *D,* for discovery, and the right side *P,* for peripety.

C: In every great work there is a complication. The resolution is embedded in the complication, but in such a way that it registers only subconsciously. It is foreshadowed in the complication. For instance, in Ionesco's play *Rhinoceros,* the complication is the first rhinoceros crossing the square of a French town on a normal Sunday morning. The reaction of the people in the square foreshadows the resolution, the willingness of the inhabitants to accept the rhinoceros, and finally to become beasts themselves.

In Scripture the complication in the story of David starts before he himself comes on the scene, with the demand of the people to have a king. The resolution is foreshadowed in David's honor in refusing to kill Saul when he has the perfect opportunity and is completed in the life of Jesus, who refuses to be an earthly king, but is, instead, the servant.

R: In the great storytelling there is usually an indication of the resolution in the first sentence. In Chekhov's story *Vanka,* Chekhov states, "Nine-year-old Vanka Jukov, who has been apprenticed to the shoemaker Aliakhine for three months, did not go to bed the night before Christmas." In the resolution he finally manages to doze off, dreaming of the freedom of other Christmases before he knew the brutality of the shoemaker.

The first sentence of Hemingway's *Farewell to Arms* is, "The leaves fell early that year." In that first line we have a foreshadowing of love dying young, a hint that before the end of the plot the hero's heart will be as bare and ruined as the trees and the roads.

When young David takes his harp and sings for the anguished old king, Saul, there is a hint that David, too, one day will be old.

D: The discovery is an event that does far more than foreshadow the resolution. It makes the resolution inevitable. In *Medea*, it is Medea's discovery—that she cannot keep Creon from banishing her in order to free Jason to marry Creon's daughter—that makes absolutely inevitable the tragedies that follow.

In Genesis it is, of course, the disobedience of the human beings, making it inevitable that redemption can come only through God completely entering into the story in the life of Jesus.

P: Peripety is an unforseen event that precipitates the dénouement. It is unforeseen, but probable. It is not a coincidence. According to the dictionary it is a reversal. In fiction it is often a change from love to hate, or from ignorance to knowledge. In *Oedipus* it was the unexpected arrival of the messenger from Corinth to tell of Polybus' death. In Scripture we might look at Jonah and Jonah's surprise when the Ninevites repent, and Jonah and all of us who read his story have to think about human unforgiveness and divine forgiveness.

We are reminded by *Oedipus*, as by every masterpiece, that the hero always has a tragic flaw. Almost invariably this flaw is *hubris*, pride, as it is in King Saul, Macbeth, Faust.

It is interesting in this Trinitarian world how often the great storytellers do things in threes, because the storyteller knows that the reader can't register a thing if he's told only once. For instance, Oedipus tries to project his guilt first on Tiresias, then on Creon, then on Jocasta.

King Lear asks the same question of his three daughters. Macbeth is tempted by three witches and starts his career of murdering first with Duncan, then Duncan's servants, then Banquo. Satan offers Jesus three temptations. Peter denies Jesus three times. In John's first epistle we read: *For there are three that testify: the Spirit, the water and the blood; and the three are in agreement.*

Even a description is usually done in threes, and the third thing is usually sound. In *Madame Bovary* we read:

> Now the sky was blue, and the leaves were still. There were clearings full of heather in bloom, and the sheets of purple alternated with the multi-colored tangle of the trees, grey, fawn, and gold. Often a faint rustling and fluttering of wings would come from under the bushes; or there would be the cry, at once raucous and sweet, of crows flying off among the oaks.

It is an interesting thing, in wondering why sound comes last, to remember that in the physical world light travels faster than sound. We *see* before we *hear*.

The storyteller never goes back into the past until he has made us sure of the present. He never puts the cart before the horse, as the beginning writer tends to do. He puts the explanation *after,* the action *first.* In conversation the gesture, posture, tone of voice of the speaker is put *first*, the words *after*, as in Lewis Carroll's *Alice in Wonderland*, where we read,

> The Fish-Footman began by producing from under his arm a great letter, nearly as large as himself, and this he handed over to the other, saying in a solemn tone, "For the Duchess. An invitation from the Queen to play croquet."

In the story of David and Bathsheba, we read, *The woman conceived and sent word to David, saying, "I am pregnant."* If the speech is put first it gives the effect of a disembodied voice.

The great storyteller sets the scene immediately, never leaving us stranded in outer space. The word *scene* comes from the Greek word meaning "tent," because the first Greek plays were held in a tent. This contains the scene, and in setting the scene immediately, the storyteller focuses the action.

2 Samuel chapter 11 starts,

In the spring, at the time when kings go off to war, David sent Joab out with the king's men and the whole Israelite army. They destroyed the Ammonites and besieged Rabbah. But David remained in Jerusalem. One evening David got up from his bed and walked around on the roof of the palace. From the roof he saw a woman bathing. The woman was very beautiful.

The scene is superbly set for David's adultery with Bathsheba.

In *Sir Gawain and the Green Knight* the scene is set thus:

King Arthur lay at Camelot upon a Christmas-tide, with many a gallant lord and lovely lady, and all the noble brotherhood of the Round Table. There they held rich revels with gay talk and jest; one while they would ride forth to joust and tourney, and again back to court to make carols; for there was the feast holden fifteen days with all the mirth that man could devise, song and glee, glorious to hear. Halls and chambers were crowded with noble guests, the bravest of knights and the loveliest of ladies, and Arthur himself was the comeliest king that ever held a court.

In *Madame Bovary* we have our perfect example of attention to the literal level. As a matter of fact, *Madame Bovary* is often referred to as the perfect novel, and I have read it several times to try to learn from it. But it is not a lovable novel just because it is perfect. I learn more about love from *Anna Karenina*, which is full of imperfections. However, there is much about the technique of fiction to be learned from *Bovary*. Every page is fully developed with sensory details. Flaubert also gives us our perfect example of the long view and the short view.

A long view:

Daylight, coming through the windows of plain glass, falls obliquely on the pews, and here and there on the wall from which they jut out at right angles is tacked a bit of straw matting, with the name of the pew-holder in large letters below. Beyond, where the nave narrows, stands the confessional, and opposite it a statuette of the Virgin: she is dressed in a satin gown and a tulle veil spangled with silver stars, and her cheeks are daubed red like some idol from the Sandwich Islands.

A short view:

As he crossed the roofed market he stopped behind a pillar to stare for the last time at the white house with its four green shutters. He thought he saw a shadowy form at the bedroom window; then the curtain, released from its hook as though of its own accord, swung slowly for a moment in long slanting folds and sprang fully out to hang straight and motionless as a plaster wall. Leon set off at a run.

Flaubert makes his long views as detailed as his short ones. The fundamental difference between a long and a short view is in Time. A short view is located in Time as well as in Space. The master snatches the telling moment (David rose from his bed and walked on the roof)—the moment that may stand for many other moments.

Viewpoint: the storyteller must establish a viewpoint as soon as possible. For most of the story of David we see it from his point of view, his honor in refusing to kill Saul, his lust in taking Bathsheba, his repentance, his grief at the loss of their baby. When David is told that the child has died, he

> *got up from the ground. After he had washed, put on lotions and changed his clothes, he went into the house of the LORD and worshiped. Then he went to his own house, and at his request they served him food, and he ate.*

Point of view is often difficult for the beginning writer. There are three (three again!) customary ways to tell a story:

1: First Person Narrator

This may seem the most straightforward and easy way to tell a story. Actually it is supremely difficult. The narrator may be a villain, a hero, a moron, a madman. He may be ignorant of things the reader must know. He may reveal the truth through telling lies. F. Scott Fitzgerald tells *The Great Gatsby* in the first person. "In my younger and more vulnerable years my father gave me some advice that I've been turning over in my mind ever since."

Milton's "Lycidas" is also written in the first person:

Bitter constraint and sad occasion dear
Compels me to disturb your season due:
For Lycidas is dead, dead ere his prime,
Young Lycidas, and hath not left his peer.

Milton knew Scripture, and might not have been able to write about the death of Lycidas had he not been familiar with David's song of grief for Saul and Jonathan, also in first person:

The beauty of Israel is slain on your high places!
How the mighty have fallen!
Tell it not in Gath,
Proclaim it not in the streets of Ashkelon . . .
How the mighty have fallen in the midst of the battle!
Jonathan was slain in your high places.

2: *The Concealed Narrator*

Flaubert's *Madame Bovary* (again) is the perfect example of this. I find it a comfortable point of view for this particular time and place in our history. Action moves swiftly from this point of view and can reflect the continuing changes in the world around us and the way it affects our lives. Much of David's story is told from the point of view of the concealed narrator, straightforwardly, as in the adultery with Bathsheba or, much earlier in Scripture, in the story of Adam and Eve.

Scripture, in fact, uses all points of view, and we can learn much of storytelling from the biblical narrator.

3: *The Omniscient Narrator.*

This is a very ancient method. Homer used it in *The Iliad* and *The Odyssey.* Tolstoy use it in *Anna Karenina;* Dickens, Thackeray, Stendhal all used this point of view, and it was certainly very popular with the Victorians, where the storyteller knows everything: "Had she only realized, dear reader, what lay on the other side of the door, she would never have opened it." Many works written from the point of view of the omniscient narrator are leisurely and long. Alas, nowadays if I am given a book of six or seven hundred pages I hesitate to start it; where am I going to find the time?

Longevity is seldom the problem of the beginning storyteller, who often scants the literal level. The inexperienced writer often starts a story in disembodied space, instead of being specific, as for instance, Faulkner is in the beginning of *Intruder in the Dust*, which starts,

> It was just noon that Sunday morning when the sheriff reached the jail with Lucas Beachamp, though the whole town (the whole county, too, for that matter) had known since the night before that Lucas had killed a white man.

All the facts are given us swiftly, those four important Ws:

> *Who* the story is about.
> *What* the person is doing.
> *Where* the person is doing it.
> *When* the person is doing it.

In reading the writers I most admire, I have noticed that they do not put a lot of ideas into one sentence, but usually have one point in each sentence. For instance, Thomas Mann in *The Magic Mountain* uses three sentences to tell us three things (three again):

He was dressed for out-of-doors, in sports clothes and stout boots, and carried his ulster under his arm. The outline of the flat bottle could be seen on the side pocket. As yesterday he wore no hat.

Romain Rolland in *Jean Christophe* does the same: "The day after Rosa was alone. They had given up the struggle. But she had gained nothing by it save resentment from Christophe." And yet once again we realize that the great storyteller shows us what is going on, rather than talking about it.

Beginning a book can sometimes be the most difficult part of the whole enterprise. The first paragraph of a novel should set up the entire story. Often I have had to write my way into a story, and when I have arrived at the beginning, then I cut the paragraphs or even pages which preceded it. These were not wasted effort; they were necessary to get me to the beginning of the story, but then I must have the courage to cut them out. This book about story began, originally, with the beavers making a lake for us at Crosswicks, and it wasn't until long after last July 28 that I knew where to begin.

The storyteller must learn the craft in order to seek the truth.

◆ ◆ ◆

In the spring of 1990 I gave a talk at Wheaton College in Illinois. Wheaton has always been a "safe" place for me, where I have felt that my stories have been loved and understood, and where I have learned much about God's love. Clyde Kilby and Mel Lorentzen "discovered" me as a writer who is a Christian, and their understanding has always been a great treasure to me. I have been going to Wheaton for a quarter of a century, and it is a special place, a place where I truly have felt "at home."

On this particular occasion I was to give an open talk for the public in general as well as for the college community, and I talked about story and truth, and the talk was from my heart. It was warmly received, but when I opened to questions I had my first experience of public heckling. There were people there, noncollege people, who had come with an agenda, and who asked questions to which they did not want answers. Many of the questions came from misconceptions about my science fantasy *A Wrinkle in Time*.

When *Wrinkle* was published in 1962 it was discovered by the evangelical world as a book written about a universe created by a power of love, and entered into by Very God Elself. It was through *Wrinkle* that my happy connection with Wheaton began. When Clyde Kilby asked me if I would consider donating my papers to Wheaton I was thrilled. It was a tremendous honor to be housed under the same roof as my beloved George MacDonald, Dorothy Sayers, Tolkien, C.S. Lewis, Charles Williams, and G.K. Chesterton. And when, a few years ago, Frederick Buechner and Luci Shaw, among others, agreed to give their papers to the college, I was delighted.

So what was happening during the Question-and-Answer session that evening at Wheaton was all the more strange and unexpected, even though I realized quickly that my attackers came from the outside.

"You are writing about a medium," one woman accused.

"No, no," I said. "She's a *happy* medium."

She repeated, "You're writing about a *medium*."

"Meg was always accused of never having a happy medium," I explained, "so I gave her one. It's a play on words. It's a joke. It's funny."

The students thought it was funny. The questioners didn't.

"You are putting Jesus on a par with Einstein and Buddha," I was told. This accusation was based on the page where the children are listing those on our planet who have fought against evil. They start with Jesus, and then go on to name some of the other men and women who have sought the truth. This, I felt, was completely scriptural, in accordance with that marvelous passage of Paul's:

And we know that in all things God works for the good of those who love him, who have been called according to his purpose. For those God foreknew he also predestined to be conformed to the likeness of his Son, that he might be the firstborn among many brothers.

I tried to explain that no, I was not putting Jesus on a par with Einstein and Buddha, and I tried to quote from Paul and was interrupted with the reiteration that I was putting Jesus on a par with Einstein and Buddha until finally I had to say, "Please will you let me finish quoting Paul," which I was able to do only with further interruptions.

When I managed to finish, the attacker simply repeated, "You are putting Jesus on a par with Einstein and Buddha."

At that I replied, "Lady, I am not putting Jesus on a par with Einstein and Buddha. You are." Which the students appreciated. It was true. I wasn't. She was.

But the saddest question of all was, "Do you believe in the *literal fact* of the Resurrection?"

I replied, "I stand with Paul: No Resurrection, no Christianity. But you can't cram the glory of the Resurrection into a fact. It's true! It's what we live by!" Had the questioner not heard a word of my talk?

What the antagonists did with their slings and arrows was to turn the majority of the audience to my side, which certainly helped take the bitter taste out of my mouth. I thought that was the end of it.

But one of the attackers, a large donor to the college, wanted all my papers to be removed from the library. This woman had taped my talk, had had it transcribed and was passing it around. First of all, this isn't legal. It is a serious infringement of copyright law. And it is certainly not courteous. But worse than that, in her transcription she cut out any reference I had made to myself as a Christian, and that was deliberate misrepresentation.

The dean called me from Wheaton to talk about this and I said, "I'm afraid Mrs. X would not want me to pray for her, but that is all I know to do." Not to coerce or demand, just to offer this woman and all her anxiety and anger to God for healing love. And I don't need to know how God is going to heal. That is up to the Creator, not me. And all the while I know that I, too, am in need of that healing love.

This was not the first time my books have been attacked, nor the first time that I have written about it. But it is the first time that the attacks have been personal. I cannot pretend that it wasn't disturbing. It was. Obviously I am still wrestling with it.

The Sunday after the Wheaton dean's phone call the Epistle for the day was from Peter's first letter. He urges Christians to love one another. And he writes,

Who is going to harm you if you are eager to do good? But even if you should suffer for what is right, you are blessed. Do not fear what they fear; do not be frightened. . . . Above all, love each other deeply, because love covers over a multitude of sins. . . . Dear friends, do not be surprised at the painful trial you are suffering, as though something strange were happening to you. But rejoice that you participate in the sufferings of Christ, so that you may be overjoyed when his glory is revealed. If you are insulted because of the name of Christ, you are blessed, for the Spirit of glory and of God rests on you. . . . If you suffer as a Christian, do not be ashamed, but praise God that you bear that name.

How do I glorify God in this matter? I think the only way I know is to continue to write what is given me, to write to the best of my ability. I wrote *A Wrinkle in Time* as a hymn of praise to God, so I must let it stand as it is and not be fearful when it is misunderstood.

What is the difference between those who attack me, and me, myself? Perhaps the main difference is that my faith is not seriously threatened because it is not literal but remains open to question and revelation. It is not always a comfortable faith; it prods and pushes me. I am a little wistful about the faith of some of my friends which is deep and strong and simple and—yes—literal. And I would never wish to shake it. That would be a kind of faithlessness on my part. But I also don't want anybody to try to take away my faith because it is not exactly like someone else's.

118

And I would be quite content, I truly would, to have Mrs. X and the other attackers come to my dinner table and share a meal, because surely we are all children of God.

I do not feel that I need to protect God as the attackers that night in Wheaton seemed to feel the need to do. I don't think God needs our protection! God is All in All, and all that Love's radiance asks is our love in return, not our protection. Indeed, in him there is no darkness at all, but there is darkness in us whenever we turn our backs on love. If I am secure in God's perfect love I will have no fear, for love casts out fear.

Knowledge is changeable (as Adam and Eve found out), but truth is eternal. Therefore, any change in knowledge does not in the least threaten or affect truth. So let us trust truth, that truth that was incarnate for us in Jesus.

Story as Scripture

5

MY PARENTS GAVE ME the great gift of faith in God who is a God of love, total love. It is ironic that because of my father's precarious health and his late hours as a drama and music critic, I went with my parents on Sunday to a late church service or to Evensong and did not go to Sunday school. Unlike many people I have encountered, I have not had to spend a lot of my adult life unlearning the horrors of an angry God, horrors that are often taught in Sunday school, so that it is difficult for some people to understand that God is a God of love and forgiveness, not one who is out to punish us as harshly as possible for all our wrongdoings.

Another misconception is of Jesus as a sad, self-pitying man who is not the wild and powerful and often unpredictable Jesus of Scripture. He was, as Isaiah prophesies, a man of sorrows, yes, but he was also a man of great joy, humor, and formidable authority.

Perhaps it is because I was never fed platitudes in Sunday school, or taught about God's wrath toward our total depravity, that I approached the Bible with no preconceptions. I went to the Bible as I went to any storybook, and it is indeed the greatest storybook I have ever encountered, far more exciting than *The Arabian Nights!* The story of Joseph and his dreams was a favorite from Hebrew Scripture, and in the New Testament I especially loved Jesus' appearing to Mary Magdalene after the Resurrection.

When I was a child God was God. Because the eight- or nine-year-old child does not think in terms of sex in general, neither did I in particular, and certainly not about God. God was All in All. God filled every single human need, be it for father, mother, lover, sister, brother, friend. Even when I became a "grown-up" I never thought of the God I prayed to as exclusively male.

And because I read the Bible as a storybook, not a moral tract (which it is not), I read it with pleasure (surely God's Word should be pleasing to us!), and I read it for fun. I read it as play, not work, and surely that is how it ought to be read. Jesus had a marvelous sense of fun, of play. It is one of the sorrows of the Fall that work has become drudgery, rather than play. My actor husband and I were blessed that our work was also our play.

I also read the Bible stories for comfort. I was not a successful child at school. At home there was constant tension caused by my father's war-injured lungs and his long years of dying. I took my grief to the Bible for healing. I cannot think of any human grief that is not expressed for us in the Bible, from the very beginning stories in Genesis.

Misunderstanding between husband and wife: Adam and Eve. And, of course, Hosea, though Hosea was not one of the books of the Bible I read as a child. I had to be older before I could understand Hosea's grieving for his unfaithful wife and loving her nevertheless. His whole book is a hymn of mourning, an icon of that healthy grief that makes whole rather than destroys.

Anguish over children: Adam and Eve again. Even worse than Abel's death must have been knowing their first-born child to be a murderer. This, too, I was going to have to wait to understand. All I knew as a child was that I often disappointed my parents, and that brought them grief. But their focus was more on the things I did that pleased them than on my faults, and I am grateful for that affirmation. Some parents define their children by negatives, by who they are not. ("Why didn't you call me?" "Why aren't you more like your sister?" "Why can't you be more polite?") My parents defined me by who I was ("You have such pretty handwriting." "Thank you for waiting for me." "I'm glad you enjoyed dinner."), and that helped me to grow in a healthy way.

King David's children caused him much grief: Amnon, his first born, with unbridled lust raped his half sister Tamar; Tamar's full brother, Absalom, was outraged and had Amnon killed. Then he turned against his father, and Absalom's death pierced David through the heart.

Childlessness: Three women of the Bible—Sarah and Elizabeth and Hannah—went through many years of being barren. So did my mother. I was a child who came late to my parents. Being barren in biblical times carried with it an onus that it doesn't have today. Sarah, Elizabeth, and Hannah not only mourned their inability to bear a child, but had to bear the scorn of their friends and neighbors and even their husbands.

It wasn't until I had children of my own that I understood my mother's joy, Sarah's joy, and Elizabeth's, and Hannah's at the birth of a child. Moses' older sister, Miriam, is a heroine, given less credit than she deserves for her courage in putting Moses in the basket of bulrushes, offering him to the Egyptian princess, getting her mother to be his wet nurse; for her dance of joy; for the wisdom she shared with her brothers.

There is also Moses' rage at the golden calf, his wild expression of grief and anger at the faithlessness of his people and their lack of obedience to the God who had saved them and led them out of Egypt.

The grief over faithlessness is sounded over and over again in the Psalms and all through the story of King David himself. There is also grief at untimely death: David's nephew, Asahel, cut down by Saul's captain because he will not turn aside when warned. In *Certain Women* Nik, the playwright, shows Asahel's mother's grief in the scene where the elder brothers bury their youngest brother. Then there is David's grief at Saul's madness and folly, his grief at Saul's and Jonathan's deaths. Much of the grief and anger are worked out in the Psalms, yet always there is the final affirmation that God can forgive us and love us no matter how faithless we are, if only we will stop and turn to our Maker.

And who is our Maker? I have trouble with the God in Deuteronomy who is far too often the God we think of as the God of the Old Testament, the tribal, local god who wants his people not only to take over the land, but to get rid of everybody in it, and if they don't do it he will curse them:

The LORD will send on you curses, confusion and rebuke in everything you put your hand to, until you are destroyed and come to sudden ruin . . . The LORD will strike you with wasting disease, with fever and inflammation, with scorching heat and drought, with blight and mildew. . . . [Y]ou will eat the fruit of the womb, the flesh of the sons and daughters the LORD your God has given you.

I shudder. That is not the God who so loved the world that he sent his only begotten son, because we are so beloved. The God of retribution is a limited, primitive, human view of God, as our view of God is always limited, and human, and probably still pretty primitive. Moses, Miriam, and Aaron lived in a very primitive world of people and gods vying for power, and sometimes we seem to have learned little from their stories.

So it is all the more extraordinary that Jesus renounced personal power. He made it very clear that the power was his heavenly Father's, not his.

Once when I was in England I saw a splendid TV series on the life of Jesus. When the Pharisees were trying to trap him by asking whether or not it is right to pay tribute money to Caesar, the actor playing Jesus laughed heartily and said, "Give me a coin!", turning away anger with laughter. Turning things upside-down and inside out as usual.

To some people it is terrifying to look at any Bible story in a way different from what was taught in Sunday school (and are *all* Sunday school teachers truly and fully qualified to teach the Word of God to children?), but Jesus did that all the time. Matthew quotes Jesus:

You have heard that it was said, "Eye for eye, and tooth for tooth." But I tell you, Do not resist an evil person. If someone strikes you on the right cheek, turn to him the other also.

125

And if someone wants to sue you and take your tunic, let him have your cloak as well.

What do we think of that? Do we obey the old Law, or the law of Jesus?

A recovering fundamentalist said to me that she had been taught never to question anything that anyone in the Bible did or said, because they were all holy people of God and could do no wrong! There are many of them who were holy people of God, but they did much wrong! God's people then and now are human and fallible. Both Abraham and Isaac passed their wives off as their sisters. Jacob, with his mother's prompting, cheated his brother out of his birthright and their father's blessing. Joseph's brothers tried to kill him, and Joseph treated them like a cat playing with a mouse. Moses murdered and lost his temper. God's chosen people worshiped the golden calf. David committed adultery with Uriah's wife and then had Uriah killed. All the disciples ran away from Jesus in the Garden in his hour of desperate need.

And so it goes. The people of God are not all good and moral people. They do terrible things. But they know that they are utterly dependent on God, and if they do anything that is good, it is because God pushes them into it and helps them every inch of the way. They do not feel that they have to protect God from other people; they know that they fail God but they pick themselves up (with God's help) out of the mud and try again. And they rejoice. David danced for God, leaping with joy around the ark.

There are many fascinating women in Scripture, as complex as the men, and many of them break all our preconceptions of what women ought to be. (Whose "ought"? It does not seem to be God's.) In Matthew's genealogy, four women are listed as being Jesus' fore-bears, and all four break the accepted patterns of their society. Rahab the harlot: outside society. Tamar: Tamar gave birth to twins after she had lain with her father-in-law, completely breaking all societal rules. Ruth: Ruth was a Moabitess, and the Moabites descended from Lot's daughters who, after the destruction of Sodom and Gomorrah, got their father drunk and slept with him in order to preserve his bloodline, an act that was and is abhorrent. Bathsheba: Bathsheba, the fourth, is referred to as the wife of Uriah, the man King David had killed after he and Bathsheba had committed adultery. All four of these women from whom Jesus came were outside society, beyond the pale. Someone examining the family genealogy would be shocked to find forebears such as these.

What does this have to tell us? God is constantly breaking human rules in order to offer the greater rule of love, speaking through people shunned by society. Was Mary of Magdala socially acceptable? There is no indication whatsoever in Scripture that she was a prostitute, but she did have seven demons, demons that Jesus drove out of her. It was to this Mary that Jesus first showed himself after the Resurrection. Mary of Bethany and Mary of Magdala probably came closer to understanding the nature of Jesus than anybody else, able to expect from him the unexpected, and to accept it with joy.

The stories in the Bible have nourished me all my life, as has the poetry, the long lists of laws, the history, and even the begats. (In my little play *The Journey with Jonah*, I named the three little rats on the sinking ship Huz, Buz, and Hazo, out of the begats!) During my morning and evening reading of Scripture I do not skip. If it's there, it's there for a reason, and I read it all, every bit of it. If we read Leviticus with an open heart we will see that the message is not to burden people with an overwhelming number of laws, but to call us to be God's holy people. The laws are there to help us, not to hinder.

But it's the stories that have always drawn me. When I was a child (as now) there were stories I found difficult, such as that of the workers in the vineyard, where those who had worked only an hour were paid as much as those who had worked all day in the heat of the sun. It wasn't fair! Like most children, I wanted things to be fair, even though life had already taught me that unfairness abounds. I think many of us still feel like the child stamping and crying out, "It's not fair!" Those who have worked all day long should certainly be paid more than those who came in at the last minute! But Jesus is constantly trying to make us understand that God's ways are not our ways, and that God's love is far less selective and far greater than ours. "Is thine eye evil because I am good?" God asks in Matthew's Gospel after he has finished paying all the workers the same wage. When God blesses those we deem unworthy, does our jealousy make our eye become evil? Are we, like the elder brother, like Jonah, upset at God's forgiveness? Daily I need a deep and penitent awareness of how much greater God's love is than my own.

It is not coincidence that Jesus so often uses Samaritans as protagonists for his stories, knocking out our exclusiveness by bringing the social outcasts into the inner circle and showing them as warmer of heart than the socially acceptable.

The story of Gideon was a favorite fairy tale for me, with Gideon being the least of his family, and his family being the least of all the tribes (somebody else socially unacceptable). And I have always loved the world of

Ezekiel, with those incredible whirling wheels and the dry bones that God brought together to live again. The story of Esther is full of excitement and beauty, and violence, too, and I anguished over Jepthah's daughter. Yes, a vow is sacred, but wasn't this young girl's life even more sacred? And what about Herod having John the Baptist beheaded because of a casual vow he had made when Salome's dancing pleased him? People don't make that kind of vow nowadays, do they? At least not in the Western world. At least not often. Haven't we learned that God does not want to be bargained with?

A story I found especially troublesome was that of Abraham and Sarah and Isaac. How could a God of love demand the sacrifice of the son he had promised to Abraham and Sarah? What kind of cold-blooded testing was that? Did Sarah know about it? Surely not! No mother would let her husband take her child to be used as a holocaust. If I felt a hint of that when I was a child, it became stronger when I was a mother myself. Sarah would say, "No, Lord, there are things that even you do not ask."

If there is more than one way of interpreting the parable of the Good Samaritan, there may well be more than one way of interpreting God's strange demand of Abraham, and I came across a completely new exegesis one winter when I was conducting my annual writers' workshop at a beautiful Episcopal monastery overlooking the Hudson River.

One year my first assignment was for the participants to pick any woman in Scripture (with the exception of Mary) at a time of crisis and decision, and write a story about her. We got some wonderful stories, and then I asked the writers to pass their stories to the person on the left, and that person was to rewrite the story from the point of view of someone else in it. At the end of the class one young woman came to me complaining, "Madeleine, I got Sarah and Abraham and Isaac, and you know I've written and written about them, and you've told me never to write from the point of view of God."

I laughed. Indeed it is not a good idea for the finite human being to try to write from the point of view of the infinite God. But I knew that this young woman was well grounded in Scripture, that she was a fine writer, and I trusted her ability to meet a challenge. "Go for it, Judith. Write from the point of view of God."

The next day she came in with a dialogue between God and the archangel Raphael, the physician of God. Raphael is very pleased with Abraham's response to God's demand, and begins extolling Abraham's virtues to God. And God is not enthusiastic. The more Raphael praises Abraham, the less enthusiastic God gets. Finally Raphael says, "But God, you put Abraham to the test and he passed."

God replies, "He did not pass. He failed. He chose law over love."

And all kinds of lights flashed on for me.

(Of course. Abraham failed, and God kept right on loving him and gave Abraham everything he had promised. We all fail God's tests over and over again. We failed most horribly when God came to live with us in the person of Jesus of Nazareth.)

The dialogue between Raphael and God continues until God tells Raphael to go, and Raphael says, "Yes, ma'am."

Perhaps it does take the feminine in the Godhead to understand that Abraham failed.

I told this story at a parish weekend, and some people were scandalized. Why? This interpretation does not change a line of Scripture. And the writer, a Jewish Christian, grew up in the tradition of the Midrash, stories written to explicate Scripture. One of the wonders of story is that it is alive, not static. A story that meant one thing to me when I was forty may mean something quite different to me today. Certainly I understand Sarah better now than I did when I was a child, or even when I was a child-bearing woman, having my babies during the normal age-span. We bring our own preoccupations and preconceptions to story, our own wounds, our own joys, and therefore our responses are going to vary. That does not invalidate them. The stories of Jesus' healing are particularly poignant to me right now, while I am still in the midst of my own healing. I was not able to reach out and touch the hem of Jesus' garment, but those who loved me touched it for me.

◆ ◆ ◆

The Resurrection meant more to me after I had encountered death, the death of my grandmothers, the death of my father; and I saw the Incarnation in a new way after the birth of my children. And certainly the two years that I have spent working on *Certain Women* have influenced the way I see the story of King David. King David and his *joie de vivre*, his willingness to admit his sins and repent, and his many loves, is very alive in my heart.

The biblical narrator brings David into the story in two different ways: Saul, when he fell into his terrible fits of depression, was advised to have someone play the harp for him, and one of his servants said, *"I have seen a son of*

Jesse . . . who knows how to play the harp," and Saul had
David sent for.

> *David came to Saul and entered his service. Saul liked him*
> *very much, and David became one of his armor-bearers. . . .*
> *Whenever the spirit from God came upon Saul, David would*
> *take his harp and play. Then relief would come to Saul; he*
> *would feel better, and the evil spirit would leave him.*

An evil spirit from the Lord troubled Saul. The Lord
hardened Pharaoh's heart. Does the Lord indeed do such
things? Or do we blame the Lord rather than ourselves?
In Jesus' time someone with Saul's problem would have
been considered to have an evil spirit, and I find this
more believable than God sending the evil spirit within
him. And it has always fascinated me that the evil spirits,
the demons, recognized Jesus as the Messiah, even when
the people around him did not. Would Saul today be
considered a manic depressive? Whatever caused his
problem, David was called in, and his harp music
brought Saul back to quiet and reason.

David's second entrance into the story is the famous
scene of the giant Goliath being slain by young David
with a slingshot and a pebble. It's a wonderful scene,
Goliath shouting his challenge, David replying, and his
brothers furious with him because they think he'll shame
them by getting killed by the giant. David is outfitted
with Saul's enormous and cumbersome armor, which he
very sensibly takes off. His slingshot has served him well
against animals who have tried to kill his sheep, and
serves him well against Goliath. *As Saul watched David*
going out to meet the Philistine, he said to Abner, commander

of the army, "Abner, whose son is that young man? . . . Find out whose son this young man is."

So again, David is brought into the story. He and Saul's son Jonathan become friends in that marvelous way among men in story—and occasionally in real life. Ironically, such friendships often come out of times of war, not the faceless war of today where bombs are dropped and missiles sent to people who are unseen and unnamed, but wars where the enemy had a face, and your comrade could save your life. My father made deep, lifelong friends in the First World War, that last war where there was any sense that the enemy had a face, was a human being, loved his family, and probably believed in his cause. Erich Maria Remarque's book *Three Comrades* came out of that terrible war which, instead of shocking us out of war, started a century of war. I have a vague memory of a cartoon with two people looking at one of the early guns, and the caption was, "This is so ghastly we'll never have another war."

David and Jonathan fought side by side and, to begin with, their weapons were primitive, because when Samuel anointed David, the Jews were still in the Bronze Age; David ultimately took them into the Iron Age. The Philistines, the enemy, sharpened the swords and sickles for the Jews because they wanted them to be dependent, incapable of sharpening their own tools and unable to move into what, for the Jews, was the future.

Saul, who never made the move out of the Bronze Age, was quickly jealous of David, not so much because of his friendship with Jonathan as his popularity with the people. Saul, with good cause, was afraid for his throne, and afraid that Jonathan would not inherit it.

When the men were returning home after David had killed the Philistine, the women came out from all the towns of Israel to meet King Saul with singing and dancing, with joyful songs and with tambourines and lutes. As they danced they sang: "Saul has slain his thousands, and David his tens of thousands." Saul was very angry; this refrain galled him.

It is easy to see why Saul was displeased, was jealous, was fearful. The next night when David played for him, the evil spirit came again upon Saul, and he cast his javelin at David, but David ducked out of the way and avoided being killed, and continued to *behave himself wisely in all his ways* (1 Samuel 18:15, KJV). And Saul *was afraid of David, because the LORD was with David but had left Saul.*

Can we hold the image of God in our hearts when we are consumed, as Saul was, with jealousy?

Jonathan was not jealous. He knew that David would be king and that he would not, and he was not jealous. He loved David with all his heart, and there, perhaps, is the key. True friendship is of the heart, and we have almost lost that concept as we have become more and more genitally oriented.

The deep friendships in my life are, for me, what keep the stars in their courses. Not only did Luci and Marilyn come to be with me in the hospital, but as soon as I got back to Crosswicks, Pat flew up from Florida to be with me and nurse me. There were other wondrous offers of help from friends who were willing to set aside their own plans if they could be of use to me.

This is the kind of friendship I believe David and Jonathan had. Isn't that enough? More than enough?

134

◆ ◆ ◆

The loss of our deep understanding of friendship is reflected in the rather frantic attempts to remove from our thinking the image of God as Father (usually an angry father). When God is called Mother, that is as sexist as Father. Because I had both a mother and a father I could respect, they were my image of mother and father, and this did not carry over to God. Indeed, I never thought of God as being either male or female. In the language of prayer I sometimes refer to my Maker as Abba/Amma (Amma being the intimate feminine for mother, mama, as Abba is father, daddy). Abba/Amma is much softer and far more personal than Father/Mother. But in my own mind there has never been an image of a God of either sex. For some reason I thought of this while I was in the hospital, where I was often wakeful for most of the night. And I wondered if I did not need a metaphor for God—not an image, not even an icon, but a metaphor.

And one came to me. In my responsiveness to God I am the infant in the womb, totally nourished, fed, warmed, completely cared for, but with no image of the Caregiver. That, for me, is a workable metaphor. And it does take it completely out of the realm of sex.

At the time that metaphor came to me I was almost as helpless as the baby in the womb, and that may have helped precipitate this understanding.

One sad result of the eating of the fruit of the tree of the knowledge of good and evil is that we have, as a result, depended too much on knowledge, and not enough on wisdom. We are, all of us, male and female, supposed to contain within ourselves the qualities of each. The people I know who use their intellect to the fullest, while never losing the intuitive and the imaginative, are indeed luminous.

It's not easy. If we (as *Sophia*, wisdom), are willing to understand that fact and truth are not necessarily the same thing, we will be feared and criticized. But perhaps fact and truth are like male and female; we need both to make the image of God.

The battle of the sexes is not so much a battle between men and women as a battle within our own selves. Dare we use our intellects fully at the same time that we trust our intuitions?

It is all of the deepening truths that are beyond provable fact that help us to be human and, ultimately, mature and loving human beings, daring to open ourselves to the truth that will make us free.

◆ ◆ ◆

David was not afraid of the truth, and so his love of God was both spontaneous and joyous, or anguished and penitent. But God was very present in David's life, as much after Samuel anointed him king as when he was a shepherd in the hills with his sheep.

Although David was still without his throne or crown, telling no one (as far as we know) about his anointing, he grew nevertheless steadily more and more of a threat to Saul, and Jonathan stood by him, trying to make peace, helping David to flee when fleeing was the only alternative.

Saul, in his wiliness (since the flung javelin had not worked) said to David,

"Here is my older daughter Merab. I will give her to you in marriage; only serve me bravely and fight the battles of the LORD." For Saul said to himself, "I will not raise a hand against him. Let the Philistines do that!"

But the Philistines did not kill David as Saul had hoped, and he gave his daughter, Merab, to another. Michal, Saul's younger daughter, loved David, and when Saul heard this he was pleased, thinking that he would have another chance to get rid of David. David, very properly, told Saul that he was a poor man and could pay no bride price for Michal, but Saul asked for a hundred foreskins of the Philistines, again hoping to have David killed by enemy. But David brought Saul two hundred foreskins of the Philistines, so Saul had to give him his daughter, Michal.

It does not seem to have been a happy marriage. Michal was torn between her father and her husband, and in helping David to escape Saul's wrath by lowering him out a window, she also lost him, at least temporarily, because David had to flee as far from Saul as possible. Jonathan was again a true friend to David, helping him in every way that he could. David gathered himself an army and brought his parents to Mizpeh, asking the king of Moab to care for them until David would *learn what God will do for me.*

In the scriptural story we see Saul disintegrate further into madness, self-pity, rage, even accusing Jonathan of conspiring against him. It is a sad story of the decay of a man who could have been great, but who was threatened by greatness.

David, unlike Saul, was not self-conscious about God's call to him. He honored Saul as God's anointed, but he also knew himself to be called, and he was willing to follow that call without pride. His pride showed itself in other ways, his adultery with Bathsheba, for instance, and his seeing to it that Uriah was killed. He was, too often, self-indulgent, but he did not turn away from paying the price. As Nik, the playwright, and I lived with the story of David, he became very dear to our hearts.

Story as the Lord's Prayer

6

WHEN I SAY MY PRAYERS at the end of the day, I am coming to terms with the events of the day, with the story of my day. Part of the Offices of Evening Prayer and Compline is the Lord's Prayer, and this prayer is in a way the story of our Maker. I say this prayer at least thrice each day and usually more often, and it is amazing how I discover something new in it every time.

Our Father. Yes, a lot of people have trouble with limiting God to Father, and so do I, but in the Lord's Prayer it has never seemed to me to be a limitation. Jesus is talking about his Father, talking out of the particular time and space in which he was born.

The word *God* itself is an offense to many. The great Jewish philosopher Martin Buber has something to say about the use of the word *God*, which has helped me through several periods of rational doubt, during which the word has been so smeared that it has seemed almost useless.

Martin Buber once visited a famous old philosopher. He had been offered the use of the philosopher's study, but one morning when he got up early to correct the galley proofs of the preface to one of his books, his host was already in his study. Buber explained to him that he had the galleys in his hand, and the old man asked if he would read the preface to him. Buber did so, and when he had finished, the philosopher cried out with growing passion and grief, "How can you bring yourself to say 'God' time after time? How can you expect your readers will take the word in the sense in which you wish it to be taken? What you mean by the name of God is something above all human grasp and conceptualization. What word of human speech is so misused, so defiled, so desecrated as this! All the innocent blood that has been shed for it has robbed it of its radiance. All the injustice that it has been used to cover has effaced its features. When I hear the Highest called 'God' it sometimes seems blasphemous."

"The kindly eyes flamed," Buber said. "The voice itself flamed. Then we sat silent for a while facing each other. The room lay in the flowing brightness of early morning. It seemed to me as though a power from the light entered into me. What I answered, I cannot today reproduce, but only indicate. Yes, I said, it is the most heavy-laden of all human words. None has become so soiled, so mutilated. Just for this reason I may not abandon it. Generations of men have laid the burdens of their anxious lives upon this word and weighed it to the ground; it lies in the dust and bears their whole burden. The races of men with their religious factions have torn the word to pieces; they have killed for it and died for it, and it bears their finger marks and their blood. But where might I find a word [other than God] to describe the Highest? . . . If I took the purest, most sparkling concept from the innermost chamber of the philosophers, I could only thereby capture an unbinding product of thought. I could not capture the presence of Him whom the generations of men have honoured and degraded with their awesome living and dying. I do indeed mean Him whom the hell-tormented and heaven-storming generations of men mean. Certainly they draw caricatures and write 'God' underneath; they murder one another and say 'in God's name.' But when all the madness and delusion fall to the dust, when they stand over against Him in the loneliest darkness, is it not the real God they implore? . . . Is it not He who hears them? And just for this reason is not the word 'God' the word of appeal, the word which has become a *name*, consecrated in all human tongues for all times? We must esteem those who interdict it because they rebel against the injustice and wrong which are so readily referred to 'God' for authorization. But we may not give it up. . . . We cannot cleanse the word 'God' and make it whole; but defiled and mutilated as it is, we can raise it from the ground and set it over an hour of great care."

"O God," an eighty-plus aunt of mine kept saying as I helped her get ready to take a taxi to the hospital—the last journey she would ever take. "Oh, God help me, God help me," she said over and over again.

God is the strange and desecrated name I have been taught to call my Creator. Some of my friends spell it G-d, knowing that we cannot know the true name. But the cry, *O God*, comes instinctively to my heart when I am frightened or unhappy. I have no illusion that it is the true name, that name of names too terrible and mighty to be uttered by mortal tongue. The word Jehovah is nothing but a made-up word, put together from some Hebrew consonants, and in some translations of Scripture the word *Lord* replaces *Jehovah* or *Jaweh.* I have prayed, "O God!" for lo, these many years. And it is enough. Perhaps one of the joys of heaven will be to hear the real name of our Maker.

So, just as Buber felt he could not give up God, I feel that I cannot give up Father, especially at the beginning of the prayer Jesus taught his disciples. *Our Father.* The word *Father,* as the word *God,* transcends all that we have done to it, just as with our rigidities we have almost demolished beyond recognition the words *Christian* and *religion.*

Our Father which art in heaven.* And where is heaven? It too is a word which has been abused. The good go to heaven and the bad go to hell. But who are the good and who are the bad? Only God knows that, and when we try to make such judgments we invariably blunder. It is God who is in heaven, who, perhaps, *is* heaven. Surely it is not a place that is either up or down. Heaven is wherever and whenever God is present; when he is present within us, then heaven is within us. If we do not begin to live in heaven now we will not be able to recognize it later—in fact, we may confuse it with hell. But trying to define heaven is like trying to define God. It is, I believe, that place where our souls continue to be taught to grow in love and wisdom, and how that teaching is to be done I do not know. Where is Hugh, now? Where is Tallis? God will not forget them; el holds them in the palm of the protecting hand.

*King James Version used for the Lord's Prayer passages in this chapter.

Our Father which art in heaven, Hallowed be thy name. How do we hallow a name that we do not rightly know? We can start by having a sense of reverence and awe whenever we speak to or refer to God, Abba/Amma, Maker, Creator. When Luci was with me in the hospital she commented ruefully about the language of the workmen outside my window. They were certainly using the Lord's name in vain, but it was not a deliberate vanity. "It's just their paucity of vocabulary," I said. Such casual, careless language is not good, but it is far less evil than deliberate cursing, consigning someone to hell, rather than leaving that judgment to God.

Too often we try to hallow our own names, falling into the easy trap of hubris. We need to honor our names, but only God's is to be hallowed. Our human names are tied to our families. They are given us, and honored at our baptisms. We need to respect them, and we need to be careful what we do in our own names.

When I write, when I speak, my beginning prayer is always that of the psalmist: that I may be got out of the way and not hinder God; only then, when my own willfulness and pride are vanquished, can God use me as co-creator.

Many years ago, when Jim Morton came to be dean of the Cathedral of St. John the Divine in New York, he asked Tallis and me to give the Wednesday Evening Lenten Meditations. I was challenged and awed, and I asked Tallis, "What shall I be thinking about? What are we going to talk about during Lent?" He looked at me impatiently. "Go away. Don't bother me. You're better when you don't think." And that was all I could get out of him, though I kept begging him to tell me what I should be thinking about.

Ash Wednesday came; he still had told me nothing. We went to St. Saviour's Chapel, behind the high altar, for communion. Then we had soup and bread, and then Tallis and I sat down, side by side, with everybody else facing us, and I still had no idea what was going to happen. Finally he pulled a small black book of deep Russian meditations from his pocket, each a couple of minutes long. He read the first one. Then he said serenely, "Now Madeleine will give you a *parenesis* of this." A *parenesis*: an example drawn from nature. I didn't have time to get in my own way. I didn't have time to think. I simply responded to the Russian meditations, one after another, for the next hour.

When it was over, I said to Tallis, "You have a lot more faith in me than I have."

He grinned. "I'm always right. You're much better when you don't think."

And that is true. It doesn't mean that I must never think. It doesn't mean that he hadn't been training me for a good many years. It doesn't mean that I didn't have a full barrel to draw from. It does mean that the creative actions do not come from the cognitive part of the brain alone, but from a much larger area. When I write, I realized, I do not think. I write. If I think when I am writing, it doesn't work. I can think before I write; I can think after I write; but when I am actually writing, what I do is write. This is always the instruction I give at writers' workshops: "Don't think. Write." And I put a time limit to the assignments. "You may not work on this for more than an hour. If you're not finished at the end of an hour, that's all right. Stop." It's a lot easier to write without thinking if there's a time limit.

One workshop participant said to me one morning, "I thought what you were asking us was absolutely impossible. But then I woke up at two o'clock and I did it." And she smiled with delight at what she had done.

To relinquish our conscious, cognitive selves is an act of hallowing. It should be true of any activity, not just writing stories. It should be true of the doctor, and too often it isn't. Those who must make instant life and death decisions are put in the position of being God, and being God is woefully addictive. The great physicians are those who know that it is not their mortal hands which heal, but God's hand using the human one. It is God's name that should be hallowed, not ours. When we put ourselves before God then inevitably we come to grief—one of the most common griefs of all.

Thy kingdom come. That is what co-creation with our Maker is all about, the coming of the kingdom. Our calling, our vocation in all we do and are to try to do is to help in the furthering of the coming of the kingdom—a kingdom we do not know and cannot completely understand. We are given enough foretastes of the kingdom to have a reasonable expectation. Being a loved and loving part of the body; praying together; singing together; forgiving and accepting forgiveness; eating together the good fruits of the earth; holding hands around the table as these fruits are blessed, in spontaneous joy and love, all these are foretastes.

Thy will be done on earth, as it is in heaven. God's will. Do we always know what it is? I'm afraid not. At least I don't. Often I get caught up in oughts and shoulds that are not necessarily God's will. When I capitulate to too many oughts and shoulds I overdo my physical strength and that is not God's will. As I continue to recuperate from my accident it is very difficult for me to know when (as Ma Katzenjammer said) too much is enough. I do more than my healing body is ready for; I get exhausted;

I have been willful rather than obedient, and the line between the two is not easy to discern.

On occasion King David substituted his will for God's will, and with all the good will in the world. Once he had built himself a palace in his holy city of Jerusalem, he felt that it was not fitting for himself, a mortal king, to live in a palace, while God's tabernacle was kept in a tent. David said to Nathan the prophet, *"Here I am, living in a palace of cedar, while the ark of God remains in a tent."*

Nathan comes into the story abruptly. Samuel the prophet has died. Another prophet is needed, and so the biblical narrator produces Nathan.

Then Nathan said to the king, *"Whatever you have in mind, go ahead and do it, for the LORD is with you."*

But it happened that night that the word of the Lord came to Nathan, saying,

"Go and tell my servant David, 'This is what the LORD says: Are you the one to build me a house to dwell in? I have not dwelt in a house from the day I brought the Israelites up out of Egypt to this day. I have been moving from place to place with a tent as my dwelling."

Trying to put God in a house is to misunderstand, to anthropomorphize (as usual). When Nathan told David what God had said, David accepted God's words and sang joyous praise. To try to put God in a house is to try to imprison the Lord of the Universe. It cannot be done. The house of God becomes more important than the God within—as happens in some churches. There are times when I wish that we had no church buildings, that we met in each other's homes. But then I remember churches where I have felt blessed by the presence of God, because we have not built a house for God, but a house for ourselves where we can be quiet and wait for God to come to us. I feel this in the great, beautiful space of the Cathedral of St. John the Divine in New York, and I feel it in the much smaller congregational church in Northwest Connecticut.

When I pray, in church or without, in my prayer corner at home, or on the street as I walk to and fro, I pray that God's will may be done, and I pray it especially fervently during those many times when I am not able to discern God's will. Is this man the right man for the young woman I love? Or vice versa. Can this marriage be saved? Can this life be saved? Should I say *Yes* or *No* to this request? Often I do not know, and so I throw myself upon God's will.

Thy will be done on earth, as it is in heaven. Heaven is not a place name. Heaven is wherever God's will is being done. When, occasionally, it is done on earth, then there is heaven. It is the most difficult thing in the world for most of us to give up directing our own story and turn to the Author. This has to be done over and over again every day. Time and again I know exactly how a certain situation should be handled, and in no uncertain terms I tell God how to handle it. Then I stop, stock-still, and (sometimes with reluctance) end by saying, "However, God, do it your way. Not my way, your way. Please."

And God's will, no matter how fervent our prayers, is not always done. We human creatures abuse our free will, set it over against God's will. Sometimes when we may truly be doing God's will, it is thwarted because of the abuse of free will by others. My faith is that ultimately God's will *will* be done, and I know to my rue that when I am willful I am obstructing that will. At my occasional best, I am lovingly obedient to what I pray is the will of God. Loving obedience should never be difficult;

we are not being coerced, or manipulated. Loving obedience is doing the Lord's will with enthusiasm— doing the Lord's will filled with the Spirit of God.

Give us this day our daily bread. Not next year, not tomorrow. Today. Jesus is emphatic about the importance of the present day, without over-concern for the morrow. My grandmother was fond of quoting, "Sufficient unto the day is the evil thereof." Scripture reminds us of the beauty of the flowers, beauty that they cannot work for or earn, but which is given to them by a loving Creator, a Creator who will take care of us if we are not over-anxious about the morrow, thinking that we have to take care of it, do it ourselves.

Like many people, I have a tendency to project. As a storyteller, I am trained to say, "What if—?" But while this is important for story, it can be crippling in real life. If I am too worried about what may or may not happen tomorrow, I cannot concentrate on what is happening today. Sometimes when we are caught up in tragedy we are better able to live in the moment than when things are going along normally. Both Luci and I knew this when Harold and Hugh were dying. We were blessed by being allowed to live in the now, the very moment.

While I was in that difficult English boarding school, when I was twelve to fourteen, on Sunday afternoons we were allowed to spend two hours in our bedrooms—the only time we were allowed there except to sleep or change our clothes. I always brought with me enough books to keep me busy for two weeks rather than two hours. When I travel I still bring with me too many books. This is not a bad kind of projection. It does no harm, other than making my bag heavy to carry. But it is a reminder. Don't live five hours from now. Live now, fully, creatively, lovingly.

Give us this day our daily bread. Not mine, but ours—everybody's. Our responsibility to the starving world is implicit in that sentence. As long as any part of the body is hungry, the entire body knows starvation. But again, we do not need to think of our obligations in terms of success; we would fail to do anything at all if we knew we had to succeed. We simply do what we can; we offer our little loaves and fishes and leave the rest to the Lord.

The story of the loaves and fishes is sometimes explained away in a reasonable sort of manner. It was something like a potluck supper, I have been told. The people who had been listening to Jesus were so moved by his words that when it came time to eat, those who had brought picnics with them shared their food around.

The reasonable explanations don't really make much sense. Jesus took the stuff of nature, bread and fish, and working from what already existed, multiplied it. He refused to turn stones into bread, which he could have done. But stones are not bread; they are stones. Instead, when he fed the multitudes, he took the loaves, he took the fish, and there was enough for everybody. In John's Gospel it is pointed out that a lad came up and *offered* what he had, and this act of offering was essential for the miracle.

Another important part of the miracle is Jesus' concern for the fragments, because he is always concerned about the broken things, the broken people. Only when we realize that we are indeed broken, that we are not independent, that we cannot do it ourselves, can we turn to God and take that which he has given us, no matter what it is, and create with it.

In my neighbourhood in New York the past few years have brought out many panhandlers, people begging for money. One night I was walking home with one of my granddaughters, and she said, anxiously, "Gran, what do you do about the panhandlers?" At that moment a young woman came up to us, begging for money for food.

We were standing outside a small cafe near our apartment. I said to the woman, "Come on in here, and I'll buy you some food."

She said, "What I really want is Chinese food."

I said, "It's late, and I'm on my way home, and I'll buy you food here."

"They don't like me in there."

"They'll like my money. I'll buy you some food. What would you like?"

"Well, I really want to go to this Chinese restaurant . . ." (it was several blocks away).

I said, "Good night," and walked on. I turned to my granddaughter and said, "That's what I do about panhandlers. She did not want food. She wanted money."

How do we distinguish the people with scams from those who are truly hungry? It's not always possible. In the past year more and more people have accepted my offer of food, and I am grateful that I am able to buy them hamburgers or sandwiches or whatever they want. It is not enough. It is never enough. But it is what I can do. And I try not to forget that the churches and synagogues in my neighbourhood have coordinated their soup kitchens, so that every day there is always a place where hungry people can get a hot meal.

Some may be hungry physically, but are hungrier spiritually, and try to assuage their anguish and emptiness with drugs. Some of my friends give money. "If they want drugs, let them have them." Something in me does not want to do that. Food, not drugs, are what I am willing to offer. Am I right or wrong? I am not sure.

It is no coincidence that Jesus follows *Give us this day our daily bread* with *Forgive us our trespasses, as we forgive those who trespass against us.* Am I trespassing against those who ask for money by offering food? I do not know. Am I adding humiliation by offering food, by assuming that my money will be misused? I don't know. But many of the people who ask for money want it for drugs, not food. Is there any other way to tell them apart? I don't know. Forgive me.

As we forgive, so are we forgiven. Jesus makes that point more than once. If we cannot forgive, we close ourselves off from forgiveness. Quite often the person we find hardest to forgive is our own self—because we are taught by the world to set up false idols of ourselves, to have unrealistic expectations of what we ought to be. This is reflected in the lack of penitence in the present Episcopal Prayer Book.

Perhaps the 1928 Prayer Book was over-heavy on penitence, but proper penitence is not groveling in humiliation. Proper penitence is repentance. When we are truly penitent, we are able to accept forgiveness, and then we are able to glorify the Lord. Over and over again I pick myself up out of the dust and try again, praying to become healed and whole and holy by the grace of God, not my own virtue. Proper penitence is being able to forgive ourselves, because only if we are able to forgive ourselves are we able to forgive others.

Refusing to forgive ourselves is succumbing to temptation, and the next line of the Lord's Prayer is: *And lead us not into temptation, but deliver us from evil.*

We beg the Spirit not to lead us into the wilderness to be tempted, as the Spirit led Jesus after his baptism, because we know that we are not immune to temptation.

"Save us from the time of trial," one of the new translations says, which is more or less the same thing. We know that we are fallible. Jesus' temptations were a testing of his dual nature as human and divine. We are human, and so we ask that we may be delivered from the plausible temptations of the evil one. We know that we are not immune; we have seen kings and princes, and princes of the church fall for the temptations of the evil one over and over again. The more power and responsibility we are given, the more we must resist the temptations. If we're willing to give up that do-it-yourself kind of autonomous control, the Spirit will not lead us beyond our power to recognize and resist the tempter.

There seems to be a good deal of nostalgia for the "wonderful days of the sixties"; but while there were many needed awakenings, there were also many evils. When we moved back to New York in 1960, to the upper west side of the city where I still live, not one of the stores had to be protected at night by a grille. The proprietor went out and closed the door; that was all that was necessary. Nobody had to be "buzzed in" anywhere. Now, in Diocesan House at the Cathedral, where the beautiful, oak-paneled library is, where I am the volunteer librarian, one has to be both buzzed in and announced. It is not safe to leave the door open.

In 1960 Broadway was still the Great White Way. It was in that decade that the pornographic movies came in, the massage parlors, all the abuses of eroticism. Crime increased radically.

But perhaps what is saddest is that our recognition of many evils, racism, sexism, ageism, poverty, illness, was followed by do-it-yourself-ism. With the best will in the world we thought we could do it all ourselves. That seems to me to be the problem of the New Agers. They have a case of the sixties.

But we couldn't do it ourselves. We had horrible and ambiguous wars. We built sterile housing developments that encouraged crime. We fell into all the temptations of hubris, all those temptations that Jesus rejected.

The fact that the tempter succeeds so often in being irresistible is a source of grief to us, and that grief is necessary preparation for help in resistance. Today one of the temptations is to feel that we must be either political-ly correct, social activists, or that we must be withdrawn from the world in order to pray. Why should these two be exclusive? Won't our action more likely be God's will if we have prayed about it first? Won't we be more likely to correct some of the terrible social inequities with which we are surrounded if we ask ourselves what Jesus would have done, and how? Don't we need to withdraw from the world for a while to ask God what we should do? It is a temptation to gallop in and try to make everything all right, without really knowing what that everything is.

Deliver us from evil.

O God, please. Please, deliver us from evil.

Some of my friends believe that my accident last July 28 was a manifestation of evil, not just the evil of the truck driver who was not paying attention, but the evil which is always out to destroy, annihilate, uncreate.

That was one of the problems of the sixties. There was much good in our awareness of the terrible needs of minorities, but wherever there is good the echthroi rush in, trying to undo it, and one of their easiest weapons is pride: You're wonderful! Of course you can take care of integration and poverty and everything else if you just try hard enough.

Well, it's not that easy.

Certainly my accident felt echthroid. Whether it was or not I do not know. But I will be succumbing to the echthroi if I do not turn it over to God. Right now it is very difficult for me to turn my physical weakness to God, to understand that I am not completely healed. Those hematomas up and down my left side are enough of a reminder. They are getting smaller, and when they are completely gone maybe I will have more right to be impatient. When I do my leg exercises I see the bruises that still remain. When they are gone maybe I will have more right to push myself into a full schedule.

O God, deliver us from evil.

I listen to the news and I shudder. War. Crime. Lust. Drugs. Disease. Riots. One cannot listen to a news report and not be aware of the evil with which we are surrounded. Unfortunately good news is not news, and that in itself is part of the evil, for there is good news, love, and marital fidelity, and friendship, and compassion, and concern. All these combat the evil and should not be ignored or forgotten.

It is an odd quirk of the human memory that it is especially vivid and retentive during times of pain and stress. I remember watching the evening news one day after coming home from the hospital where my husband was dying. Tucked in with all the bad news was a charming story of a major highway in Tokyo that was completely shut down for the length of time it took a mother duck and her ducklings to cross the eight lanes on their way to water. There must have been many delightful little slices of life on the news since then, but that is the one I remember.

For thine is the kingdom, and the power, and the glory, for ever. Amen. So be it.

God's. Not ours. The minute we want it to be ours—and that's one of the temptations, after all—it's grief. Grief for us. Grief for God.

The kingdom and the power and the glory. Where are they?

It's been pounded into our heads in the last decade or so that God is neither up nor down; hell is not below nor heaven above. When the astronauts on the moon looked at the earth, there was no up nor down.

I'm not sure what all the shouting is about, because a God worth believing in is obviously not limited by space or time or place. God includes all time and all space. The God of Creation made it, called it good, and it belongs to the Creator.

But even if we know that God is not up and is not down, humankind lives by images, and it is sometimes through our earthly images that we catch glimpses of the heavenly. We live on a planet that is bound by the laws of gravity. Gravity pulls us down; levity raises us up. Our images come because of the laws of gravity. We sing:

Lift up your hearts!
We lift them up unto the Lord!

Yea, Amen, Alleluia! There is joy in those words for me.

But of course, God is not up, therefore we might as well say:

Throw down your hearts.
We throw them down before the Lord.

No. It won't do. We do have genetically bred images within us, sown by generations beyond our memory. We lift *up* our hearts in joy. God is the *light* of the world, and the darkness cannot comprehend it.

Ultimately the heart's desire is to move beyond images.

Meister Eckhart says: "Thou shalt apprehend God without image, without semblance, without means. But for me to know God thus, without means, I must be very He, He very me."

When we receive the bread and the wine we pray that God may be in us, and that we may be in God.

We say the Lord's Prayer; we tell God's story, as Jesus has told it to us. We turn to a Love that is far beyond our conscious understanding. It is more of a miracle than the multiplication of the loaves and the fishes.

It is how we live and move and have our being.

Story as Community

7

WHEN WE SAY THE LORD'S PRAYER we do not say it alone, no matter how physically alone we are. We say it in community, the community of the disciples who asked Jesus to tell them how to pray, the community of everyone who has said this prayer in every language throughout the centuries, the community of those who happen to be praying it at the moment we are, whether we are together in church, or whether we are praying alone in our rooms.

From the ends of the earth I call to you,
I call as my heart grows faint;
O set me upon the rock that is higher than I. (Coverdale)

Sometimes when I am feeling isolated I need to be on that rock so that I may have the vision to understand that

I am not alone. When I tell my stories, I may be alone at my computer, but storytelling is always an act of community.

Bedtime has been for me a special community time of storytelling. When my children were little, community was very visible, at home, school, church. But it had special meaning for me as we sat around the dinner table and held hands for grace. And, after the meal was eaten, the dishes done, there was the special time of getting ready for bed, brushing teeth, getting into night clothes, and then gathering together for prayer and story. I liked to start bedtime early so that it could go on longer. We read wonderful stories from books which had been mine as a child, and some of which had been my mother's. When Hugh and I were raising our family we were not near a bookstore and we did not have extra money for new books. But we already had many shelves full of books. Great stories do not lose their appeal; they can be read over and over, with undiminished enjoyment.

Perhaps community is especially important to me because I did not have it as a child: first, an only child in a big city, and then an only child in Europe where my parents wandered in the Alps trying to find a place where my father's injured lungs could breathe with some kind of ease.

I began to know community when we returned to the United States and I was sent to a second boarding school, Ashley Hall, where I was happy in the nurturing atmosphere of the world of school—the first time that school was community for me, rather than a place of isolation that had to be endured.

Then there was the community of college, and after that the community of the world of the theatre where I was fortunate enough to find work. Being in a play is somewhat like being part of a great orchestra, and though my roles were the equivalent of the triangle in the orchestra, even the triangle is needed.

My first *conscious* understanding of my need for community was the community of marriage, of our growing family, a family of open doors. Because we lived outside the village proper, playmates for our children had to be fetched and carried, and we usually had at least three extra for the weekends.

Then there was the community of the church, the white-pillared, tall-spired church that stood directly across from our general store in the center of the village of Goshen. It was, for Hugh and me, a return to the church community. We had never left God, but we had rebelled, each of us, against our particular religious establishment. When our children were born we recognized that we needed to move back into a church community, and our church became the center of our lives, as well as the geographical center of the village.

It was within the community of those who worked for the church, sang in the choir, taught Sunday school, visited the sick, that I first experienced a truly Christian community. I doubt if I will ever experience it in the same way again, because there are very few villages around today as small as ours was then; it, too, has grown.

Years later, reading for who-knows-how-many times the Book of the Acts of the Apostles and coming across the passage where we are told that in the early days of Christianity you could tell the Christians by their love for each other, it struck me forcibly that for almost a decade I had experienced this kind of love.

Does that decade sound idyllic? It wasn't. For many reasons it was one of the most unhappy periods of my life. But I did experience Christian community, and it was this that kept much of what happened—illness, death, rejection—from being destructive. I know that I'm a better writer now because of the conflict and frustration of those years, my most difficult years as a writer, full of rejection slips, and I don't want to minimize any of the pain.

I don't remember ever living without conflict of one kind or another, and I'm not at all sure that life without conflict would be desirable. Perhaps conflict is the tightening of the violin string so that the bow, moving across it, will make music. But the string must be loosened periodically or it will break.

My choices have always reflected my need of community. A writer must write alone, but I need to have this solitude encircled by community. I can understand the community of marriage, of family, of religious communities, church community, the community of close friends, only in the context of human failure. It is only when I am able to acknowledge my own failures that I am free to be part of a community, and part of that freedom is to be able to accept that the community itself is going to fail. At the very least, it is going to change, and it may die, and this, in worldly terms, is failure.

The church in our village offered me community and so redeemed my failures as wife, mother, writer. That church is very different today, but that does not change what it gave to me then. It still has much to give me today.

My church in New York provides a different kind of community. We are a young and enthusiastic congregation, diverse in our approach to God, but this very diversity can be a strength as long as it does not become divisive. One of the ways in which the church offers community is through what is called house churches. We meet once a week in our own geographical neighbour-hood with others from the congregation, a small group of anywhere from four to twelve, and share singing, Scrip-ture, prayer—voicing our needs, our thanksgivings, and our requests. In an enormous city like New York such a house church can give us that intimate community that began to vanish as the small farms died and more and more people moved to the cities.

The people in Jesus' day lived in small communities where people knew each other, and my mother, growing up in what is now a large Southern city, also knew com-munity. Her friends were mostly her cousins.

The cousinly relations can be important indeed. I think of young Mary, receiving the announcement of the angel, becoming pregnant with God—what a terrifying prospect! How much support did she receive from her immediate family? Joseph, through the ministry of the angel, accepted the incredible story and did not turn her away. But others may not have been equally willing to believe the unbelievable. What about her parents? We are not told how they reacted. Even if they told her they believed her, it may well have put a terrible strain on them.

So Mary left home and went up to the hill country to her cousin, Elizabeth.

I know my mother was hurt,
that she did not understand.
Despite my Joseph's keeping me
she could not hide that she felt shamed.

Mothers and daughters are too close.

So I went up into the hill country
to my cousin Elizabeth—as old
as my mother, but because she was not
my mother, she was not too close to
understand.

When I was little my cousin
never laughed at me because I thought
I talked with God.
She did not tell me not to make up tales,
never warned me not to blow up my own importance.
Because she knew my littleness before God's thunder
she took me on her lap and rocked me.

So I went to her, to the hill country,
not so much to rejoice with her because
she, too, was bearing within her womb
a miraculous babe, but to ask for comfort,
her understanding that the voice
I heard had told me true about
the father of my son.

Oh, Elizabeth, my cousin, friend,
My son is grown.
Your son is dead, and mine . . . .
Elizabeth, Elizabeth, I need you now.

I, too, am blessed with cousins, and in the South we claim each other even if the cousinship is remote. It is still a tie that is strong.

King David had cousins, nephews. His army chief of staff, Joab, was his nephew. He had close friends who remained loyal to him even when it seemed that his son, Absalom, had taken everything from him. And it was this loyalty in the end that prevailed against the ugliness of civil war. I have often wondered what kind of community David's wives had, living together in a harem, presided over, I suspect, by Abigail, the wife who was older, wiser than the others. Without community they might have been mortal enemies. David had a marvelous way of loving people enough so that they could love each other as well as him, the king.

Friendship is powerful through the Bible, though I wouldn't want to have friends like Job's. Ruth, who was a forbear of Jesus, had a friendship with Naomi that was not unlike the friendship between Mary and Elizabeth.

I am also blessed with a community of friends. We meet to eat together on a regular basis, because sharing bread and wine is an essential part of community and the time when we tell our stories.

Many of the stories delight me! My friend Laryn leads conferences and often has to spend the night alone in a motel. One evening when she had finished her job and gone to her room, the phone rang. She answered. It was an obscene phone call. When the man called her a third time, Laryn, being Laryn, said earnestly, "I'm really worried about you. I think you must be very lonely. What I would like to do with you is pray with you, right now . . ." There was a click on the other end of the line, and no more phone calls. I find myself wondering if Laryn's loving response didn't make a difference to that sick person. He probably was lonely indeed, cut off from any kind of nurturing community.

It is no coincidence that the people who are most aware that they are strangers and sojourners on the earth are the people who are most able to open their doors to the stranger and to receive the blessing the stranger brings. So we should not be surprised that Jesus, despite his awareness of his own migrant condition and his need for solitude—for time to be alone with the Father—also had a close community of disciples and friends. He had no permanent address, appearing and disappearing with disconcerting suddenness. It is only when we are not rigid in our expectations of our communities and when our doors are wide open, that he may choose to come, with the stranger, into our midst.

Story as Joy

8

AWHILE AGO I was at a very large evangelical Christian conference in a Midwest city. After one of my talks a young woman came up to me and said, "You really seem to enjoy your faith." She added, with a wry smile, "And that immediately makes you suspect." I must have looked startled, because she said, "Oh, yes, it's true."

She was a nice young woman, and she was not accusing me. Nevertheless it was an accusation, and I've been thinking about it ever since. Do I, in fact, enjoy my faith? And if I do, what does it mean? That trip to the Midwest was the first trip I'd taken since the accident. I was still weak, still in considerable pain. And yet I was being accused of enjoying my faith! On the whole, I was pleased, because it was an affirmation that my faith was not failing me when things were anything but good. My faith, however, did not prevent bad things from happening. It was, in mortal terms, no protection.

And in immortal terms? St. John of the Cross says that in the evening of life we shall be judged on love. Have we been loving in this life? Has our faith in the Maker of the Universe been so joyful that we have been able to pass that joy on to all we encounter? And how are we to pass on that joy?

We hear a lot about evangelism today and how the church must pay more attention to evangelism. But mostly evangelism is not what we tell people, unless what we tell is totally consistent with who we are. It is who we are that is going to make the difference. It is who we are that is going to show the love that brought us all into being, that cares for us all, now, and forever. If we do not have love in our hearts, our words of love will have little meaning. If we do not truly enjoy our faith, nobody is going to catch the fire of enjoyment from us. If our lives are not totally centered on Christ, we will not be Christ-bearers for others, no matter how pious our words.

What is a religion like where faith is not enjoyed? I remembered a friend telling me that her mother grew up in strict Lutheran country. "If it was fun, it was sin," she said. "It was as simple as that."

Even today there are schools where the students have to sign a pledge saying, among other things, that they will not play cards or dance. Personally, I'm a terrible card player, and I hate gambling, but I've played cards for fun with my grandchildren, and it *has* been fun. When my husband and I went on vacation we played cribbage, and a kind of double solitaire called "Spite and Malice," and you were supposed to be as spiteful and malicious as possible with your partner, and that was fun, too, because it was a game. My husband was a solitaire player, and he would sit on our bed playing solitaire, with a script in front of him, and learn his lines while moving the cards in his game. The people in my family who play solitaire are those who are good with numbers, who prepare income taxes and do all kinds of mathematical things I can't do. For them, it is a way of expanding the numerical parts of their brains, and it seems to work well. There's nothing inherently wicked about it. In fact, what is not particularly enjoyable for me, was very enjoyable for my husband. My minor mathematical bent comes out in my struggles with Bach fugues on the piano.

As for dancing, my clumsiness has made me a poor dancer, but I remember with great pleasure one summer on Nantucket Island when I was playing in a lovely summer theatre. After the show was over and the audience had left, we cleared the stage, put on records of Viennese waltzes, and danced peasant fashion, our arms around each others' waists, and I did much better at this than at ballroom dancing. And it was fun. And quite often it was joy. Fun can frequently be the doorway to joy.

Is the ban of cards fear of gambling? That your faith is not strong enough to keep you from the snare of gambling? Gambling seems to be a disease, like alcoholism, but, thank God, not everybody has it. We've had some hilarious family games of poker-playing with ancient chips. I don't like gambling any more than I like smoking, and I dislike smoking because it gives me terrible allergies and is a known health hazard; it's a sin not against moral rectitude but against ourselves, which is what really makes it immoral. And dancing? Yes, it can be very erotic, but sex has been around since Adam and Eve, and dancing can be a healthy way of expressing it. Dancing between man and wife can be a great joy. A popular song when I was young was "Dancing Cheek to Cheek," and yes, it was erotic, and I didn't like it unless I really liked my partner, and it did not lead to sexual license.

Almost everything good can be abused, but that doesn't make the original good any less good, and if it's fun, it may well be joy in the Lord and in Creation, not sin. When we deny our legitimate pleasures we are denying the Incarnation, for Jesus came to affirm, not to deny. He enjoyed eating with his friends, and shared food is always sacramental for me. Even good food can be abused, and over-eating can cause all kinds of problems, but that does not mean that all eating is therefore wrong. The confusion of excess with moderation must please Satan enormously.

Yes, I enjoy my faith, and enjoying my faith frees me to enjoy all the lovely legitimate pleasures of life. Indeed, enjoying my faith helps me to discern which pleasures are legitimate and which are not.

Story, telling story, listening to story, has been such a large part of my enjoyment, of my legitimate pleasure, that it's difficult for me to realize that this is not necessarily generally true. All children, I believe, love story, enjoy story, *need* story. "Tell me a story!" they beg. And then, alas, the grown-up world tells us that story is not true and is only fit for children, who should outgrow it. If story is not true, is it fit for children? Children love story *because it is true*.

And Jesus knew and loved story. When he and his disciples plucked corn and ate it on the Sabbath, and were reprimanded for this, Jesus reminded his accusers of the story of David eating the priestly shewbread from the temple when he needed food.

The story of David and the shewbread is full of depths that Jesus understood and expected his listeners to recognize. David was fleeing from Saul. He asked Ahimelech, the high priest, for food, and all Ahimelech had to give him was the temple shewbread, so David took that. He was also not entirely honest with Ahimelech, telling the priest that Saul, the king, had sent him on a secret mission, rather than telling him the truth—that he was fleeing the king's anger. Both David and Ahimelech paid heavily for this lie. Doeg, Saul's chief herdsman, was there, and reported the incident to Saul, who sent for Ahimelech and his priests and accused them of conspiring with David against him. Ahimelech, more honest than wily, replied, *"Who of all your servants is as loyal as David, the king's son-in-law, captain of your body-guard and highly respected in your household?"*

For this honesty Ahimelech and all his priests were killed:

Doeg the Edomite turned and struck them down. That day he killed eighty-five men who wore the linen ephod. He also put to the sword Nob, the town of the priests, with its men and women, its children and infants, and its cattle, donkeys and sheep.

Only Abiathar, one of Ahimelech's sons, escaped, and fled to David, who promised to protect him.

Jesus, in referring briefly to David's taking the shewbread from Ahimelech, knew the entire story, and he expected his listeners to recognize it, too. Do we? Are we as scripturally literate as Jesus expected his listeners to be? I am grateful yet again to my Episcopal parents who knew, loved, and shared the great stories of the Bible with me.

I don't know how to go to bed without reading, and what I want to read at bedtime is story, good story about interesting people who do brave and honorable and sometimes impossible deeds, and this gives me the courage to be braver myself and to dare things I might otherwise hold back from.

"You really seem to enjoy your faith," the young woman said. Yes, I hope I do. So what is it about my faith that I enjoy? I enjoy it because I believe it to be true, not necessarily factual, but true. If it's factual I don't need faith for it. I enjoy my faith because I believe that God created this wondrous universe out of love, and that God had fun in the act of Creation—hydrogen clouds and galaxies and solar systems and planets capable of sustaining life, and fish and birds and beasts and us human creatures. And then God rested, and I, too, enjoy my day of rest and (occasionally and wonderfully) several days of rest when I go on retreat.

I enjoy my faith because it is full of story, marvelous story, and sometimes terrible story. I have just finished reading *Alone* by Admiral Richard E. Byrd, the incredible story of his desperate months alone at the South Pole. But out of his aloneness came new revelations of his enjoyment of his faith:

The day was dying, the night being born—but with great peace. Here were the imponderable processes and forces of the cosmos, harmonious and soundless. Harmony, that was it! That was what came out of the silence—a gentle rhythm, the strain of a perfect chord, the music of the spheres . . . I could feel no doubt of man's oneness with the universe. The conviction came that the rhythm was too orderly, too harmonious, too perfect to be a product of blind chance—that, therefore, there must be purpose to the whole.

Later in the book Byrd describes his anguish, physical and mental, when he is slowly being poisoned by carbon monoxide from a faulty stove:

The dark side of a man's mind seems to be a sort of antenna tuned to catch gloomy thoughts from all directions. I found it so with mine. It was as if all the world's vindictiveness were concentrated upon me as a personal enemy. . . . Eventually my faith began to make itself felt; and by concentrating on it and reaffirming the truth about the universe as I saw it, I was able again to fill my mind with the fine and comforting things of the world that had seemed irretrievably lost.

Byrd's faith affirmed my own as I read his story.

Jesus taught by telling stories, witty stories, bitter stories, funny stories. I turn to the Bible every morning and evening because it is a great storybook and I never tire of great stories.

But story, like cards and dancing, can be two-edged. Jesus talked of a two-edged sword, and our proclamation of the divinity of Christ can indeed be that. We can give people life with our own heralding of Jesus in our lives, but we must never forget that we can also deal death. We are called on as Christians to affirm and to offer life, but sometimes we can use Jesus to wound; life-giving words can become murderous words of death. During the terrible fires that burned hundreds of houses in Oakland, California, occasionally a single house would be spared, surrounded by the ruins of burned houses. In front of one house that was still standing, in the midst of smouldering foundations of houses that had been totally destroyed, was a large sign: THANK YOU, JESUS.

That sign stabs my heart. One child said to his parents, "Jesus must hate us. *Our* house got burned."

In the evening of life we shall be judged on love. What kind of love caused that THANK YOU, JESUS sign to be flaunted in front of people whose homes had been destroyed? What kind of judgment of love will be given those people who put up that sign? Surely if my house had been spared I would have been awed and grateful, but I pray that I would not have used Jesus' love in self-righteous pride. During Hurricane Bob, when the power in northwestern Connecticut stayed on, my heart ached for those areas where there was no power. At the same time, I was truly grateful for my tiny night-light. If I could have offered some of my power to those without it, I hope I would have.

Share what you have, John the Baptist urged. If you have two coats, don't gloat; give one of them away. If you have enough food, share it with those who are hungry. Rejoice in the love of God. Indeed, yes, enjoy your faith, but not to the exclusion or hurt of other people. I know of one family in Oakland whose house was burned, and they are people who have always enjoyed their faith, and I believe that they still do, because enjoying our faith is enjoyment in the ultimate, rather than the temporary.

 It is enjoyment in an ultimate victory that can be expressed only in the high language of poetry, not the low language of fact. What can we prove about Christ's coming in glory? Nothing. It is far beyond the language of limited proof. Indeed, our entire faith rests on a joyous acceptance of the factually impossible. When we celebrate Christmas we are celebrating that amazing time when the Word that shouted all the galaxies into being, limited all power, and for love of us came to us in the powerless body of a human baby. My faith is based on this incredible act of love, and if my faith is real it will be expressed in how I live my life, but it is outside the realm of laboratory or scientific proof. God—the holy and magnificent Creator of all the galaxies and solar systems and planets and oceans and forests and living creatures—came to live with us, not because we are good and morally virtuous and what God's creation ought to be, but precisely for the opposite reason, because we are stiff-necked and arrogant and sinful and stupid. We have indeed strayed from God's ways like lost sheep.

God still loves us so much that Christ, the second person of the Trinity, the Word, came to live with us as one of us, and all for love.

It's a tough word, love. That love that God showed us at Christmas is beyond our finite comprehension. We can only rejoice. It is glory! It is what makes our hearts sing! It is what makes us enjoy our faith! It blasts the limpness of a factual interpretation into smithereens. Dr. Paul Nathanson, a researcher at McGill University's Center for Medicine, Ethics, and Law, writes,

> My theory is that the churches are secularizing, and they are jettisoning myth and ritual, the imaginative elements. The Bible is mined for statements to legitimate moral or political stances, but it is no longer taken seriously as something to stimulate the imagination and evoke the sacred.

When I receive Communion I am partaking in the most sacred myth and ritual of the Christian church (and let us remember that myth is about *truth*). When we receive the bread and the wine we receive the truth of Jesus' promise, the truth of his love. We don't need to get hung up on words like *transubstantiation*, which tend to take the Eucharist out of the truth of myth and into the wimpiness of fact. What happens when we receive the bread and wine is a mystery, and when we try to explain it in any kind of way we destroy our own ability to partake in the truth of this marvelous and eternally mysterious ritual.

When we receive the bread and the wine we are indeed taking into ourselves Christ's love, that love that will be finally expressed in the Second Coming.

Yes, we are meant to enjoy our faith; I do truly believe that. But our enjoyment involves acceptance of our mortality, of the Cross, and the even deeper wisdom of our immortality. Getting literal about the mighty acts of God in the life, death, and resurrection of Jesus Christ leads to dead ends.

When Christ was born as a human baby, he ensured that he would die, because death is something that comes to every human being. But because Jesus Christ was wholly God as well as wholly human, he rose from the grave, to the astonishment not only of the Roman overlords and the powerful Jews in the Sanhedrin, but to the astonishment of all those who had been with him during his earthly life. The Resurrection, too, is beyond the realm of fact (Do you believe in the literal fact of the Resurrection? No! I believe in the Resurrection!) and bursts into the realm of love, of truth, for in Jesus, truth and love are one and the same.

God's tough love did not stop with the birth in Bethlehem. It shone all through the life of Jesus. The Gospels show him as a strong and uninhibited man who enjoyed his friends, most of whom weren't "the right people"; he enjoyed his great gift of healing; he turned water into wine at a wedding feast; and he enjoyed his faith, even when no one understood him or why he was on this earth or what he was offering us. How terrible it must have been for him that no one understood him—not the disciples, not his friends, not Mary of Magdala, or Mary of Bethany. No one. And he kept on loving, even in his time of total abandonment.

The story of Jesus is indeed great story, but it goes far, far beyond the realm of provable fact and into the realm of mystery and marvel.

A few evenings ago two parents were putting their small child to bed. The child fervently thanked God for all the good things that had happened that day, and then added, "And God did it all with his left hand, too!" This child happened to be right-handed, and the curious parents asked, "Why God's left hand?" And the child replied earnestly, "Jesus was sitting on his right hand."

The parents were able to move their little one beyond this literalism, but it is a groove of literalism many people remain stuck in, and that is, indeed, taught in some churches. However, if we take Scripture seriously rather than literally, we discover it has little to say about "moral or political stances," and instead constantly "stimulate[s] the imagination and evoke[s] the sacred" (Dr. Paul Nathanson).

One of many things the Bible stories have taught me is that God loves me, just as I am. I don't have to struggle for some kind of moral perfection impossible to attain. It is the biblical protagonists who, like us, far from perfect, show us how to be truly human. I don't believe that God deliberately made me with one leg considerably longer than the other, but that is how I am, and I am loved that way, resultant clumsiness and all. I knew that God loves me as I am, so I was able to accept the wondrous truth that my husband did too—one result of enjoying my faith! For we cannot give love if we cannot accept it.

Does enjoying my faith imply protection from the slings and arrows of outrageous fortune? No. It did not stop my husband from dying prematurely. It did not stop a careless truck driver from going through a red light and nearly killing me. My faith is not a magic charm, like garlic to chase away vampires. It is, instead, what sustains me in the midst of all the normal joys and tragedies of the ordinary human life. It is faith that helps my grief to be creative, not destructive. It is faith that kept me going through the pain at the very portals of death and pulled me, whether I would or no, back into life and whatever work still lies ahead.

It is faith that what happens to me matters to God as well as to me that gives me joy, that promises me that I am eternally the subject of God's compassion, and that assures me that the compassion was manifested most brilliantly when God came to us in a stable in Bethlehem. God gave us the wonderful story of Jesus, and that story dignifies my story, your story, all our stories. As we read it in the Gospels we see that Jesus was not only a great storyteller, he also came in for much frightened and irrational criticism. He was accused of having fun with his friends. His enjoyment of his faith, too, was suspect! This joy came from his constant awareness of his Source. And it is that awareness of our Source that takes away our fears and not only allows us, but prods us, even commands us to enjoy our faith.

John the Baptist proclaimed that Jesus would baptize us with the Holy Ghost and with fire, and that fire is the fire of love, not the fire of a literalistic version of hell, but the fire of love, right here, right now. We are called to

love each other, and that call is not for an easy, sentimen-
tal love, but for tough love, love that knows when to say
No rather than *Yes*. I have slowly learned that when God
says *No* to my most earnest prayer, that *No* may well be
the prelude to a wonderful *Yes* I couldn't even have
begun to predict. If I am to enjoy my faith I have to trust
the *No* comes from love, not anger. I have discovered that
many people who do not enjoy their faith are afraid of
God, afraid because they view God as an angry parent
who must constantly be placated lest he vent his anger
with unreasonable and irrational noes because we don't
deserve the yesses. If I felt I had to deserve God's *Yes*
answers I'd be miserable, indeed. God says *Yes* whenever
possible because it is our Maker's pleasure to give us
pleasure. We are loved because we are God's and that
love is shown most gloriously through Christ's presence
in our world and in our lives.

Story as
Good News

9

THE FOUR GOSPELS tell us the story of Jesus, and that is Good News indeed. The Good News is what the word *gospel* means. We read the Gospels with joy, not with long faces.

We read the Gospels with joy because in human terms the story they tell is impossible. Jesus said, "With man it is impossible. With God nothing is impossible."

In human terms, how can we understand the great good news of the Incarnation? How can we understand the all-powerful, immortal God putting on mortality, sharing with us life and death and all that comes in between, and then offering us the radical joy of the Resurrection? Oh, indeed, yes, in human terms what God offers us is impossible, and it is when we try to limit it to the possible that we get into trouble, terrible trouble.

When we limit God's mighty acts to the possible we can castigate and sometimes kill other Christians because their understanding of Christ is not exactly like ours. We can be terrified of Roman Catholics and refuse to have any statues or images in our churches. We can deny ourselves the nurture of symbol and sacrament because their potency is fearful. Sometimes when I am asked if I am a New Ager, I reply, "No, I am an Episcopalian," understanding that Episcopalianism is as alien to my questioner as the New Age! When we try to define and over-define and narrow down we lose the story the Maker of the Universe is telling us in the Gospels. I do not want to explain the Gospels; I want to enjoy them.

And that is how I want to read and write the story. This does not mean that story deals only with cheeriness, but that beneath the reality of life is the rock of faith. I ask God to set me upon a rock that is higher than I so that I may be able to see more clearly, see the tragedy and the joy and sometimes the dull slogging along of life with an assurance that not only is there rock under my feet, but that God made the rock and you and me, and is concerned with Creation, every galaxy, every atom and subatomic particle. Matter *matters*.

That is the promise of the Incarnation. Christ put on human matter, and what happens to us is of eternal, cosmic importance. That is what true story affirms. Someone asked me why all my stories have happy endings, and I replied, "They don't. Joshua is killed in *The Arm of the Starfish* and he's not going to come back to life. Neither are Maggie's parents in *Meet the Austins*. Ron, in *The Other Side of the Sun* is shot by Aunt Olivia in order to prevent an even worse death."

No, many of my stories do not have happy endings, but I suspect that what made the reader ask that question is that despite the tragedy of life, the stories affirm that it matters. It matters to us; it matters to our Creator. Ultimately there is meaning to tragedy, even if we may not know what it is in this life. Story helps us dare to take seriously Jesus' promise that every hair of our head is counted—one of the Maker's joyous exaggerations. Or is it exaggeration? Are there angels whose job is to do such counting? What has happened to Christianity that there is so little joy? (Not mere happiness. Joy. Someone told me that the difference between happiness and joy is sorrow.) Why do we forget the promise of the rock under our feet? Why is there so much fear, so much antagonism, so much judgmentalism? Why do some people read story looking for something to criticize rather than applaud? It is a human tendency to draw together when a common enemy can be found. If there is no real enemy, or if the real enemy is too fearful to be faced, then one has to be made up. That frightens me more than the real enemy.

During the fifties there was hysterical terror over communism, with Senator Joseph McCarthy pointing a quivering finger at those he accused of being communists, out to overthrow the United States. I am sure that there were indeed communists out to overthrow the United States, but those weren't the ones he was accusing. Instead he pointed at artists. Actors were out of work for years, hungry, unemployable, because somebody had decided they were communists. Perhaps a few of them were; we had just finished a war in which Russia was our ally; communism seemed to offer a message of hope for the oppressed, to be a real antidote to Nazism and facism. But I doubt if the actors who were attracted by the philosophy of communism were out to overthrow the United States. In one of my journals written during that period I've pasted in two articles from the *New York Times* about a major Hollywood studio scrapping its plans to produce a movie of Hiawatha. HIAWATHA MAY AID REDS, the headline reads. HERO IS IN FAVOR OF PEACE. I am equally horrified by the present-day equivalent, which seems to me to be equally hysterical and unrealistic.

In the fifties if you cared about peace you were a communist; in the nineties if you care about peace you are a New Ager. For people who have to have an enemy, the new enemy is the New Age (whatever that is; I'm still not sure). The books I've read which are against the New Age tell me more about the people who are against it than about the New Age itself. From what little I have found out about it, it strikes me as being a twentieth-century form of Gnosticism, with a touch of Mary Baker Eddy, and I am not particularly interested. I was sent one book by a New Age guru and tried to read it; I didn't find anything terrifying in it; I simply found it so dull that I couldn't finish it.

I got a little more idea of what New Ageism might be in Marion Zimmer Bradley's editorial to her fourteenth *Fantasy Magazine*. In it she says, "I get furious when some sloppy New Age type asks me (casting her eyes to heaven) why I 'chose to manifest diabetes.' By me that's just another way of 'blaming the victim.'"

If that's New Ageism, I'm against it, too. I did not manifest the carelessness that made a truck driver run through a red light. But it is not enough to terrify me into seeing the New Age as some kind of terrible evil.

Why am I so concerned about this? Because the hysterical need for a common enemy is an enemy of story. If the only way we can believe that our faith is valid is by <u>accusing another faith of being false</u>, then our <u>faith is shaky indeed.</u> Communism was a religion, a powerful religion while it lasted, but proving that it was a false religion (which it was and is) did little to affirm the love and joy of faith.

After I had given a lecture at an evangelical conference, a woman came up to me after one of my talks, saying, "I heard you were a New Ager, but now that I've heard you speak I can't think what they meant."

I laughed and said, "Neither can I. Although I *am* an Episcopalian."

"Well, I think I'm going to buy one of your books now."

"Thank you," I said. "And I really hope you will enjoy it."

There was enough talk about me and the New Age that I asked one group of several hundred people, "Can any one of you tell me what the New Age is, and why my books are supposed to be New Age books?"

No one could.

That was interesting.

Someone suggested, "Unicorns are a New Age symbol."

I replied, "Unicorns are a Christ symbol, and they are also scriptural."

Astonishment. Unicorns in the Bible? Heaven forbid!

But they are. "Just read the Psalms," I suggested. "You'll find unicorns there pretty quickly. But they're also in Deuteronomy, Isaiah, Numbers, and Job for starters."

"Oh."

"What about rainbows?" someone else asked.

"What about them?"

"Aren't they a New Age symbol?"

"The rainbow is the sign in the Bible of God's covenant with his people," I said. "Why are you letting fear take away symbolism which has been part of our Christian imagery for thousands of years?"

"Isn't it Satanic?"

"What?"

"The New Age."

"I don't know. I do know that there is Satan worship in the world and that it is dangerous and that it terrifies me." But I have a suspicion that looking for Satan worship in the New Age movement is like looking for those who would overthrow the United States among actors. It's accusing the wrong people and ignoring the truly dangerous ones. And they are dangerous indeed.

Why am I being accused of being a New Ager? It's beyond me, unless meditation, imagination, poetry, joy in the Creator and Creation are considered to be New Age.

Well, I thought, *I'd better look up a book on the New Age and find out what it's all about.*

One of my godchildren got a book from her assistant pastor about the New Age and gave it to me. The problem is that it wasn't really about the New Age. It was about Anti-New Agers. It was a scary book. My friend said, "Madeleine, someone remarked that you were very honest in your presentations and that you ought to know who your enemies are. I don't think your enemies are the New Agers, I think they're the Anti-New Agers." The book she gave me didn't scare me about the New Age because it didn't tell me much about it. It scared me about those who hysterically oppose the New Age, because it's as irrational as refusing to make a movie about Hiawatha because Hiawatha upheld peace.

The writer of this pamphlet says, in explaining the ethics of the New Age Movement, "Most people in the New Age movement are ANTI-WAR/ANTI-NUCLEAR pacifists." (The capitalization is his.) And I wondered: Can one be a Christian and not be anti-war, and anti-nuclear warfare? Why is peace, once again, a sign of the enemy instead of a sign of the Good News?

In a book and music catalog there was a listing of New Age records, which included Pachelbel's Canon! Pachelbel, one of the composers who influenced Johann Sebastian Bach, would be astounded!

Many of the symbols which are now purported to be New Age, or, even worse, signs of devil worship, are Christian symbols. Indeed they may be misused and distorted by groups which are not Christian (a black mass is a blasphemous distortion of the Christian Eucharist), but that does not mean we need to toss them out and hand them over to the enemy! Give up the rainbow as a glorious sign of God's covenant with his people? Never! Give up the crescent moon and the stars and call them symbols of Satan rather than visible signs of the glory of God's creation? Never! The enemy can't have them unless we weakly and thoughtlessly relinquish our very own heritage.

This does not mean putting on blinders and pretending that the enemy is not there. He is, horribly, powerfully there. Indeed there is devil worship in this country, and it is evil and terrifying. But we only help it to spread when we label serious thinkers, such as Teilhard de Chardin, devil worshipers. (Yes, gentle Teilhard was listed as a devil worshiper in one anti-New Age book.) Just as Senator Joseph McCarthy looked under the wrong beds, ignoring the communists who were indeed seeking the overthrow of democracy, so I believe that the anti-New Age people are also looking under the wrong beds and ignoring the real horror of Satanic rituals. I talked to a young man who was struggling to recover from the horror he had endured as a child, being made a participant in such rituals, which were a dark and vicious travesty of Christian holy rites. Shuddering, pale with remembered fear, he told of the slaughter of babies. The anti-god requires blood, human blood.

What upsets me most, I think, is that the anti-communists were *against* communism, rather than *for* democracy. And the Anti-New Agers are *against* the New Age rather than *for* Christ. Isn't this being *against* rather than *for* the frame of mind which produces terrorism? Isn't it, in itself, a kind of terrorism? The terrorists who blew up a plane full of people felt holy in their action; a religion that not only condones but commands murder of "unbelievers" is a fearful thing. As I read the Gospels, one of the strongest messages is *for*; for love, for warmth of heart, for that love which dissolves hate and coldness of heart. When our religion brings hate to our hearts, it becomes terrorism, not religion.

When I am asked if I have accepted Jesus Christ as my Lord and Savior, it is usually an accusation, not a true question. It is an accusation which strikes me as impertinent, because it usually comes in the context of a Christian conference at which I am a speaker. And I know from the tone of voice of my accuser that my answer of Yes is not going to be accepted. We have to be very careful that when we invoke the name of Jesus, it is always a call to love and not a weapon of anger and judgmentalness. When I say "Thank you, Jesus," I must be very careful that I know what I am saying.

It must give great pain to Christ that so much damage has been done in his name, ever since the beginning. And yet, somehow or other, the Church continues, stronger than those whose zeal would destroy it. It comforts me to read the Acts of the Apostles, because the early followers of Christ were so like us, quarreling with each other, reinterpreting and misinterpreting the words of Jesus, and yet, ultimately, serving Love rather than themselves and their own opinions.

As for the New Age—didn't it begin in a stable in Bethlehem two thousand years ago, when Christ came to make all things new?

So I must hold to the Good News and not let myself be trapped in the same trap as the Anti-New Agers! I asked a large group at the Midwest conference: "If your faith is secure, what are you afraid of?"

If my faith is secure, what am I afraid of?

The answer is, of course, that my faith is not as secure as it ought to be. Finite Madeleine is often far from certain of the infinite God who (nevertheless) rules my life. I know to my rue that I am not as good a Christian as I ought to be. Too often reason gets in my way. How can I understand the unreasonableness of the Incarnation, an act of love beyond my fragile mind to comprehend?

If that Rock that is higher than I is solid under my feet, why am I perplexed and hurt when I am accused of being a New Ager?

Am I afraid that maybe I am, without knowing it, all that I am accused of?

Yes, I care about our planet and I am pained at what we are doing to destroy it. Yes, I care passionately about peace. Saving the whales matters to me. I read a recent "Christian best seller," a novel, in which the reader is given a clue that one minister is a bad guy, a New Ager, "Because he cares about the family of man and saving the whales."

We are also warned that *meditation* is now a "bad" word, a New Age word! In Genesis, Chapter 24, Isaac *went out to the field one evening to meditate*. Wasn't Jesus meditating when he left his friends and went away to a desert place to be alone with the Father?

I suspect that the fear and condemnation of meditation comes because it is difficult for us to let ourselves go, to put our entire lives with absolute faith in a God we cannot in any way control. We live in a society which is sold on control, and tries to sell it to us. But the only way we can brush against the hem of the Lord, or hope to be able to work with our Abba/Amma in the telling of our story, is to have the courage, the faith, to abandon our control and to give it entirely to the Creator.

I am sad that this novel (which I read with deep sadness in my heart) is a best seller among Christians, because it is, to me, pornographic, in that it treats people as objects, not subjects. It draws people together through fear and hate, not love. But if I am upset about it, is it because I feel myself accused? Not so much accused of being a New Ager, as accused of my own lacks of love, my own angers, my own looking at people who disagree with me as objects, not subjects.

Jesus was accused of all kinds of behavior that went against the law, but mostly he turned anger away softly rather than falling into the same trap as his accusers.

Do I want to be like Jesus, or like the Pharisees and Sadducees? Or the Anti-New Agers? (And I remind myself, not all the Pharisees were legalistic and narrow-minded. They were serious scholars and willing to be open to what Jesus was saying even if, like Nicodemus, they came to him at night.)

If my faith is secure, then I should not be surprised when I am criticized or misunderstood. And I must not expect of myself super-human virtue. Virtue is not the sign of a Christian! Joy is. When my feelings are hurt, I am not joyful.

I heard from my son-in-law, Alan, of one young man who was an atheist because of his father, who was a devout and virtuous Christian. Alan asked, "Was your father full of joy and light?"

"No, he was a miserable bugger."

That is why, to this young man, misery and Christianity were synonymous.

When I turn to the Good News and accept it joyfully, that does not free me from human emotions. "Are you angry?" my doctor and friend asked me after my accident. And I wasn't. Not then. I didn't have time or energy for anger. All my attention was focused on healing.

I'm still healing. I still wear out easily; I still need a nap in the afternoon. But I found out that I *am* angry. I'm angry not so much at the irrationality of the accident or the carelessness of the truck driver as at the fact that the insurance companies expect me to pay for it. Me! The man who hit me was minimally insured, and his insurance didn't cover a tenth of the hospital bills, much less all the other costs, doctors, medication, lost time, lost income.

I found out how angry I was when I walked into my apartment late one afternoon, ready to lie down for my nap, and picked up the ringing telephone. I was exhausted; my side ached; I should have ignored the phone and just let it ring. But I lay across the bed and reached for it. Someone was calling from San Diego to ask me why I hadn't paid my ambulance bill.

"I haven't received the ambulance bill."

"We sent you three."

"I have not received one."

The woman at the other end of the line checked the address, which was correct. "I still have not received a bill," I said. "Now that we're paying more for stamps, delivering mail is no longer part of the job description of the postal worker. In any case, it is the man who ran through the red light and hit me who should be paying for this bill."

"We must be paid. It's the law. We'll put a lien on your house."

"Fine. Go ahead. I'll go to jail where I can write books in peace and quiet." I certainly don't want to make money from the accident. No amount of money could compensate me. But I don't feel I should have to pay for it.

But that's life. Postal workers are no longer in the business of delivering mail. Insurance companies are no longer in the business of paying for the insured. The only way I can get the money from the insurance company, I am told, is to sue them, in which case my premiums will be raised so that there will be little point in carrying insurance. Why have I been paying for it all my life when, the moment I need it, I am badgered with phone calls from San Diego demanding payment for bills I have never received? Yes, I am angry. I am furious!

I said, "If it came before a jury, I'd win, because they'd be on my side." I was told that yes, they'd be on my side, but they couldn't go against the law. The law is that the bills must be paid, and if I'm the one who has to pay them, that's tough, but that's life.

Nobody ever promised fairness. That this is grossly unfair should not surprise me. And it's okay for me to be angry as long as I move through the anger and let it go. This blatant inequity is peripheral to the Good News, which is central. Part of that Good News to me is that God laughs gently at my anger, and does not become angry at me in turn. Instead, God reminds me of my tendency to disproportion, and prods me towards that marvelous peace at the center of things. When I look inward, I am grateful to find that the peace is still there. The anger will go; I know that it is inordinate, and that one reason I over-reacted to that telephone call was that I was over-tired. It is not possible to come partly back into the world; you're either taken out of it, or shoved all the way back in it, and all the way in was my choice, so I must accept the price of fatigue and the pain of a still healing body. Despite it, the peace of the Good News will not disappear, and that is what matters.

In his life on earth, Jesus was not treated fairly, was he? And he is still often treated unfairly. Should we be surprised when it happens to us?

One of the things the secular world tries to teach us is that we should never be angry, that all anger is destructive. As we look at the world around us we see that much anger is indeed destructive, especially in our over-crowded cities. I still shudder at the story, factually true, of a fifteen-year-old boy sitting on a bench outside Columbia University, talking and laughing with a friend. He was an attractive young man, acolyte at Corpus Christi Church, honor student, with lots of friends. A stranger came up to him and demanded, "Why are you laughing?" The boy looked up, surprised. "I'm just laughing . . ." At which the other took out a gun and shot him. Dead.

That's destructive anger. There are many examples of it. Pick up any paper from any good-sized town or city, and there will be examples.

♦ ♦ ♦

Probably the first, instinctive reaction to something going wrong is outrage. One morning when my husband woke up with a hot, inflamed foot and we called the doctor who immediately diagnosed blood poisoning, I was furious—furious at the diagnosis, furious at my husband for being so inconsiderate as to have blood poisoning, particularly at a time when I myself was over-tired and needed taking care of, rather than the other way around. Part of my anger was to mask my fear that something might be seriously wrong with someone I love. Part of the anger was because once more I had been forcibly reminded of the precariousness of all life—that we can never take an ordinary day for granted. We can't help falling for the seductive promises of the world that we have a right to security. And when that nonexistent security is threatened we respond with anger.

When we have moved through the first response of anger, it is replaced by grief, healthy grief. Real grief accepts that there is no security. No one can promise us that in mortal, temporal terms nothing bad will happen. The implied promise of the insurance commercials is that no rape or murder or fire or accident can touch us—as long as we pay our insurance premiums.

Unhealthy grief usually has qualities of resentment. Or self-pity. Or sullenness.

I have a hunch that anyone with a strong and lively faith is not immune to the anger which is the first reaction to injustice, but the anger when worked through will not be destructive but will lead to healthy grieving and accepting.

♦ ♦ ♦

The way we handle our little griefs, the petty irritations of daily living, is an indication of the way we're going to handle the larger griefs. Life in New York is full of petty irritations; for instance, it's almost impossible to get across town without getting stuck in what seems like an interminable traffic jam. For the petty irritations I turn to a nursery rhyme which I find not only helpful but theologically sound:

> For every evil under the sun
> There is a remedy, or there is none.
> If there be one, try to find it.
> If there be none, never mind it.

If I'm stuck on a crosstown bus, or if I've taken a taxi to try to save time and it's even slower than the bus, I repeat that rhyme to myself and sit back and relax. I realize there's absolutely nothing I can do about the traffic; if I'm going to be late there's nothing I can do about that, either. So why waste energy getting furious and frustrated?

The larger angers I try to turn to God. Like the psalmist, I bellow at life's unfairness and God's apparent refusal to do anything about it. And our Maker absorbs and heals all our angers, though the world gives us little legitimate outlet for them.

Many years ago when my husband and I left New York to raise our family in the country, and he was taking over the general store in the village, Hugh spent the day with an old country storekeeper in a neighboring town. The old man took him down to the cellar and showed him a large wooden lolly column in the middle of the cellar, holding up the sagging floor. Beside the lolly column was a baseball bat, and the old storekeeper told Hugh that when he'd had customers to the teeth, he'd go down to the cellar and have at the lolly column with the baseball bat, until he was fit to face human nature once more. That was a good lesson for us both.

Most of the scriptural protagonists had cause to learn a lot about unfairness, their own, and that of others. It was unfair of Saul to try to have David killed by sending him into battle against the Philistines. And yet David did the same thing when he had Uriah placed in the heat of battle, and David did not have Saul's excuse of insanity. Later, when Bathsheba's baby died to pay for David's sin, surely that was unfair!

When my young children stamped and complained, "But it isn't fair!" I would reply, "Who promised you fairness? Of course it's not fair." And when they wanted revenge, I'd ask, "That's being just like the person who was unfair to you. Is that what you want to be like?"

And when I stamp my interior foot and say that the insurance companies aren't fair, aren't I being just like a small child? Yes, the insurance companies are in the business of making money, lots of money, and not in the business of helping the people they promise to help. If I need a reminder that we live in a fallen world, that's a good one. People have been making money out of other people's misfortunes, illness and death, for millenia. Why should I think that I should in any way be exempt from unfairness? And yet this irrational demand for fairness has been within me for a long time; it is hard to get beyond it.

So what's the Good News?

It is that God loves me even when I am outraged! And God wants me to know all of my story, not just the pleasant parts. We do tend to want to rewrite our stories, turning ourselves into models of perfection which would probably bore our friends to pieces.

A number of years ago at a writers' conference I got to talking with the leader of the nonfiction workshop. At least—he *said* that he did not write fiction, but then he told me about ghostwriting the "autobiography" of a famous European prima donna. They had long talks about her life, and he kept trying to find out what had happened to her between the ages of twelve and eighteen.

"But nothing happened. I was a good girl at St. Cecelia's convent."

"But something must have happened."

The prima donna shook her head. "I was a good girl at St. Cecelia's Convent."

This didn't strike him as exciting enough, so he invented a count who adored her with an undeclared passion. The count and the young girl spoke of love only with their eyes. Theirs was a pure flame of undefiled love.

When he sent the prima donna the manuscript he expected an angry reaction. Nothing. Later, at a large autograph party he heard her say, "The count was really taller and he had black hair."

The apocryphal count had become part of her memory. He was somebody who ought to have happened. As far as the opera singer was concerned, he had become real.

When my granddaughters were little they had the same uninhibited kind of memory. I used to make up stories for them, about Princess Charlotte and Princess Madeleine, and they would demand, "Tell us a story we've never heard before. Tell us a story we don't remember."

My six-year-old grandson, in his playtime, dons costumes. He enlarges his life by becoming a pirate, a turtle, a knight. And that is good. He is experimenting with his story. But far too often we diminish ourselves instead of expanding ourselves. We tidy ourselves up, removing the uglier characteristics, but that is, ultimately, dehumanizing. The good news is that God loves and wants all of us, at our best and at our worst, because it is out of this extraordinary mixture that God weaves the warp and woof of our souls.

Is there, then, no bad news? Oh, yes, there's much bad news, and much of it is a result of our refusing to look at our whole selves, to read our whole story. If we edit and revise, then we are able to rationalize our anger, our vindictiveness, our vengefulness instead of accepting that these feelings are within us, but do not have to be acted on, and can, with God's help, be overcome and forgiven. Maybe not immediately, maybe not entirely, but we can, as the psalmist affirms, be purged in the fire like silver.

I have a pleasant (though not playable) imaginary scenario of going to the small jail in Litchfield, on a pleasant street, and next door to the bank. There, with no normal day-to-day responsibilities, I can refuse to pay the ambulance bill and instead I can sit and write my books. That scenario is not going to happen. I'm going to have to pay whatever amount of my hard-earned money is legally necessary, and I'm not going to like it. But I'm not going to stay stuck in my annoyance. Already my first howl of outrage is past. This is the way of the world, and aren't we taught that although we are *in* the world we don't need to be *of* it?

The bad news is that I have had to face my anger. Or is that bad news, after all? The good news is that I know that God loves me anyhow. The literary protagonists who have meant the most to me have had all kinds of faults and flaws; they have been far from perfect; had they been perfect I would not have been able to recognize myself in them. I see myself in Mary Lennox in *The Secret Garden* because she is selfish and nasty and human and, in the end, love breaks through the selfishness, as it can with all of us. I sympathize with Viola in Shakespeare's *Twelfth Night* because she gets herself into the terrible predicament of seemingly hopeless love with Count Orsino; most of us human beings have blundered in love at some time or other in our lives! I do not recognize myself in Victorian Elsie Dinsmore because she is too perfect and knows it. I agonize with King David's daughter, Tamar, when her brother lusts after her, then abuses and abandons her. And I agonize with David's inability to act to right the wrong, which is not unlike Hamlet's.

In story I recognize my own humanness, and the call to become more fully human—not perfect, but human— bearing within me the image of my Maker.

The Gospels are story, the Good Story, the story we are called to share with humility and joy.

Story as a Creative Act

10

THE POWER OF LOVE that called forth the universe, calls on us to create, too—not out of nothing, for only God can do that—but with what the Creator has given us.

All art, good, bad, indifferent, reflects its culture. Great art transcends its culture and touches on that which is eternal. Two writers may write the same story about the same man and woman and their relationship with each other. One writer will come up with art and the other with pornography. There is no subject that is not appropriate for the artist, but the way in which it is handled can sometimes be totally inappropriate. True art has a mythic quality in that it speaks of that which was true, is true, and will be true.

Too much concern about *Christian* art can be destructive both to art and to Christianity. I cannot consciously try to write a *Christian* story. My own life and my own faith will determine whether or not my stories are Christian. Too much Christian art relies so heavily on being Christian that the artist forgets that it also must be good art.

When we write a story, we must write to the absolute best of our ability. That is the job, first and foremost. If we are truly Christian, that will be evident, no matter what the topic. If we are not truly Christian, that will also be evident, no matter how pious the tale. When I am working on a book I move into an area of faith that is beyond the conscious control of my intellect. I do not mean that I discard my intellect—that I am an anti-intellectual gung ho for intuition. Like it or not, I am an intellectual. The struggle is to let my intellect work *for* what I am working on, not against it. And this means, first of all, that I must have more faith in the work than I have in myself.

Scientists are now discovering that the cognitive part of the brain is not necessarily the most used part. Ideas, be they scientific or artistic, come when the cognitive mind is at rest, and suddenly it will awaken to an idea that has been given it by the interior, creative, often unrecognized area of the brain. When the storyteller insists on being in control of the story, then the story has no chance to take off and take the writer with it into strange and unexpected places.

I do not always choose what I am going to write. Sometimes I feel called to write on subjects I really don't want to tackle. That's when I most need to listen to the story with humility and virtue, virtue in the ancient sense of the word, which has little to do with moral rectitude. True virtue means strength. And in one etymological dictionary, virtue is defined as *that which is necessary*. So let us spell it *vertue*, to differentiate it from self-conscious virtue. In biblical language it means creative power—*creative* power vs. that dominant power that Lord Acton warns us will corrupt us. When the woman with the issue of blood touches the hem of Jesus' garment, he knows someone has touched him, because he feels the *vertue* drain from him. So, indeed the act of creation is virtuous, as the Word shouting the galaxies into being was virtuous. Indeed, our *vertue* may involve a sudden acknowledgment of our wrongdoings. Indeed, our sin.

I was upset at the Bible college's statement of faith that emphasized God's wrath at my sin and depravity, not because I think I am sinless, or because I am never "crooked or wrong" (my etymological dictionary's definition of depraved), but because I believe that God is calling me away from sin and depravity, both of which kill the creative element in us, and towards creativity, humility, and vertue.

If I dwell constantly on my sin and depravity, and am thereby constantly fearful of God's wrath and indignation, I make it impossible for myself to move out of sin and depravity into joy and creativity. This does not mean that I forget what I have done that is wrong. Adam, in *The Arm of the Starfish*, must live the rest of his life knowing that he was at least partially responsible for Joshua's death. But his calling is not to dwell on this terrible awareness, but to move on and to live the rest of his life as creatively as possible.

King David's life was changed forever because he succumbed to temptation with Bathsheba, and then tried to get out of the mess by having her husband killed.

He confessed in an anguish of repentance, and Nathan the prophet told him,

"The LORD has taken away your sin. You are not going to die. But because by doing this you have made the enemies of the LORD show utter contempt, the son born to you will die."

So it wasn't just what David had done; it was the example he had set. People who have accepted positions of public trust are particularly responsible not to give occasion to the enemies of the Lord to say it's okay to dump your wife, to sleep around, to evade income tax. Fulfill yourself, that's what the world says is important.

But the people I know, in literature and in life, whose chief concern is fulfilling themselves, are always empty.

The rules are not the same for all of us; we'd like them to be, but they are not. I am free to have a glass of wine at a dinner party. My surgeon friend who is on call and may have to operate on someone that night is not. I have committed myself very publicly in my writing about marriage and marriage vows. Hugh and I used to laugh and agree that it was a good thing that we didn't want to get divorced, because we couldn't. I believe that those who are ordained to the ministry are also called to set an example in their daily living.

A man in a position of public trust said to me that he was unhappy with his marriage, that he could not stay in it and keep his integrity. This may sometimes be true. Too often it means, "I cannot stay in this marriage and have my own way."

Someone else told me of a monk who, after ten years in a monastery, had recognized his homosexuality, and left the monastery because he felt he could not stay there and keep his integrity. I asked, "Why was it harder for him to be a celibate monk as a homosexual than as a heterosexual?" Didn't keeping his integrity once again mean, "I cannot stay here and have my own way"?

If the public persona and the inner man (or woman) are not close together, there is trouble, and there is certainly loss of integrity. It is only as we recognize our sin and depravity and turn to God for healing (not wrath) that we are enabled to sin less frequently. If we set ourselves up as models of rectitude and make ourselves believe that we have perfect morality, we are apt to fall on our faces, as have some televangelists and many politicians. Moral rectitude may come naturally to angels, but not to us human beings.

King David's public and private selves were close together, despite his adultery, and that is why his repentance was real. Ultimately he truly became a king, but not until after he knew himself a sinner, after he had suffered civil war with his son Absalom, and grieved for the death of those closest to his heart. Then, at last, he became "royal David," a true king. *We went through fire and water*, David, the psalmist sings. *But you brought us out into a wide place.*

"My God, my God!" David cried. *"Why have you forsaken me?"*

And Jesus, on the cross, echoed King David's words.

Story is seldom true if we try to control it, manipulate it, make it go where we want it to go, rather than where the story itself wants to go. I do not control my stories, and most of the writers with whom I have talked agree with me. We listen to the story, and must be willing to grow with it. But how do we know that the story is right?

We've lost much of the richness of that word *know.* Nowadays "to know" means to know with the intellect. But it has much deeper meaning than that. Adam *knew*

203

Eve. To know deeply is far more than to know consciously. My husband *knew* me. Sometimes he knew me far better than I know myself. In the realm of faith I *know* far more than I can believe with my finite mind. I *know* that a loving God will not abandon what has been created. I *know* that the human calling is co-creation with this power of love. I *know* that *neither death nor life, neither angels nor demons, neither the present nor the future, nor any powers, neither height nor depth, nor anything else in all creation, will be able to separate us from the love of God that is in Christ Jesus our Lord.*

The powers of darkness would like to keep us from this knowing, and it is possible that we can permit them to blind us, because we are mortal and flawed. But Love is always more powerful than hate, creativity than destruction. When I falter and fear I turn to story to return me to light. God's story, God's wonderful, impossible, glorious story of the mystery of the Word made flesh.

♦ ♦ ♦

After President Coolidge retired, he and Mrs. Coolidge lived a quiet life together, away from politics and political problems. One rainy Sunday Mrs. Coolidge had a cold, and decided to stay home from church. When President Coolidge returned, she asked him what the preacher's sermon had been about.

"Sin."

"What did he have to say about it?"

President Coolidge, ever laconic, replied, "He was agin it."

We're all "agin" sin, and yet we're all deep in it, because it is an intrinsic part of human nature, and until we are aware that we're sinners, it isn't really possible for us to be "agin" it.

And what is sin?

As I read and reread the great stories in the Bible it seems more and more clear that sin is separation from God, and one way to separate ourselves from God is to over-define God. If Jesus was like us, but sinless, it wasn't that he never did anything the moral majority of his day considered wrong. Indeed, he did many things that they considered sin, such as breaking the law by healing people on the Sabbath. But he was never separate from the Source, while we, of our essence, separate ourselves over and over.

The first great story in the Bible, after the wonderful paean of praise to Creation, is a story of separation from God, the story of Adam and Eve in the Garden. It doesn't really matter who was the first to eat of the fruit of the tree of the knowledge of good and evil. What is important is that in going against God's wishes, they separated themselves from their Maker. Both of them.

Like many of the tales in Scripture, the story of the expulsion of the human beings from the Garden is an ambiguous one. It is a story not of punishment, but of separation, the two human beings' separation from God, and separation from their own natures. Suddenly Adam and Eve became aware of knowledge—intellectual knowledge, and they weren't yet ready for all that they learned. It was out of chronology and inconsistent with God's time. Perhaps, in God's time, when Adam and Eve were ready, God would have called them to the tree and said, "Eat." But they took matters into their own hands and ate too soon. Their intellectual and spiritual development was sundered.

We are still paying for that sundering. We know with our intellects far more than we know with our spirits. We know how to make war and to kill; how to build factories and make slaves of those who work in them; how to allow immense wealth and terrible poverty side by side; how to be judgmental and intolerant and exclusive and unforgiving.

And so Adam and Eve were prematurely expelled from the Garden. I suspect that sooner or later they would have had to leave, that God would have gently shoved them out, as the mother bird pushes the fledgling from the nest. But the timing would have been right. They would have been ready to fly.

But, prodded by the serpent, they took time into their own hands and broke it. When we look for a way to heal this brokenness, God offers us story, and sometimes the story is so extraordinary that it is difficult for us to understand, especially if we try to understand, as Adam and Eve did after they had left the Garden, with mind alone, and not with heart and spirit.

After the first separation from God in the Garden, the next story is of an even more terrible separation: murder. Cain killed Abel. And this kind of separation has gone on ever since. At its worst this sin of separation is murder, literal murder; occasionally it is hysterical folly. Last summer before going to Oxford for a conference I re-read Elizabeth Goudge's *Towers in the Mist*, set in Oxford at the time of Queen Elizabeth, and I had forgotten the terrible things Protestants and Catholics did to each other, each group as brutal as the other, depending on which was politically in power.

The story of Romeo and Juliet is a story about this kind of irrational separation, as are the Narnia Chronicles, as is *The Brothers Karamazov*. As we read of the pain caused by separation, we are offered healing. And that is why I love the stories in Scripture, for they are prescriptions for healing, even when they are incomprehensible, such as this marvelous passage from Ezekiel:

> *I looked, and I saw beside the cherubim four wheels, one beside each of the cherubim . . . the four of them looked alike; each was like a wheel intersecting a wheel. As they moved, they would go in any one of the four directions the cherubim faced. . . . Their entire bodies, including their backs, their hands and their wings, were completely full of eyes, as were their four wheels. . . . Each of the cherubim had four faces: One face was that of a cherub, the second the face of a man, the third the face of a lion, and the fourth the face of an eagle.*

This is from the tenth chapter of Ezekiel, and the cherubim, man, lion, and eagle are reprised in John's Revelation. What are we to make of these extraordinary wheels? of the glorious cherubim? There are many marvels in this book as well as terrible prophecies of doom and destruction and, ultimately, God's promise of love, forgiveness, and regeneration. In Chapter 37 the Lord says to Ezekiel, *"Son of man, can these bones live?"* Dry, dead bones, with no life in them. Ezekiel answers, *"O Sovereign LORD, you alone know."* Then the Lord says to Ezekiel,

> *Prophesy to these bones and say to them, "Dry bones, hear the word of the LORD! This is what the Sovereign LORD*

says to these bones: I will make breath enter you, and you will come to life."

And the Lord God lays sinews upon the bones, and flesh, and skin, and they live again.

This is strong stuff. This is mythic stuff, great creative story that moves beyond fact into the redemptive truth of myth.

Elijah, like Ezekiel, is a mythic figure, larger than life. He challenges the gods of Baal, laughing their prophets to scorn when Baal cannot kindle a fire, whereas Elijah's God ignites wood over which buckets of water have been poured until it is soaked, saturated. And Elijah's fire blazes and burns brilliantly. Then Elijah slays, single-handedly, all the prophets of Baal.

Later, the Lord God tells Elijah to

"Go out and stand on the mountain in the presence of the LORD, for the LORD is about to pass by." Then a great and powerful wind tore the mountains apart and shattered the rocks before the LORD, but the LORD was not in the wind. After the wind there was an earthquake, but the LORD was not in the earthquake. After the earthquake came a fire, but the LORD was not in the fire. And after the fire came a gentle whisper.

Or, as the King James Version has it: "a still small voice." We have to listen if we want to hear God, to listen through all the noise and the storm and the turmoil, to hear that still small voice.

At the end of Elijah's life, a chariot of fire appears, and horses of fire, and *Elijah went up to heaven in a whirlwind.* What a wonder!

Strong stuff. Mythic stuff.

It is all through both Testaments, this wondrous creative wildness of God, this strong stuff not to be understood in the pale language of provable fact. Jesus, like
Elijah, stands *on the mountain in the presence of the LORD*
and takes with him Peter and James and John, and extraordinary things, incomprehensible things, come to
pass. Jesus' clothing becomes shining, and Elijah himself
appears to Jesus in the brilliance, and so does Moses, and
the three talk together, breaking ordinary chronology
into a million fragments. And then a cloud over-shadows
them, as it over-shadowed Moses on the mount, and the
voice of God thunders out of the cloud.

Strong stuff. Mythic stuff. Story. True story.

A misinterpretation of Peter's Epistle sees him as
warning us against myth, or what he calls *cleverly invented stories*, and he tells us that he saw what happened
on the Mount of Transfiguration; he was an eyewitness,
and he himself heard the voice of God coming out of the
cloud. True. But he didn't have the faintest idea what was
going on, as Mark reminds us: *He did not know what to say,
they were so frightened*. And in his bewilderment he
wanted to build three tabernacles, to put Jesus, Elijah,
and Moses into boxes where they would be safe. But
safety was not the reality of the Transfiguration. Glory
was.

Yea, verily! Those who are terrified of story jump on
that one line of Peter, out of context, and cry out: "Beware! Stories are lies! If you can't prove it, literally, don't
believe it."

But faith is *the substance of things hoped for, the evidence
of things not seen*. The language of proof is needed for
knowing how much money we need to buy our food for
the week or what our rent is. It is necessary, but it is not
for our faith, for the wondrous joy we live by. Most of

what makes life worth living lies beyond the world of provable fact. God can be neither proved nor disproved. Did God make the universe? While in the language of provable fact we have neither proof nor disproof, in the promise of Scripture we can cry out a resounding Yes!

Yes, indeed, let us beware of the *cleverly invented stories* that we see in television commercials every day, and let us look for that truth that will make us free, and that is frequently expressed in myth—true myth, not the *cunningly devised fables* (KJV) of floor waxes that are better than other floor waxes, or pain killers that will deaden all our physical aches, or all the other false promises that are constantly being offered a gullible public, and that the public (including Christians) far too often swallows wholesale. Why do we swallow those false promises given us by the media and yet boggle at the truth of Ezekiel, or Elijah, or the unreasonable, overwhelming Love of God in Christ Jesus?

Just as we are losing vocabulary in these last years of the twentieth century, we are losing myth and the creativity of myth—myth as truth, not lie; myth as that truth promised by Jesus to make us free.

Rollo May in his book *The Cry for Myth* tells us that it is myths that give us our sense of identity. They make possible our sense of community. They undergird our moral values (and this is particularly important if we truly want to understand what moral values mean). And they are our way of dealing with the inscrutable mystery of Creation.

May continues,

Our powerful hunger for myth is a hunger for community. The person without a myth is a person without a home. . . . To be a member of one's community is to share in its myths. . . . [In church, our] rituals and myths supply fixed points in a world of bewildering change and disappointment.

Conversely, the current "clinging to cults and our neurotic passion to make money is a flight from our anxiety, which comes in part from our mythlessness."

We have a deep need for heroes in this anxious age where drug use has increased to epidemic proportions. Rollo May points out that we have confused celebrities with heroes, and that is disastrous. David was a hero, not a celebrity.

And what about Jesus? He was certainly not a celebrity! He shunned everything that would have marked him as a celebrity. Satan offered to make Jesus a celebrity. But Jesus showed us true heroism. And how did he teach? Yes, once again: Jesus taught by telling stories, parables, myths, and his stories were true, though not everybody could hear them. Jesus came to show us through his stories what it is to be human and what it is to be heroic and to understand heroes. He told stories to show us how to counteract our sins and imperfections with love, rather than anger; to show us how to rejoice, to laugh, to heal; and the world couldn't stand true humanness, and tried to kill it.

If Jesus came today, would we be any braver, any more open, any more willing to give ourselves to his love, than were those who cried out, "Crucify him! Crucify him!"? Would we be any more willing today to allow him to love all kinds of people, even those we don't much care about?

That, of course, was part of the problem—Jesus' friends. They were not the right people. He went to the wrong dinner parties (his first miracle took place at a big party). He loved children, and let them climb all over him with their sticky little hands and dirty little feet. He even told us that we had to be like little children ourselves if we wanted to understand God, and yet the world (and too often the church) taught then, and still teaches, that we have to outgrow our childhood love of story, of imagination, of creativity, of fun, and so we blunder into the grown-up world of literalism.

Literalism kills the stories of Jesus, and comes close to killing us. Literalism makes no demands of us, asks of us no faith, does not cause us to grow. Story pushes and shoves us and then helps us out of the mud puddle. Sometimes I remind myself of the little boy who was going to be late for school for the third day in a row, and he set off in a total panic, running as fast as he could, and panting out, "God help me! God help me!" He stumbled and fell into a mud puddle, and he looked up to heaven and said, "I didn't say push!"

God pushes, and often pushes through story.

God also pushes through our prayers, and for me the disciplines of writing and praying are ever closer and closer together, each a letting go of our own will and an opening up to the power of God's will. We pray that our own will may reflect God's will and that we will be given the discernment to know when it does not.

When I listen to a story, trying to set it down faithfully, the two disparate parts of myself, the mind and the heart, the intellect and the intuition, the conscious and the subconscious mind, stop fighting each other and begin to collaborate. They know each other, as two people who love each other know each other. And as the love of two people is a gift—a totally unmerited, incomprehensible gift—so is the union of mind and heart.

The storyteller knows complete dependence on listening to the story. One of the current buzz words today is *codependence* which means, as far as I can tell, that you have to get your sense of self from someone else, rather than from God's image within you.

Codependence is certainly to be avoided, but sometimes fear of it leads people to be wary of any kind of dependence. Once again I remember Dean Inge of Saint Paul's saying, "God promised to make you free. He never promised to make you independent." The freer I am, the more I am aware of my interdependence, with my family, my friends, the people I sit near in church, or even those I pass on the street. And I am dependent on faith in God, who pushes me in my work, sends me to places I am not at all sure I want to go.

I listen to my stories; they are given to me, but they don't come without a price. We do have to pay, with hours of work that ends up in the wastepaper basket, with intense loneliness, with a vulnerability that often causes us to be hurt. And I'm not sure that it's a choice. If we're given a gift—and the size of the gift, small or great, does not matter—then we are required to serve it, like it or not, ready or not. Most of us, that is, because I have seen people of great talent who have done nothing with their talent, who mutter about "When there's time . . . ," or who bury their talent because it's too risky to use.

Yes, it is risky. We may not hear the story well. We may be like faulty radios, transmitting only static and words out of context. But I believe that it is a risk we have to take. And it is worth it, because the story knows more than the artist knows.

It is nothing short of miraculous that I am so often given, during the composition of a story, just what I need

213

at the very moment that I need it. When I was roughing out *A Swiftly Tilting Planet*, trying to find a structure for the family, home for Thanksgiving and facing a nuclear war, I opened the mail one day and there was a card from the holy island of Iona, in Scotland, with the words of Patrick's Rune, that glorious rune that became the structure of the book. It led me to a lot of research I hadn't expected, and it was hard work, but it was also exhilarating, a lot of fun.

I can't explain how these gifts come to me—at least not in the language of provable fact, but that is the language of human control, not the language of faith. And acceptance of the wonder of such gifts helps me to understand what Ezekiel is saying, or Daniel, or Matthew, Mark, Luke, and John! I read their stories with sublime wonder, with rapturous joy, acknowledging that reality cannot be organized by us human creatures. It can only be lived. Indifference goes along with perfectionism and literalism as a great killer of story, and perhaps indifference is nothing more than a buffer against fear.

When I was in Egypt I asked the guide why there were so many cobras, crocodiles, vultures, in the temples. The reply was, "The people worshiped what they feared."

This same kind of fear is behind much bibliolatry today. Many fundamentalists—not all, thank God, but some—worship the Bible, which is largely terrifying, and so they try to tame it by putting it into their temple, as the Egyptians did with the cobras, crocodiles, vultures. How are we to understand Elijah's ascending into heaven in chariots of fire drawn by horses of fire? Has anyone ever seen such a thing? How is it to be believed? What are we to make of Jesus in a blaze of blinding glory on the Mount of Transfiguration? Or Moses with his face shining so brilliantly after he has talked with God on another mount that the people can't bear to look at him? These marvelous mysteries cannot be understood in the language of literalism or inerrancy, and all such attempts to tame and restrict the glory are deadly. Deadly indeed.

How can we understand in terms of literalism the glory of the Creation of the universe, Jonah in the belly of the large fish, Daniel in the lions' den, or angels coming to unsuspecting, ordinary people and crying out, "Fear not!"

Literalism is a vain attempt to cope with fear by quelling Scripture, attempting to make it more palatable, less wild and wonderful. Would the angels cry out "Fear not!" if there were nothing to fear?

Story makes us more alive, more human, more courageous, more loving. Why does anybody tell a story? It does indeed have something to do with faith, faith that the universe has meaning, that our little human lives are not irrelevant, that what we choose or say or do matters, matters cosmically. It is we humans who either help bring about, or hinder the coming of the kingdom. We look at the world around us, and it is a complex world, full of incomprehensible greed (why are we continuing to cut down our great forests that supply our planet with so much of its oxygen?), irrationality, brutality, war, terrorism—but also self-sacrifice, honor, dignity—and in all of this we look for, and usually find, pattern, structure, meaning. Our truest response to the irrationality of the world is to paint or sing or write, for only in such response do we find truth.

In a recent article in a medical journal (given me by my friend, Pat, the physician), Dr. Richard F. Ott writes that "throughout time, myths have provided meaning for the life of the individual and his society. They have also provided the ability for people to experience the mystery of life by participating in the rituals of myth." How marvelous is the ritual of the Holy Mysteries, the Eucharist, where we joyfully eat Love! For me, one of the most potent phrases in the Episcopal Book of Common Prayer is "in the mystery of the Word made flesh . . ." It is a mystery that cannot be understood in terms of provable fact or the jargon of the media. Mystery, unlike magic, can be understood only mythically.

When we lose our myths we lose our place in the universe. Dr. Ott points out that "our sense of self-worth has become based on what we possess, and our language has evolved to reflect this. We not only have material possessions, we have children. When we cannot sleep, we have insomnia. We have even replaced 'my head hurts' with 'I have a headache.'" We have sex rather than making love. We even "have" the Bible.

How do we get rid of this "have, have, have" mentality and return to "I am, I will be, I am hopeful, I love, I am joyful?" The "I have" complex has led to a litigious society in which malpractice suits are crippling medicine. Why was it necessary for my family to employ a lawyer in San Diego before the insurance company of the truck driver who ran the red light was willing to pay even the minimum he was insured for? Dr. Ott says that

the Japanese have a fraction of the numbers of lawyers that we have because the myths behind their culture have meaning to them. We need not contrast their [scientific] successes in the last 20 years, as it is common knowledge. Yet the Western mind seems incapable of understanding what lies behind these successes.

Jesus was not a Westerner. He did not have a Western mind, which is perhaps why he is so frequently misunderstood by the Western mind today. He was not interested in the righteous and morally upright people whom he saw to be also hard of heart and judgmental; he devoted himself to those who knew they were sinners and broken, and who came to him for healing. His birth was heralded by angels and visited by adoring shepherds, and it horrifically resulted in the slaughter of all Jewish infants under the age of two.

If Jesus was a threat to Herod two thousand years ago, he is still a threat today, because he demands that we see ourselves as we really are, that we drop our smug, self-protective devices, that we become willing to live the abundant life he calls us to live. It's too strong, so we react by trying to turn him into a wimp come to protect us from an angry Father God who wants us punished for our sins: not forgiven, but punished. And our response of fear hasn't worked, and we're left even more frightened and even more grasping and even more judgmental.

Let's recover our story because we'll die without it. It's a life-giving story—this magnificent narrative we find in Scripture—if we are willing to read openly and to read all of Scripture, not just passages selected to help us prove our point. The God of Scripture can sometimes seem brutal, seen through the eyes of the early biblical narrator, who is looking at the Creator through crudely primitive eyes. But the God of Scripture is also the God who refused to nuke Nineveh, even though that's what Jonah wanted; who forgave David for a really staggering list of wrongdoings; who wants only for us stiff-necked people to repent and come home; who goes out into the stormy night for the one lost black sheep; who throws a party when the Prodigal Son returns; who loves us so much that God did indeed send his only begotten son to come live with us, as one of us, to help us understand our stories—each one unique, infinitely valuable, irreplaceable.

Jesus. The God who came to us as one of us and told us stories. How marvelous! The life of Jesus has been called the greatest story ever told, and that is true, but one of Satan's cleverest successes has been to make us distrust story. But God's stories are great gifts to us, gifts to help us understand what it is that the Creator wants of us.

God wants a lot. Satan is much more easily pleased, or that's what he'd have us believe. God wants everything, and calls us to have faith in what, if we are truly Christian, is impossible—at least in terms of morals or perfectionism or qualifications. It is not only secular humanists who have trouble believing in the Incarnation. Honest struggle with the truth of the Incarnation is more creative than taking it for granted. How can we smugly accept, without feeling wondrous awe, the infinitely small seed within Mary that grew, as all of us grow in our mother's wombs, until it was ready to be born as a human baby?

In the fascinating study of modern physics we learn that energy and matter are interchangeable. So the sheer energy of Christ, for love of us, put on the matter of Jesus—ordinary human matter. What love! It is beyond all our puny efforts in clay, or stone, or music, or paint, or ink, but that love is behind our artistic endeavors, no matter how insignificant.

The Incarnation hallows our human lives. We've heard the story of Jesus so often that our ears have become blunted. Story reawakens us to truth, the truth that will set us free. Jesus, the Story, taught by telling stories, quite a few of which on the surface would appear to be pretty secular, but all of which lead us, if we will listen, to a deeper truth than we have been willing to hear before.

I suspect that the story about President Coolidge and sin is factual as well as true; I think it probably really happened. But it's the truth of the story that matters. Yes, we're "agin" sin, and we know ourselves to be sinners, but forgiven sinners, sinners loved by God.

John writes in his first Epistle,

How great is the love the Father has lavished on us, that we should be called children of God! And that is what we are! . . . Dear friends, now we are children of God, and what we will be has not yet been made known. But we know that when he appears, we shall be like him, for we shall see him as he is.

What a wonderful story! What wonderful good news! Let us respond by looking fearlessly at our own stories, so that we may, with God's help, create a story that will be pleasing to our Maker.

Once upon a time . . . And it came to pass . . . Yes! We are about to hear a story; we are about to be part of the great creative action of the universe.

Story as a
Redemptive Act

11

WHEN MY FATHER DIED I was seventeen and still too young to understand this complex man who had struggled valiantly with illness during my entire lifetime. I never knew the vibrant person whose life was smashed by World War I when his lungs were irrevocably damaged by mustard gas. I knew a few marvelous stories about him. One of my favorites concerns a print of Castle Conway in Wales, which was on the hall of my parents' apartment in New York and which is now on my living room wall. One hot summer evening before that terrible war broke the back of this century, my mother looked at my father, sighed, and said wistfully, "Oh Charles, it's so hot! I wish we could go to Castle Conway."

"Come on!" My father took my mother's hand, led her out the door, into a taxi, down the docks, and onto a ship, without so much as a toothbrush.

The father I knew lived with pain, physical pain, and the pain of being unable to do the work he loved, traveling all over the world as a foreign correspondent. When his last attack of pneumonia finally killed him, I was stunned, but somehow not surprised. I had known, when he and my mother put me on the train from Jacksonville to Charleston to start my senior year at Ashley Hall, that my father was more frail than I had ever known him, that his coughing was worse, that the pain in his eyes was dark and deep.

I recorded this death in my journal. Straight. "Father died."

Later I wrote it as a story, very much out of my own experience of this death.

Still later, after I had graduated from college and began to recognize in myself characteristics of my father, I wrote about it again, in the death of the mother of the protagonist of my first novel, *The Small Rain*, far from the facts of this death, but close to the truth of what it meant to me.

That was the first, though certainly not the last time that God has helped me redeem pain through story.

Writing *A Wrinkle in Time* was a redemptive experience for me, a working out of a great deal of pain from a decade that had been extraordinarily difficult. It was my first effort in a genre now called "science fantasy," and science fantasy is not far from fairy tale, that world which delves deep into the human psyche, struggling to find out at least a little more of what we are all about. We are indeed mysterious creatures, and the more rational we think we are, the more irrational we are likely to be, for we are not made up of reason alone. Reason alone produces characters like IT, the archetypal villain in *Wrinkle*, IT, who is brain alone, with no heart, no imagination, no mystery.

In fairy tales there are doors that should not be opened, boxes that must remain closed. And human curiosity being what it is, we open doors, like Bluebeard's wife; and we open boxes, like Pandora; and we eat forbidden fruit, like Eve. Now we have to live in a world that is irrevocably changed by what was in those secret rooms and what has escaped from the mysterious closed boxes and by the loneliness that came from being forever expelled from the Garden.

When we human creatures opened the heart of the atom we opened ourselves to the possibility of terrible destruction, but also—and we tend to forget this—to a vision of interrelatedness and unity that can provide a theology for us to live by.

My daughter-in-law's uncle was one of the scientists in New Mexico who exploded that first test atom bomb on the desert sands. When they did this they did not know—they truly did not know—whether or not it was going to start a chain reaction that would just go on and on until it ended up destroying the entire planet. With incredible courage—or was it foolhardiness?—they exploded that first atomic device and saw the first mushroom cloud. And the planet will never be the same again.

The discoveries made since the heart of the atom was opened have changed our view of the universe and of Creation. Our great radio telescopes are picking up echoes of that primal opening which expanded into all the stars in their courses. The universe is far greater and grander and less predictable than anyone realized, and one reaction to this is to turn our back on the glory and settle for a small, tribal god who forbids questions of any kind. Another reaction is to feel so small and valueless in comparison to the enormity of the universe that it becomes impossible to believe in a God who can be bothered with us tiny, finite creatures with life spans no longer than the blink of an eye. Or we can simply rejoice in a God who is beyond our comprehension but who comprehends us and cares about us.

It is easier for a single human being to be open and willing to change than it is for an institution, but if enough of us single creatures are open to God's amazing revelations, our institutions will ultimately come along with us. Long before the church institution was ready, many individuals were willing to accept that the earth is round and is a planet circling a parent sun in one of countless galaxies. An institution, be it religious, medical, legal, or educational, tends to move very slowly, holding onto the status quo, afraid of rocking the boat, loath to accept that familiar ideas may have to be left behind. We shouldn't wait for the institutions to do the changing, but be willing to change ourselves, for in the end it is we who make up the institution, and if we become more open, more loving, more interdependent through the lavishness of God's love, then we can and will make a difference.

The universe as we are beginning to understand it is far stranger than we could have imagined. Much of it is dark matter, which we cannot see, and about which we can only speculate. Perhaps this dark matter is the galactic equivalent of the dark side of the human soul. This invisible, dark world is the natural world of the storyteller. In the beginning of *King Lear*, the old king ignores his darknesses completely, and the rest of the play deals with his moving more and more deeply into the shadows, and finally out into the light. *Lear*, like *The Tempest*, is a fairy tale, with scenes of ominous skies with brilliant light occasionally breaking through. Fairy tales, if we are not afraid to translate them, show us the night side of ourselves and what happens if we ignore it. Bruno Bettelheim has shown us the Freudian aspect of these tales, but there are other and even deeper levels. Wouldn't we all have opened the forbidden door, the box that held so many terrible things, but which also contained much good? Would we have closed our ears to the serpent and refused to eat the fruit?

The secrets of the atom are not unlike Pandora's box, and what we must look for and hold onto is not the destructive power but the vision of interrelatedness that is desperately needed on this fragmented planet. We are indeed part of a universe. We belong to each other; the fall of every sparrow is noted, every tear we shed is collected in the Creator's bottle.

In the fairy tale we find hope of interrelatedness, and sometimes this hope comes because fairy tales deal forthrightly with brokenness. One reason that children are given fewer fairy tales today than when I was little is that many fairy tales are violent, and they involve risk. Why we shudder at the violence in fairy tales rather than the violence of everyday life at the end of this century is beyond me. The violence in fairy tales pales beside the violence that children watch daily on television. Yes, the fairy tales offer risk, but "no risk, no fairy tale." Failure is not only possible, it often strikes. And even when the poor peasant boy or the lovely stepchild succeeds, there is risk first. The young man may not make his way safely through the magic thicket. The power of the evil fairy may be stronger than that of the benevolent godmother. If the princess kisses the beast, he may devour her. Will the frog really be saved from the wicked spell and turn into a prince?

In fairy tales, and in life, there is risk—risk of failure, of horror, of death. But there is no despair. Rather, there is an unspoken affirmation of the ultimate happy ending.

But before we can affirm this all-rightness, we must first deal with all-wrongness. It is in these dark and unknown waters that fairy tales have their home. Although we tend to think of fairy tales as light and crystal clear—glass slippers, enchanted mirrors, vast parties in great ballrooms—they speak to us, ultimately, of dark things. No one is more aware of the disastrous aspects of overweening human pride than the teller of fairy tales. No one is more aware of our inevitable insecurity, loneliness, horror. But the teller of fairy tales, ancient or modern, is also aware of the infinite value of the human being, of the extraordinary fact that we often accomplish the impossible.

Therefore, the fairy-tale teller must convey a far deeper sense of verisimilitude than the writer of slice-of-life stories which deal with a much more limited reality. In George MacDonald's *The Princess and Curdie* we believe that the stairs in the castle which Irene must climb to her godmother are there, that they would be there even if George MacDonald had never written about them; we must believe it is quite possible that one day we may be asked to plunge our own hands into that terrible, burning fire of roses. The fairy-tale writer tells about a world more real than that of every day. When I am deep in a story and am interrupted, I am jerked out of the "real" world into a much more shadowy world.

It is only recently that fairy tale, fantasy, myth, have been thought of as being exclusively for children. Originally they were not written for children at all. Myth is the foundation of conceptual thought. These so-called children's stories are aware of what many adults have forgotten—that the daily, time-bound world of provable fact is the secondary world, the shadow world, and it is story, painting, song, which give us our glimpses of reality.

When the beautiful princess who has slept within the enchanted castle for a hundred years is roused from her sleep, we are given a hint of resurrection. Before resurrection comes sleep (as the Christians in Acts called death) and darkness. And then comes the call, "Sleepers, awake!"

Jung talks about a memory which is more than our own, private memory, which reaches out and touches the memory of many centuries, and fairy tales reveal this universal memory. If we didn't, all of us, share in the memory of our ancestors, every generation would have to invent the wheel and the needle all over again. We are human animals because of the extraordinary but little-appreciated fact that we can look back to our past, unlike the other beasts, and we can look forward to our future.

In folklore it is usually accepted that infants in their cradles understand the language of angels and fairies and all supernatural beings, and that as they grow up they lose this gift, except in rare cases. The seventh son of a seventh son may keep this gift and then will often have to hide it. But it is freely acknowledged that there is something rare and lovely about a princess who can actually walk through the forest speaking to the animals and trees. Perhaps she awakens our sleeping memories of Eve.

True story calls us to be part of the universe as it heals us. When I am feeling wounded and broken I do not turn to do-it-yourself books or self-help books or even inspirational books, but to story. During my lonely childhood I learned about myself and those I encountered through fairy tale. In a fairy tale, animals may talk, princes may be turned into frogs, princesses may sleep for a hundred years, but we must believe the story, and believe not only with our conscious minds, but with all of ourselves, with our intuition as well as our intellect, our hearts as well as our minds.

All the elements of the fairy tale are waiting within us: the quest; the younger son; the true princess; the benevolent king; the elder brothers (or sisters); the witch, or wizard; the wise old woman; beasts and monsters; the happy ending. The fairy tale reveals a truly nonsexist world, because we are all, male and female, both the younger son and the true princess—as well as the monster we'd rather not recognize.

At our birth we are all, willy-nilly, started on the Quest, our quest for being, for the meaning of our own particular life. Why are we here at this moment in time, in this particular geographical space? What direction should we take? Dare we go into the dark woods? What is the meaning of the quest? What is our task? What is the value of our life? Does it matter? Does anybody care?

These are questions all adolescents ask, and they are questions we should never stop asking. But the questions come more easily if we are prepared for them in childhood by fairy tale, fantasy, myth.

Who am I? is one of the most painful and penetrating questions.

And the fairy tale assures us, regardless of our gender, "You are the younger son. You are the true princess. You are the enchanted beast. You are more than you know."

But we must accept our marvelous complexity before we can understand this. Fairy tales speak in a language which does not need to be translated for us by specialists, a language easily understood by children, if only we are open to it and are not afraid of reality. For fairy tales speak of the real world, the world beyond plastic credit cards and traffic jams and word processors that suddenly gobble up half a chapter of what we are writing.

If we open ourselves to story, to fairy tale, fantasy, myth, novel, we cannot help being aware of the ultimate unexplainableness of the deepest depths. We know we are on a quest, but we do not know the entire nature of the quest, nor where it is going to take us.

The great Sufi master Nasrudin went into a small store and said to the shopkeeper, "Have you ever seen me before?" "No, never," the shopkeeper replied. "Then how do you know it's me?" the Sufi master demanded.

We start the Quest, uncertain of who we are, and where we are going. For many of us, we start our quest unknowingly, in our cradles, at the time of our baptism. I am grateful for my infant baptism, because I know that it was entirely a gift. I didn't ask for it. I did nothing to earn it. I was given my name and the gift of my direction. We are headed towards the coming of the kingdom, and what we do or do not do will hasten or delay that day.

That is a staggering responsibility, and we dare to continue along the path only because God calls us by name, and bids us come. And I cannot be healed or made whole or holy unless God calls and keeps calling me by name, and unless I hear and heed the call.

◆ ◆ ◆

Once there was a man who was a Namer. That is what he was called by God, to be, and to do. Out of the earth, in the days of the beginnings, the Lord God formed every beast of the field and every fowl of the air and brought them to Adam to see what he would name them: and whatever Adam called every living creature, that was its name.

Adam's vocation as a son was to be a Namer; that was how he was to co-create with the Maker of the Universe. If you name somebody or something, you discover that the act of Naming is very closely connected with the act of loving, and hating is involved with unNaming—taking a person's name away, causing anyone to be an anonymous digit, annihilating the spirit.

When we are unNamed, we are broken; all around us we see fragmented, mutilated people. And the world offers little help for healing, for knitting up the "raveled sleeve of care."

That is why it is important for us to take time for prayer, for being with our Amma/Abba who loves us, all of us. That is why it is important to take Paul's exhortation to pray at all times with the utmost seriousness.

The prayer of the heart is a short petition from Scripture which includes the name of Jesus and which becomes part of the rhythm of our heartbeat and of our breathing. It is sad that this prayer of Jesus has become suspect among some Christians. I think that much of the fear comes because even in the church we have accepted the safe world of the elder brother, rather than the dangerous world of the Quest of the younger son and the true princess. We have been taught that we must be in control of ourselves and our lives, and it is difficult for us to let ourselves go, to put our entire lives with absolute faith in a Master of the Universe whom we cannot in any way control.

And indeed the prayer of the heart is nothing to be taken lightly or dabbled in. Like anything else worthwhile, it is fraught with danger and risk. It is an offering of love, and when we love we are vulnerable. And the temptation is to run away. When I held on to the words, "Lord Jesus Christ, have mercy on me," after the truck smashed the little car I was in, I knew myself to be totally dependent on God's mercy.

We say the "Our Father" prayer so frequently that we forget that it begins with *Our Father, who art in Heaven, hallowed be thy Name,* and in hallowing the name of God we also Name ourselves.

The psalmist affirms that God calls all the stars by name, all of the stars in all of the galaxies. And God calls us by name, each one of us, and sometimes—no, often—el calls at night, when the elder brothers let loose their attempts at control, and we are most free to listen and hear.

Does it matter that your name is Tom or Eliza or Donald or Jane? A friend said to me, "When God calls me by name, I'm sure it isn't George." Perhaps not. But when God called young Samuel it was not by a strange or unknown name. Perhaps el didn't use the name, Samuel, but what Samuel heard was "Samuel!" And he answered, "Here I am."

God called Isaiah by his own, earthly, human name. I'll venture a guess that when God speaks our name it might just as well be a new name. But it was recognizable, and the men and women of the Bible didn't sit around waiting for some esoteric, secret name to be revealed to them. They heard their own names, and they answered to them: "Here I am, Lord. Send me."

When Adam and Eve refused responsibility for their own actions ("The woman made me." "The snake made me."), they stopped being younger sons. It is the elder brother, not the younger son, who tries to dump the blame on somebody else. It was the Second Adam who took up the story that the first Adam could not finish.

The Second Adam, Jesus—a name of great power. When you give someone your name, you give that person power over you, and we've forgotten this. We jump too lightly into first names—on television talk shows, for instance—without thinking.

Our names are more than we know, just as we are more than we know. Jesus said, *"I thank thee, O Father, Lord of heaven and earth, because thou hast hid these things from the wise and prudent, and hast revealed them unto babes"* (KJV).

And Scripture tells us,

For ye see your calling, brethren, how that not many wise men after the flesh, not many mighty, not many noble, are called: But God hath chosen the foolish things of the world to confound the wise; and God hath chosen the weak things of the world to confound the things which are mighty. (KJV)

Those are the words which the guardian angel, Mrs. Who, quoted for Meg Murry, and I find that being able to accept myself as foolish and weak is very comforting, for if I can recover some of the openness of my child self, which is still within me, then perhaps I can understand, even if just a little, what it is to be killed to the world and Named forever in the kingdom.

The storyteller must open the listening ear vulnerably, willing to be condemned as foolish and weak, for of course the world looks down on the foolish and the weak.

So do we look to the world and its shallow expectations, or the incredible demands of God? Paul of Tarsus asked God three times to take his affliction from him—and if I know Paul, it was probably thirty and three—and God replied calmly, "No, Paul. My strength shows best in your weakness."

In story, isn't it usually the weak one, the foolish one, who ends up doing what the worldly and strong people fail to do?

The world looks down on the weak and glorifies the strong. It ignores our wholeness. The result of this is that we have become fragmented, broken creatures. The vocation of the storyteller is not to worry about the expectations of the world, but to bear the pain of redemption.

Redemption is indeed often painful. It was for King David. Almost everything had to be taken away from him—wives, children, friends, kingdom—before he was stripped of pride and vanity and self-indulgence and became truly royal. In his old age he moved from the role of the younger son and into that of the wise king who rules over his kingdom with humility, prudence and power.

Indeed, we are the youngest son, all of us, male and female.

The younger son (and of course Cinderella is a younger son, and so is Snow White, and so is Sara Crewe, and so is Meg Murry) succeeds in the quest where the powerful elder brothers fail. The younger son realizes, if only intuitively, that the Quest is a cosmic one, involving the healing of the whole creation which *has been groaning as in the pains of childbirth right up to the present time. Not only so, but we ourselves, who have the firstfruits of the Spirit, groan inwardly as we wait eagerly for our adoption as sons, the redemption of our bodies.*

The mystics throughout the ages have known that meditation involves letting the mind expand. Theologian William Johnston writes of "a loss of self, and entrance into altered states of consciousness, a thrust into dimensions beyond time and space, in such wise that not only man's spirit but his very psyche and body become somehow cosmic." Just as the great suffering of the mystic is his sense of separation from his end, which is the resurrection, so the great suffering of the universe is separation from the end towards which it is straining and striving.

The mystic, who is always a younger son, knows that we wrestle not against flesh and blood, but against the hierarchies, the establishments, the authorities, against principalities, against powers, against the rulers of the darkness of this world, against spiritual wickedness in high places.

It is not an easy quest we are sent on, and it is fraught with dangers. How dare we set out on it? We dare only if we know that power, and high I.Q.s, and moral rectitude are not really what we need, for *God chose the foolish things of the world to shame the wise; God chose the weak things of the world to shame the strong.*

When St. Paul was busy persecuting the Christians, when he cheered the stoning of Stephen, he was indeed an elder brother. But the elder brother, like Paul, can be changed. My son-in-law, Alan Jones, contrasts *metanoia*, conversion, repentance, with *paranoia*. Before his conversion on the Damascus Road, Paul, the elder brother, might be described as being in a state of *paranoia*, out of his right mind. And after his conversion from the elder brother to the younger son, he was in a state of *metanoia*. He was completely turned around and, as younger son, was in his right mind.

Contrition, penitence, turning again, are part of becoming who we are, of becoming Named. This contrition doesn't mean wallowing masochistically over the depth of our sin or beating our breasts in order to be "sinfuller" than thou. It does mean a willingness to be turned, to allow God to turn us so that we may be healed.

We are broken creatures, and yet this is not in itself a terrible thing. Refusing to admit it is what is terrible. *The sacrifices of God are a broken spirit. A broken and contrite heart, O God, you will not despise,* sang King David in Psalm 51. The younger son is usually considered by the older siblings to be so stupid that they feel he's a drag on them as they set off on the Quest, so they leave him alone in the darkest part of the forest, in order to get on with the business of the world. They expect to succeed and to succeed through their own power and control. And they are not generous. Many of Jesus' stories point this out. When the Prodigal Son returns, the elder brother is not pleased. He goes out and sulks because he does not want his father to give a party for this kid who has made such a mess of his life. The elder brothers in the parable of the workers in the vineyard are furious at the vineyard owner for paying those who worked for only an hour at the end of the day the same wages as the good elder brothers who worked all day in the heat of the sun. The elder brothers all scream for justice, fairness. And there is something in most of us that agrees. It isn't fair! we cry out. And it isn't. But God is not a God of fairness, but of Love.

Sometimes younger brothers forfeit their status as younger sons, as Adam and Eve did, and that is always tragedy.

The second Adam did not. The Father said, *"This is my Son, whom I love; with him I am well pleased. Listen to him!"* And if we listen, what we hear is that the glory is always God's, and we are bathed in it—burned in its purifying fire—and with angels and archangels and all the company of heaven we laud and magnify his Holy Name, evermore praising him and saying, "Holy, holy, holy, Lord God of hosts. Heaven and earth are full of thy glory. Glory be to thee, O Lord most High." Amen.

One of my favorite biblical fairy stories is that of Tobias and the angel in the Book of *Tobit*. This book also happens to have the only nice dog in the Bible. Tobit, Tobias's father, is blinded by some bird droppings that cause white patches on his eyes (cataracts are still a big problem in the Middle East). In desperation Tobit sends Tobias, a true younger son, off to collect some money owed him by a cousin in a far land. Tobias's mother insists that he must have a guide, and lo! Tobias meets a stranger who says he knows the way and is willing to go along with Tobias. So Tobias sets off with his dog, and the stranger, who is, of course, an angel in disguise.

They spend the night by the river Tigris—Tobias, the dog, and the angel—and in the morning when Tobias is washing in the river, a great carp leaps at him to eat him. The angel tells Tobias to club the fish, which the boy obediently does, and then to cut the fish up and take its heart and liver and gall and keep them safe.

Tobias does this, and they eat the rest of the fish for breakfast, giving the dog his fair share. Tobias asks the angel why he must keep the heart and the liver and the gall, and the angel explains that if a smoke is made of the heart and liver it will drive demons away. And if the gall is rubbed on the eyes of someone with white film, the eyes will be cured.

They arrive at their destination, and the angel tells Tobias that they will spend the night with his kinsman, who not only has the money for Tobias but also has a beautiful daughter. Tobias and the daughter meet and immediately fall in love. However, there's a big problem, because Sarah has already been given in marriage seven times, and each time a monster has killed the groom on the wedding night.

But the angel tells Tobias not to fear ("Fear not, Tobias!"), and the two are married. Sarah's mother whispers to her husband that he might as well go out and dig the grave. Tobias and Sarah go up to the bridal chamber, and Tobias makes a smoke of the heart and liver, and when the demon comes he smells the smoke and he flees to the farthest parts of upper Egypt and there the angel binds him.

The gall cures Tobit's blindness, and they all, including the dog, live happily ever after, giving much glory to God.

Pure, charming, delightful fairy tale.

Gideon, too, is a younger son, and the hero of a fairy tale. When the angel comes to him and says, *The LORD is with you, mighty warrior. . . . Go in the strength you have and save Israel out of Midian's hand,* Gideon, the typical younger son says, "Who? Me? You surely don't mean me! My father's tribe is the least of all the tribes of Israel, and I am the least of my father's house."

"You," says the angel.

First, Gideon is told to tear down the temple of Baal, which he does at night because he's afraid someone will see him. Then, still reluctant, he suggests that if he's really the one to save his people, the dew that night should fall only on a fleece of wool that he's going to put out. And the dew falls only on the fleece of wool. "Well," he says, "Just to be sure, how about if the dew falls on the ground tonight, and not on the fleece of wool?" And so it happens. So he gathers himself an army, and God looks at the army and sees that there are a lot of people. Since there are so many that they might think their success in defeating the mighty enemy is a result of their own valor, God tells Gideon to send everyone home who's afraid. About half of them go away. But God looks at those who stay and says there are still too many, so el has Gideon send them to the brook to drink, and they are divided according to those who drink from their hands and those who lap like a dog. Gideon is left with a tiny little band who couldn't possibly conquer the great horde of the Midianites with their own strength. Nevertheless, they blow their trumpets, and cry out, *A sword for the LORD and for Gideon!* and the Midianite horde is vanquished.

The story of Gideon emphatically underlines that the point of the stories of the younger son is that the younger son *knows* that he does not accomplish the Quest on his own. He *knows* that though with him it may be impossible, with God nothing is impossible. He *knows* that he cannot take the credit for the achievement, that he did not do it himself. He accepts his interdependence. He is willing to listen, as the writer must listen to where the story wants to go. The younger son, listening to the angel, to the fairy godmother, to the talking beast, listens and hears and is willing to go where he is sent, no matter how strange it may be, or how terrible.

(*"My Father, if it is possible, may this cup be taken from me. Yet not as I will, but as you will."*)

Nowadays we're surrounded by the worldly older son who foolishly considers his power to come from his own virtue (rather than *vertue*), who mistakes the real purpose of the quest, and looks for more power and more money and more everything. If he meets failure, his confidence is destroyed, and he gives up. He wants credit for his deeds; he wants to be praised for them. I don't think any of us is completely immune from liking a pat on the back, from being told we've done a good job. But that's very different from the need for constantly gathering spiritual merit badges.

Napoleon, Hitler, Tiberius—these are all examples of the elder brother, and there are plenty of others nearer to us in time. It is the elder brothers who worship golden calves, or get hanged on their own gallows (like Haman), or who pragmatically decide that it is expedient that one man die for the sake of the nation.

The younger son doesn't feel that he is entitled to any special privileges. He isn't surprised when he takes wrong turnings, makes mistakes (all those pages which end up in the wastepaper basket), those cruel reviews written (usually) by elder brothers, those unpublished books, unsung songs, unsold paintings.

And age—chronology—like sexism, has nothing to do with it. The younger son can be middle-aged, like Moses when he was sent on the Quest, or old, like Sarah or Hannah or Elizabeth.

If the storyteller follows the elder brothers he may well get on the best-seller list, but he will not be a true storyteller. Surely we want our work to be accepted, but if we write or paint or compose only with worldly success in mind, we fail. What incredible faith in his quest Van Gogh must have had to continue to paint wherever his pictures drove him, despite total lack of acceptance or worldly success. Surely he understood in the depths of his being that the foolishness of God is wiser than men, and the weakness of God is stronger than men.

Unless you turn and become like little children, you will never enter the kingdom of heaven. That child within us is the younger son.

That child within us is Christ. If we are meant to be Christ for each other, to see Christ in each other, then we must be careful that we see the younger son and not the elder brother. Jesus was born of a human mother, in a stable, not in the palace of a king. Jesus goes on the Quest on which he is sent with no proud estimate of his own worth. It's always, "Not me, but the Father." He knows the Quest is of ultimate, cosmic importance, and that it is he, the carpenter's son, who has been called. But the Quest, and the Father who sent him on the Quest, always come first, are always put before his own interests.

Jesus is also the true princess, and the true princess is within each one of us, too.

All men have within them the true princess, if they're wise enough to find her, just as all women are also the younger son, if we're willing to be open and vulnerable. A lot of sexism has been forced on us in the name of a false liberation. Perhaps the fairy tale will help us over some of the hurdles the world has put in our paths to trip us up.

Far too often we trip. The Quest is dangerous. J.E. Fison says that

There is no possibility of contact with the Divine without running the risk of being destroyed by the demonic. This is why Bible religion . . . is the death enemy of safety and certainty and knowing what's at the end of the road before you start out. It is always either bliss or perdition, salvation or damnation, the greatest curse or the most wonderful blessing in life. It cannot be the one without running the risk of the other; promise and peril must always co-exist. So long as we refuse that total commitment to the Creator by the creature, that humbling awareness of the infinite by the finite . . . we shall have no reality in our conscious experience to correspond with the words, Holy Spirit.

If we are to call on and be helped by the Holy Spirit we (and the protagonists of the fairy tale) must have great humility. My bishop remarked that one cannot have humility without humor, and they both come from the same root, *humus*—of the earth, earthy.

From humility comes strength, for only with humility can we have confidence in the Quest.

The true princess knows that only the truly strong man is able to be gentle, that tender, loving concern springs from a willingness to accept our whole selves. The world of elder brothers wants us all labeled and pigeonholed: the good people must be entirely good, the wicked must be entirely wicked. And it's never as simple as that, though we often wish it were.

I tend to put people I admire up on a beautiful marble pedestal, but no real friendship is possible until I demolish the pedestal and accept the whole person, the younger son, the true princess, and, yes, the monster.

The princess knows that to identify is to limit, to pigeonhole. To Name is to love.

◆ ◆ ◆

Of course the prototypical story of the true princess is that of the princess and the pea. Once upon a time—and the moment we say "Once upon a time" we move out of the restrictions of chronology and into *kairos,* real time, God's time—Once upon a time in the midst of a storm a young woman knocked on the doors of the palace. When she was admitted she looked thoroughly bedraggled, with her hair hanging about her wet as seaweed. Nevertheless she announced proudly that she was a princess.

The prince of that kingdom looked at her and saw that under her seaweed hair and wet clothes she was lovely, so he determined to test whether or not she was truly a princess. A bedchamber was prepared for her with a bed piled high with twenty-nine mattresses, and under the bottom mattress was placed a single pea.

In the morning she was asked if she had slept well, and she replied, "Sleep? How could I possibly sleep with something hard digging into my back all night?" And that's how the prince knew that she was a true princess.

We're all meant to feel the pea, if we're to be true princesses, and we can name some of those dulling mattresses:

What will the neighbors think?
Will it upset the congregation?
Will it affect the real estate value?
Have I put in enough sex scenes to please the public?
Did I put in enough shock value for it to sell?

We can all add our own mattresses that may blunt our awareness of the pea.

Often we're faced with questions for which there are no easy or visible solutions, and we must accept that for many reasons we don't always do the right things, and sometimes the sad truth is that there *is* no right thing to do, and so we tend to become discouraged and turn away. In Christ there is no east nor west, black nor white, rich nor poor, but in the world there is, and though Christ has overcome the world, the world often overcomes us. But have hope, take courage, don't give up.

Simply the fact that we couldn't sleep all night because we felt the hard pea of awareness under all those mattresses of indifference is a step in helping Christ overcome the world.

For the true princess who is a storyteller, our awareness must lead to our making other people aware. *Uncle Tom's Cabin* did more to make people aware of the horrors of slavery than many sermons. Arthur Miller's *The Crucible* awakened us to the danger of witch hunts (surely Senator Joseph McCarthy was an elder brother. Surely the Anti-New Agers are elder brothers.). The true princess has no guarantee that she will succeed in curing the world of the ills of greed and corruption, but if we are aware of them, then other people may be, too, and if enough people become aware, then things can change for the better.

The true princess, like the younger son, sees beyond this world and beyond chronological time to the cosmic dimension. If we think only in terms of success, then our success becomes more important than compassion; if we feel compelled to succeed, we don't have time to know anybody in the cause by name.

Jesus who was, of course, true princess as well as younger son, was *aware* of the political unrest and social inequity of his day, but he refused to lead a revolution.

He was *aware* of the outrageous position of women in his day; a woman had nothing of her own, and if her husband didn't like her, he could write a bill of divorcement, and she had no say in the matter. It's difficult to realize that this was true at the beginning of our own century in England and, to a certain extent, here in the United States. Like the world of two thousand years ago it was a man's world, and though Jesus disregarded this in his own relations with women and treated them as equals, which shocked many of his friends, he did nothing to start an Equal Rights movement. Not that I'm against Equal Rights, mind you, but I think such come *after* we are known by name, not before; otherwise the amendment becomes meaningless.

The world, which daily tries to overcome us and un-Name us and keep us from our vocation of being real princesses, wants us to think in terms of immediate worldly success; to implement instant social justice everywhere for people who are statistics, not named; to feed all the poor since the way to a man's heart is through his stomach, and if his belly is full he'll do whatever we tell him to do; to cure all ills by a magic new drug, rather than calling the afflicted person by name, and laying on hands that heal. Perhaps it takes both for healing to be effective.

When we feel the pea and start to think in terms of success, like the elder brothers, we begin to think of the *cause* of social justice, the *cause* of world hunger, the *cause* of the poor, the old, and the ill. It doesn't hurt us to be involved in a cause because we don't have to name the individual people who make up the cause or see them one by one. We may be politically correct, but we are far from being truly human.

The vocation of the real princess is not to blunt the pain of awareness by plunging into causes. H.A. Williams writes,

> Causes begin to matter more than people and the Son of God is on the way to being crucified afresh in the name of righteousness and by campaigns and committees. For how can I love my neighbor as myself unless I am deeply aware of what I am, that I am being loved into life by the Father of us all? . . . It is only the degree in which I can begin to apprehend his love for me that I can begin to apprehend his love for all men.

That is the mainspring of all Christian social action—love, not success. Having compassion. Having the courage to share in each other's joys and fears and pains, every single day.

The true princess ultimately must grow up. She cannot stay a beautiful young girl forever. Sooner or later she will become either the wise old woman or the wicked witch.

The temptations that lead away from wisdom are, as always, seductive. They have been the same temptations world without end, even before the Spirit came to Jesus after his baptism, after his Naming, and led him up the mountain to be tempted. The true princess who is on her way to becoming a wise old woman sees the temptations for what they are. She feels the pea of self-indulgence through the seductive mattresses of success without substance: don't worry about hurting others; your own fulfillment comes first. Remember your integrity! Discipline is rigid, and there's no point in praying unless you feel like it and it makes you feel good; avoid pain at all costs. Give lip service to a cause because it's "in" right now, but you don't have to be involved with any of the people who make up the cause. Be politically correct and all will be well for you.

The true princess as she becomes a wise woman learns the toughness of love. Often, when someone exclaims "I love you," what is being loved is that part of us the person wants to see, rather than all of us; and our wholeness includes many things we'd rather not see—flaws and follies, weaknesses—in fact, monsters. If the princess cannot love the monster in us, she cannot love us, for only love can release the monster from its bondage.

Sometimes the line between the wicked witch and the wise old woman can be a very fine line. There may be a moment of decision. When Gertrude, Hamlet's beloved mother, turned from her husband to her lover and conspired with him when he murdered the king, she made an irrevocable decision. She surrendered her wisdom to the temptations of lust and power. The princess faded away, the wise old woman never came to be, and the wicked witch usurped her place.

In fairy tales the witch is sometimes actual witch, sometimes wicked stepmother, and the reason there are many wicked stepmothers and very few wicked stepfathers is that in the time frame when these tales were being told many women died in childbirth, and their husbands remarried, at least partly to have someone to take care of their children.

When we are children it is hard for us to allow our parents to stop being extensions of our own needs and to become people with needs of their own. At the same time that we are clinging to them with a false dependency, we are also struggling to separate ourselves. That is why many children have fantasies of being orphans or having been switched in the cradle. As Bruno Bettleheim points out, we can work through a lot of growing up by reading or listening to fairy tales.

I know, to my rue, that if I *stay* in anger, justified or not, the decision to stay there moves me away from being the wise old woman and towards being the wicked witch. The focus of one of my current angers is the U.S. Postal disService. A horrendous number of letters never reach their destination, nor are they returned to the sender. I wrote a dear friend of my sadness at her husband's death. A month later she called to ask me if I had heard. She had never received my letter. I am grateful that she called; she could easily have thought I didn't care. And this is just one among many examples. I can be legitimately angry at this lack of integrity on the part of the postal service; alas, yes, delivering mail seems to be no longer part of the job description. I have a vision of going to the New York City main post office on 34th Street with a blow torch and blasting out the words carved in the stone, "Neither snow nor sleet nor hail nor dark of night can stop these carriers from their appointed rounds."

An assignment for one of my writers' workshops was to take any parable of Jesus and rewrite it for this last decade of the twentieth century. One of my favorite stories was of a young woman who marches up and down in front of the post office with a large sign, I JUST WANT MY MAIL! IS THAT TOO MUCH TO ASK? and refuses to leave. What a pointed and delightful interpretation of the parable of the judge and the importunate widow!

And is the importunate widow a witch or a wise woman? It all depends. Witches do not have either humility or a sense of humor; wise women can laugh.

Remember, it was by gravity that Satan fell. The princess and the wise woman know holy levity. (And of course the wise old woman is also a wise old man.)

The wise old woman, like the true princess, feels the pea of awareness, and she does not blunt this awareness with forgetfulness. She is vulnerable, but when she suffers she greets the pain with love. And because she and the younger son know each other as intimately as Adam and Eve knew each other, she knows that the very small can be as important as the very great, and that God can use the least offering of love to change the course of a galaxy.

The wise old woman knows who she is. And many of us do not, or do not want to, because we are afraid.

In the Book of Wisdom in the Apocrypha, *hagia Sophia*—the true princess, the wise old woman—is described thus: "For within her is a spirit intelligent, holy, unique, manifold, subtle, active, incisive, unsullied, lucid, invulnerable, benevolent, sharp, irresistible, beneficent, loving to humankind, steadfast, dependable, unperturbed...."

And that is a description of the princess/wise woman we are called to be. And "successful" isn't a necessary component. Love is, that Love that comes to us as sheer gift, so that we can first of all accept ourselves, and then accept that love which has been given us, and offer it out of our royal richness. Then our souls will magnify the Lord.

◆ ◆ ◆

But there are characters in fairy tales—and modern novels—who don't care anything about love. They care about power, and to get power they are willing to hurt others. Might we say that the opposite of love is power, rather than hate? Hate is often the result of impotence, and impotence is lack of power.

One of our prominent politicians was caught with a young woman to whom he was not married. We were discussing this at dinner, and I wondered why so many politicians and statesmen have been wanton about sex. My son said calmly, "Mother, it's not sex. It's power." And I think he's right.

When I was a little girl I was terrified of witches, with an instinctive fear of those who want to exercise control-ling power over others. A witch often misuses power by means of black magic, and that is terrifying indeed. The word *magic* is a difficult one because its meaning is wider than the evil misuse of superhuman or inhuman powers. For children, particularly, it can also mean *marvel*, the tiny faerie hiding in the bluebell or the cowslip; the small gnome who tends the garden and devours cookies; the dwarves who cared for Snow White; the unicorn with its healing horn; the fairy godmother who can provide Cinderella with a beautiful ball gown and a golden coach. That kind of beneficent magic is shown in Winnie the Pooh and the heffalump, or the Dun Cow, or a bull that likes flowers.

In fairy tales we accept, with a willing suspension of disbelief, good fairies, and bad ones, too; guardian an-gels; talking animals; and, with a less willing acceptance, monsters.

We'd like to think of monsters as something outside us, but there are also many monsters within, and we don't want to recognize them, any more than did the man who wanted to take the mote out of someone else's eye without seeing and removing the plank in his own.

Christians are no more immune to the monsters of jealousy and overweening ambition and resentment than anyone else. The monsters are especially strong if we're going through a period of failure, as I know from my own experience. While my books were being rejected and other writers were being published I had many battles with my monsters. Success can be equally dangerous if we take the success seriously as a reflection of our own merit, our own talent, our own control of our art. But that's the world impinging again and blinding us to the real quest which is never ours alone, but is part of all of the body of Christ and the journey to the kingdom.

In fairy tales there's enormous emphasis on baptism, all those lavish christening parties, the good fairies all coming with their gifts, hovering around the baby in the white-bedecked cradle. I believe that each baby is given, at birth, its own gift, and part of our quest into wholeness is to discover our gift, and to be willing to accept that even though it may not be what we want it to be, it is uniquely ours.

But, alas, there's always some fairy who has been left out, who, through some oversight, doesn't receive her invitation (the Postal Service either lost it or failed to deliver it). So she comes to the party with evil intent, to bestow some terrible destructive gift upon the infant. But the good fairies, the guardian angels, are stronger. Though they cannot take away the evil gift, they can turn it to good. It may take a hundred years, or more, but the fairy tale is patient with chronology in the righting of our wrongs and the coming of the eternal life in which we live happily ever after.

One of the ugliest of the monsters (the christening gift of the bad fairy or witch) is resentment. Don Gregorio Maranon, a Spanish, Roman Catholic, Freudian psychologist (what a combination!) writes that resentment does not figure as one of the deadly sins because "it is not a sin, but a passion, a passion of the mind, which can lead to sin, and sometimes madness or crime." He writes,

> The resentful person is always a person lacking in generosity. . . . The passion opposed to resentment is generosity. . . . A generous nature has, as a rule, no occasion for forgivenenss, because it is always disposed to understand everything. . . . But the only man capable of understanding everything is the man who is capable of loving everything.

For all of our monsters there is the loving forgiveness that can change the monster, free it from the spell of the wicked fairy, and liberate it to be beautiful, to be loved, and therefore capable of giving love.

We create other monsters when we have false expectations, those false expectations that are themselves monsters—false expectations of ourselves, our husbands, our wives, our doctors, our political leaders, our priests, our bishops, our pastors. . . .

Michael Marshall writes that

> The Middle Ages well knew that some of its priests were bad priests, but it never fell into the heresy of Donatism by demanding a subjective moral qualification to endorse the validity of the priestly functions.

There was also room "in a large room" for Christian men to sin and be forgiven, for a man to be sexually incontinent in his actions and yet by the affirmations of penitence to remain chaste. It was well understood that whereas a man cannot properly be a Christian if he commits worldly or fleshly sins as a matter of settled policy and without regret or desire for amendment, he can certainly be a Christian if he falls into such sins—as we all do—at times of weakness, but does his level best, through prayer and striving, to allow the Spirit of God to dwell in him and conform him to Christ.

When we label a person a sinner, when we see only the monster, then we are unNaming, we are holding back that person from any hope of becoming whole, of becoming Named.

Naming the monsters in ourselves is a different matter. We cannot get on with the journey unless we do recognize and conquer our monsters. When Jesus came to Peter after the Resurrection and said, *"Simon, son of John, do you love me? . . . Feed my sheep,"* it was *after* Peter's monster had reared its hideously ugly head, and he had three times denied his Master. One of the most heart-rending moments in all of Scripture is just after Peter's third denial, when Jesus turned and looked directly at him. And Peter went out and wept bitterly.

But he never pretended he hadn't done it.

He never pretended that it hadn't happened.

He never tried to whitewash it, or to alibi, or to rationalize.

He lived with it. And that's what we must do, too.

All the men except John were conspicuous by their absence at the crucifixion. The women, the true princesses, were made of sterner stuff. For it's usually the true princess who is able to see through the monster and transform it with love.

If that love is not given, the monster gets more and more monstrous. I know that when I am being monstrous I am being my least lovable, and yet it is only love that will stop me from being monstrous. And even at times when no human being may be able to see through the monstrousness and give me the love that will heal me, *God can*. There have been times when I have flung myself at God in rage and anguish and have felt myself loved and protected under the shadow of the almighty wings and have returned to being, because of this love. Then I can get on with the Quest, knowing that the Maker never gives job descriptions or asks anyone to list qualifications before setting out on the Quest.

The story of Esther is, as in many fairy tales, a going from rags to riches, from poverty to royalty; Esther is indeed a true princess. In the story of *Beauty and the Beast*, Beauty is the younger son. Her two elder sisters are looking for the values of this world—lots of clothes and rich husbands—and they think these things are their right, are owed them; they are "entitled," as people say nowadays. So when their father loses all his money they are bitter and resentful.

But Beauty, the younger son, knows that nothing is ours by right—not good schools, nor warm clothes, nor more than enough to eat.

On our planet more people do not have these good things than those who do in the ghettos, in India, Venezuela, Haiti. Half the world is starving; the other half is on a diet. We are not privileged because we deserve to be. Privilege accepted should mean responsibility accepted.

The younger son accepts responsibility. Beauty's love for her father is responsible and so, unlike her elder sisters, she is able to accept it when he loses all his money. And she is able to offer herself in his place to the horrifying beast. And in the end, she is able to accept the beast, to see through his hideous ugliness and to kiss him in spontaneous affection so that he is released to become the prince he really is.

Part of recognizing the monster-prince part of ourselves is accepting that we do not have to be worthy; it is remembering that God always works with unworthy people and that when something good is done, we do not do it alone. If I thought I had to be worthy I'd never start another book; I certainly wouldn't be writing this one. What we are called to do is share our own story, without pride, as a humble offering.

Another monster that would unName us is atheism. Olivier Clement says,

What we must say to the atheist of today is that however deep may be the hell in which they find themselves, Christ is to be found still deeper. What we must say to all those who are wounded by the "terrorist" God is that basically what is asked of man is not virtue or merit, but a cry of trust and love from the depths of his hell; or, who knows, a moment of anguish and startlement in the enclosed immanence of his happiness. And never to fall into despair, but into God.

For despair is perhaps the most terrible of all the monsters, leading to apathy, indifference, what the medieval theologians called *accidie*, the sloth of the soul.

The extraordinary thing is that if we are willing to plumb the depths of our hell, we find there not Satan, but Christ. But before we find Christ, we must have faced and accepted and kissed our monsters.

Christ in hell? Yes. Christ made it all. There is no place Christ's love cannot go.

In the Russian Orthodox faith one of the most holy days of the year is Great and Holy Saturday, the Saturday between Good Friday and Easter Sunday. On Great and Holy Saturday Jesus went through the gates of hell (shown in icons as the cross on which he was crucified), and harrowed it. As the farmer harrows the ground before planting, turning over the sod, so Jesus turned over hell, emptying it. According to tradition, first he pulled out Adam and Eve, and then the Holy Innocents, those children under two slaughtered by jealous Herod's soldiers. Jesus emptied hell, which would not please those who want the "terrorist" God mentioned by Olivier Clement.

Thus, since hell is emptied, all the Old Testament heroes and heroines are available for sainthood! We can have Saints Shadrach, Meshach, and Abednego and Saints Abigail and Esther and Sarah, to name only a few favorites.

For the month of August 1990 I was in Russia, going mostly to seminaries and churches, and watching the marvel of the Russian church bursting forth like water from the rock as the state returned more and more church buildings to the church. In Leningrad (now once again St. Petersburg) we went to St. Isaac's Cathedral and were told with great excitement that there had been a service there for the first time in seventy years. One of our group asked who St. Isaac's Cathedral was named after, expecting to hear the name of some early Christian saint. Not at all. St. Isaac's Cathedral is named after Isaac, son of Abraham and Sarah.

It is certainly a misreading of Scripture and of God's love that has led some people to believe that those who were born before Christ's resurrection are forever excluded from the kingdom. It is another example of literalism, more dangerous than believing that God had to accomplish everything with his left hand. Literalism tends to be cold of heart, not warm. Literalism may understand sex, but not love.

And what about hell now, for those born since the Resurrection, who have not lived by God's love, who (perhaps) have not accepted Christ? Thank God it is up to God, not me, and I am nervous around people who assume that they have a right to decide who is destined for hell and who for heaven.

There's a charming true story of a small child's literalism. One day at Sunday school the class was asked to draw pictures of Bible stories. This child drew a rectangle, with four wheels. The rectangle was obviously a cart, and seated in it were two stick figures. The cart was being driven by another stick figure. When the child was asked what the picture was about, the answer was, "It's God driving Adam and Eve out of the Garden."

God can indeed do anything needed; drive anybody anywhere, out of the Garden, and, ultimately, into the kingdom. God is not going to fail. The happy ending is going to come. It may take a few more billennia or trillenia, but God is going to succeed.

It is not always easy to affirm the final element of the fairy tale that pulls all our parts into wholeness—the happy ending. If it's hard for us to accept our monsters and love them and free them to become the beautiful creatures they were meant to be, it's even harder for most of us to believe in the happy ending. The elder brothers can never believe in it because they think it is something they have to earn, or make all by themselves. Sometimes we can accept the happy ending for ourselves but not for monsters like Tiberius and drug pushers and child molesters.

The happy ending, like the Quest, is not for the qualified, and we human beings can never quite understand the length and depth and longing of God's love for all of Creation.

Our human icon of this love of God is the love of husband and wife. Surprisingly, the *Song of Songs* is still left out of the Episcopal Lectionary, despite the fact that the church appears to think it's completely freed-up and open-minded about sex. The strongest language of love known to the human being is the language of love between man and woman. John of the Cross, Julian of Norwich—all the great mystics—were unabashed about using this language to describe their relationships with God and frequently quoted from Song of Songs.

Similarly, Isaiah sings:

For your Maker is your husband—
the LORD Almighty is his name—
the Holy One of Israel is your Redeemer.

The Genesis story of the human being's turning away from God calls forth from God the cry, *"Where are you?"*

And in Hosea, God calls out, *"How can I give you up, Ephraim? How can I hand you over, Israel?"* And again in Isaiah, the Lord says, *"Though your sins are like scarlet, they shall be as white as snow; though they are red as crimson, they shall be like wool."* And Jesus cries out, *"O Jerusalem, Jerusalem . . . how often I have longed to gather your children together, as a hen gathers her chicks under her wings, but you were not willing."*

And John says,

For God so loved the world that he gave his one and only Son, that whoever believes in him shall not perish but have eternal life. For God did not send his Son into the world to condemn the world, but to save the world through him.

When the world rejected that love and crucified it, Jesus did not lash back; he cried out in love and forgiveness.

Things are never quite the way they seem: things do not look the way we think they ought to look. Isaiah's description of Christ as the Suffering Servant bears little resemblance to the pretty young man with the beautifully combed beard and melancholy eyes we so often see depicted. But Isaiah's description rings much more true. In his own day, Jesus was a monster to many, disconcerting them with his unpredictability and the company he kept, vanishing to go apart to pray and to be alone with his Father just when people thought they needed him.

Perhaps if we are brave enough to accept our monsters, to love them, to kiss them, we will find that we are touching not the terrible dragon that we feared, but the loving Lord of all Creation.

And when we meet our Creator, we will be judged for all our turnings away, all our inhumanity to each other, but it will be the judgment of inexorable love, and in the end we will know the mercy of God which is beyond all comprehension. And we will know, as Hosea knew, that the heavenly Spouse says, *"I will betroth you to me forever; I will betroth you in righteousness and justice, in love and compassion."*

It is too good to believe; it is too strong, so we turn away, and the church leaves the *Song of Songs* out of the lectionary. But we can put it back in.

To the ancient Hebrew the love of God for his chosen people transcended the erotic love of man and woman. For the early Christian, it was the love of Christ for the church. For all of us it is the longing love of God for his Creation, a love which is too strong for many of us to accept.

There is an old legend that after his death Judas found himself at the bottom of a deep and slimy pit. For thousands of years he wept his repentance, and when the tears were finally spent he looked up and saw, way, way, up, a tiny glimmer of light. After he had contemplated it for another thousand years or so, he began to try to climb up towards it. The walls of the pit were dank and slimy, and he kept slipping back down. Finally, after great effort, he neared the top, and then he slipped and fell all the way back down. It took him many years to recover, all the time weeping bitter tears of grief and repentance, and then he started to climb up again. After many more falls and efforts and failures he reached the top and dragged himself into an upper room with twelve people seated around a table. "We've been waiting for you, Judas," Jesus said. "We couldn't begin till you came."

I heard my son-in-law, Alan, tell this story at a clergy conference. The story moved me deeply. I was even more deeply struck when I discovered that it was a story that

259

offended many of the priests and ministers there. I was horrified at their offense. Would they find me, too, unforgivable?

But God, the Good Book tells us, is no respecter of persons, and the happy ending isn't promised to an exclusive club, as many groups, such as the Jehovah's Witnesses believe. It isn't—face it—only for Baptists, or Presbyterians, or Episcopalians. What God began, God will not abandon. *[H]e who began a good work in you will carry it on to completion. . . .* God loves *every one,* sings the psalmist. What God has named will live forever, Alleluia!

The happy ending has never been easy to believe in. After the Crucifixion the defeated little band of disciples had no hope, no expectation of Resurrection. Everything they believed in had died on the cross with Jesus. The world was right, and they had been wrong. Even when the women told the disciples that Jesus had left the stone-sealed tomb, the disciples found it nearly impossible to believe that it was not all over. The truth was, it was just beginning.

It is important to remember that after the Resurrection Christ was never recognized by sight. Mary Magdalene, the first person to whom the risen Christ appeared, thought he was a gardener and knew him only when he called her by name. When the couple met him on the road to Emmaus it seems evident that he did not show them his wounds; otherwise they would have recognized him. With tender love, he showed those wounds when Thomas needed to see them.

The disciples did not bother to try to understand the resurrection body. They doubted, and then they believed. They believed something so wonderful that it changed this broken, fragmented, beaten-down little group of men and women in a moment from depression to enthusiasm, from despair to new life, vibrant and unafraid.

When Paul was asked what the resurrected and cosmic body looks like, he snapped, "Don't ask foolish questions!" How do you describe a spiritual body? You don't. Not one of the Gospel writers tried to. Paul said, *"How foolish! What you sow does not come to life unless it dies."* And then Paul, speaking more like a twentieth-century cosmologist than a first-century tentmaker, tells us that there are many kinds of bodies, many kinds of flesh. *"There are also heavenly bodies and there are earthly bodies . . . and star differs from star in splendor."* And the seed of that Pauline paradox, the spiritual body, is planted in us at our baptism.

One of my friends and I often talk about our husbands, missing their living presence. Her husband died only a year ago, and the wound is still raw. We talked today, via telephone.

"When I see him again, I will recognize him," she affirmed.

I agreed, but I said, "He may not look the way he looked in life. But you *will* recognize him."

Yes. She understood that. The seed that goes into the ground and dies does not look like the oak tree or the lilac bush or the snowdrop that comes up in the spring. But we will recognize each other, because our sight will have changed as much as our bodies: we will know each other in a deeper way than was ever possible in life, no matter how close and intimate our human bond has been.

To the Eastern Orthodox Christian, the Crucifixion, Resurrection, and Ascension are seen almost as one blinding, simultaneous event, and there is much wisdom in this, for there is far too often a tendency to focus on either the Crucifixion or the Resurrection and to ignore the Ascension entirely, or to exult in the Resurrection and forget that the Crucifixion preceded it. The Ascension underlines the cosmic quality of the Crucifixion and Resurrection, and the truth that we cannot have one without the other. Paul says, *"If only for this life we have hope in Christ, we are to be pitied more than all men."* Indeed, it would be a cosmic bad joke if our little candle flickered and went out and God did not care enough about us to complete what was begun at our birth and ratified at our baptism.

Too often pious people see Paul glorifying in the Cross, Jesus and him crucified, and forget Paul's greatest song of glory, that of the Resurrection. Without the Resurrection, glorying in the Cross becomes morbid to the point of sadomasochism. The Cross is easier to understand than the Resurrection, because the Resurrection bursts the bond of literalism and blazes with that reality that burns so fiercely and brilliantly that it is often too hard to bear. The Cross was a recorded, historical event; the Crucifixion of a man called Jesus is mentioned in a history written two thousand years ago. But the Resurrection bursts through and beyond human history and is part of God's Creation story.

Some people, in an effort to avoid all pain, try to focus on a literal Resurrection, which is a painless Resurrection. But I suspect the Resurrection may be as traumatic as birth, for it is indeed a new and cosmic birth. The Cross and the Resurrection are inseparable. There is no resurrection until there has been a death. Jesus says, "Unless a grain of wheat falls into the earth and dies, it remains alone; but if it dies, it bears much fruit."

Meditation is the practise of death and resurrection. When we include meditation as part of our daily practise of prayer we are not dabbling in New Age-ism. We are simply letting go of that conscious control we hold so dear; we are opening ourselves up to the darkness between the galaxies which is the same as the great darkness in the spaces within our own hearts. Only if we have such faith in the reality of the happy ending can we let go of everything we think of as being ourselves, knowing that the Maker of the Universe who has Named us into being is there, waiting for us, calling us into deeper being. Occasionally those who meditate (the wise old women, male and female) are given the further gift of contemplation, which is beyond human thought. And until we can let go of our conscious, cognitive selves in this way, we are not ready for the happy ending.

If we look for the happy ending in this world and according to the standards of this world, we'll never find it. We can't earn it; we don't deserve it; there's no way we can acquire it, no matter how many merit badges we manage to pile up.

And it came to pass . . . Once upon a time . . . A story is a beginning, and the very fact that we are telling a story affirms our belief in redemption.

The real princess and the younger son and their adventures—after the beast has been kissed and turned into a prince—are blessed by marriage, by the two protagonists living happily together ever after and ruling their kingdom with prudence and power.

But the beast and the princess and the journey are not without us, but within us, and we ourselves are the kingdom over which they are now to rule. The happy ending does not come automatically, and it does not come free. We must embark on the Quest, knowing that it involves great dangers. We are not protected by our goodness or our own superior powers. We know we are not qualified, and we rejoice in being servants. The happy ending begins with our recognition of our wholeness, which is symbolized for us in the elements of the fairy tale. We are much more than we know, and we can begin to find that *more* through our willingness to go on the Quest, and to welcome in ourselves the younger son, the elder brother, the true princess, the benevolent king, the enchanted beast, the wise old woman, all leading towards that redemptive fulfilling of the journey which is our story.

The happy ending is part of our calling Jesus *Lord,* and that is a sheer, unadulterated gift of the Holy Spirit, sometimes given us when we least expect it, and sometimes so gently that it is a long time before we even recognize it. Someone who loudly affirms Jesus as his personal Saviour may be further from knowing the Lord than someone who lovingly longs to be able to do so and hardly dares, knowing the enormity of such an affirmation and the incredible responsibility it brings. If we are to affirm Jesus as Lord, we must model our behavior on his, though sometimes when we ask, "What would Jesus do?" there is no easy answer.

Even when there is no answer, hoping to do what Jesus would do is still the gift of the Holy Spirit, and because God's time and our time are as radically different as the mortal body and the cosmic body, the gift begins at our baptism. As Archbishop William Temple says, the more we are enabled to start dying now, the less noticeable the transition will be when we come to our physical death which, if we are allowed to enter it knowingly, not drugged and strung up on life-support systems, can be our greatest and deepest offering of self in meditation.

Lord Jesus Christ, have mercy on me was in the rhythm of my breathing and my heartbeat from the moment the truck hit the car until I went under the anesthetic. And when, after the surgery, I woke up, Lord Jesus Christ was still with me. There have been times, during the slow period of recuperation, when I have wondered why I am still alive. Why didn't I die there and then? Why have I not visibly grown spiritually? I was truly willing to die; I was not afraid.

So shouldn't my waking from anesthesia have shown me and all my friends a new me? Shouldn't my monsters have vanished, leaving a wise old woman? Wouldn't you expect that I'd have become some sort of a saint, more deeply spiritual, after such an experience? But none of this has happened. I'm the same old Madeleine, impatient, volatile. I still ask unanswerable questions. Have I grown at all?

Yes, I believe that I have, but growth is still for me a slow process, not a Damascus Road experience. God will help me to become a wise old woman in God's good time. Maybe it is a good thing that I am still Madeleine, recognizably the same person, not only physically, but spiritually; I must still look to my monsters, recognize them, name them, ask God to redeem them.

It is time for me to understand that the true princess part of myself is chronologically behind me, and that makes it even more important that I become the wise old woman. The wise old woman is the part of you and me most able and willing to understand the Resurrection.

When I was in I.C.U., the trauma team made their rounds. In what I learned was typical fashion they stood at the foot of my bed, and I heard one doctor say, "Here we have a seventy-two-year-old Caucasian female." He began telling the others what had happened to me. He made a few factual mistakes. Finally I said, "This seventy-two-year-old Caucasian female is quite conscious, can hear everything you have to say, has a name, and no, I was not driving the car, I was in the passenger seat."

Later, one of the doctors came to me with an apology. "Sometimes we just have to play at being doctors." He smiled.

The next time the doctors were making rounds, and stopped at the bed before mine, I heard the head doctor say to the patient, "I hope you don't mind if we need to talk about you rather impersonally."

So maybe some good came out of that tiny incident, a good that in its own small way leads toward the happy ending.

For the happy ending is intrinsic to the life of faith, central to all we do during all of our lives. If we cannot believe in it, we are desolate indeed. If we know, in the depths of our hearts, that God is going to succeed, with each one of us, with the entire universe, then our lives will be bright with laughter, love, and light.

Story as Resurrection

12

THE YEAR IS TURNING to a close as I write this. I am out of the city for two weeks, at Crosswicks, rejoicing first in the confusion and excitement of Christmas—with four little boys six and under!

Now they are gone. The beds are all stripped and remade, and I am once again in my own bedroom, after having had to move out to the couch in my workroom to make room in this inn. It was wonderful to share the excitement of the children, to be together as family, but it is good to be quiet again, just the three of us, Bion and Laurie and me. The children all had sniffles; now, of course, so do we.

On the weekend, when Laurie (the physician) is not on call, we take the dogs and walk to the brook and to the beautiful pond the beavers have made for us. Hugh and I

267

longed for years for the beavers to come and make a lake for us, and now, at last, it has happened. I miss Hugh because he isn't here to enjoy it, but it is a good missing because it recalls all the good things we did enjoy together.

Right now I must think about not slipping and falling! There is enough ground cover of snow to provide traction, and I have on good hiking boots. The dogs rush ahead, double back, rush ahead again. Once we are into the woods the wind drops and it is less cold. We get to the stone bridge over the brook, which is still running under its icy edges despite the subfreezing weather. To the right of the brook is the first and smaller of two remarkable beaver dams. We follow around the rim of the frozen pond to the larger dam, an amazing feat of engineering. The pond gleams silver. The winter light slants through the trees. We don't talk much, except to remark on some particular beauty or other—the light on the icicles near the first dam, a small bird's nest in a low cleft of a tree.

Then we tramp home to make cocoa and warm our toes. And think a little about the past year. There has been considerable personal grief. It has not been a good year for many of our friends. For the planet it has been an astounding year. The world events that shared the news with Hurricane Bob when I was first home from the hospital in San Diego have continued to accelerate. There is no more Soviet Union. The communist religion has gone down the drain with unprecedented rapidity. There is now a commonwealth of nations, and what will happen in the next year is far from clear.

The bitter fighting between Serbs and Croats continues, the differences in religion making the fighting more anguished. Why is so much war muddied by

268

religion? Do not the Catholics and the Orthodox worship the same Christ, the same blessed Mother of God? And, in other parts of the world, much is shared by Catholics and Protestants. Why do different visions of God cause war between Moslems and Christians and Jews and Hindus? What is wrong, that we let our dogmas about God separate us rather than unite us?

Story helps us understand our humanness and our mortality. All grief is mourning over death—the death of a friendship, of a hope, of a career, of a marriage, of a love. If we try to circumvent the right and proper period of mourning, or repress it, then it will fester within us, and hurt both us and everybody we come in contact with.

I remember being alone in the beach house the day after my grandmother died, and sensing simultaneously her presence and her absence. And I turned to story, a book I had already read and re-read, a book in which a young woman is called to look at her own life and let it go. And her grief eased my grief.

This morning I talked with and cried with a friend who has had one physical vicissitude after another. She has every right to weep. She is one of the bravest people I know, but she needs to express grief over what is happening to her body, and everybody expects her just to go on being brave. Right now she needs to weep like a child, and such weeping embarrasses people.

There are times I, too, need to weep, because I am still paying for last year's accident with fatigue and pain. I am ashamed, though I think that's probably foolish. Sure, the world has taught us not to mourn, but that's the world we're not supposed to conform to. We've listened to the world for so long that we don't know how to mourn. We don't even know what it's about. And this denigration of mourning seems to be a twentieth-century phenomenon that came in—I'm not sure when, but during my lifetime. I remember when I was a little girl growing up in New York City, seeing houses with all the shades drawn, and a funeral wreath on the door—a public announcement that those within that building were mourning.

And I remember the prickling of unease when I saw black and white signs on an apartment door: DIPH-THERIA or SCARLET FEVER. With the discovery of antibiotics we have saved a lot of lives, but we have also come to think of death as unnecessary. We no longer have a mandated or permissible period of mourning. Though it is futile to assign a timetable for grief, it is eased if it is expressed.

When I was a child there was mourning for death; death was still respectable. There were other kinds of grief, much more hidden. The divorcee was usually depicted smoking a cigarette in a long holder; she wore brilliant lipstick and dresses above her knees and had a "come hither" look. Or was that how respectable married people insisted on looking at the divorcee, so they wouldn't have to mourn with her the death of a marriage?

We don't wear mourning for our dead anymore, sometimes not even at the funeral. What did I wear at Hugh's funeral? I do not remember. Clothing seemed totally unimportant. I don't know what I wore, except my grief.

Nowadays divorce is more commonplace than a long-term marriage, and as for those other hurts, the loss of a job, the acceptance of illness, having to move from a home—we're expected to grin and bear it and shed no tears.

But tears need to be shed, alone, and with each other.

The proper expression of grief is mortification.

The word *mortification*, like widows' weeds, has gone out of our daily vocabulary. Mortification is expensive. It is a grace that is costly.

How many of us have cried with Jo March and her sisters over Beth's death? Or with Sara Crewe when she is told that her father has died in India? But the healthy expression of grief is contrary to what the world would teach us.

If we do not allow ourselves to grieve, we cannot allow God to grieve. Surely when things go wrong with us human creatures, when a child is hit by a truck and killed, when people who love each other hurt each other, when Christians are murderous in the name of Christ, oh, surely God grieves. That is shown clearly all through Scripture.

The easiest way to discover what the world would teach us is to watch television commercials. More money is put into the commercials than into the actual shows. One year my husband was on a soap opera; he was in both a Broadway and an off-Broadway play; he was in two movies; he did a major television commercial. And he made more money from the commercial than from all the rest of the jobs put together.

I've never seen anyone grieving on a television commercial. Basically what the commercials teach us is that we are to believe in security and the instant gratification of pleasure as the greatest good in living. If we will just buy the right painkiller and the correct insurance we will be secure. And that will make us happy.

Oh?

Instead of being allowed to grieve for the precariousness of all life, we are taught to look for a security that does not exist. No one can promise that we will end a day in safety, that we, or someone dear to us, will not be hurt.

271

All too often we fall for it and go into debt to buy the latest gadget. Whatever it is, it's made to self-destruct after a few years, and it will never help whatever it is that's making us hurt.

What does help? The gift of Christ, who offers us the grieving that is healing. This kind of grieving is a gift; it helps us "Walk that lonesome valley." It involves a lifelong willingness to accept the gift, which is part of what Bonhoeffer called *costly grace*.

Costly grace is no bargain in a world offering us "bargains." But if we look for cheap grace we end up with nothing. As Bonhoeffer said,

Cheap grace is the preaching of forgiveness without requiring repentance, baptism without church discipline, communion without confession. Cheap grace is grace without discipleship, grace without the cross, grace without Jesus Christ, living and incarnate. . . . Costly grace is the Gospel which must be *sought* again and again, the gift which must be *asked* for, the door at which [we] must *knock*. Such grace is *costly* because it calls us to follow, and it is *grace* because it calls us to follow *Jesus Christ*. It is costly because it costs [us] our lives, and it is grace because it gives [us] the only true life. It is costly because it condemns sin, and grace because it loves the sinner.

We were bought with a price, and what has cost God so much cannot be cheap for us.

God took a tremendous risk when he created creatures who could make mistakes and wrong choices. We do not pay for our mistakes by ourselves; God pays with us. Forgiving us is part of that payment. Over and over God forgave his stiff-necked people; over and over he forgives us and calls us to be part of that forgiveness.

Forgiveness requires healing grief. Forgiveness hurts, as all grief must, and if it hurts to forgive, it hurts equally to be forgiven. We can feel magnanimous when we forgive—in which case it isn't real forgiveness because it does not involve grief. True forgiveness involves fellow-feeling with the one forgiven. When we *accept* forgiveness we accept ourselves as sinners, which is not popular today, even in the church.

In my own search for a church home I look for a community where there is deep and continuing forgiveness, where a path is steered between permissiveness and rigid judgmentalism. I want a community where I will find true grace, knowing that true grace is not cheap.

True grace involves knowing that people, even those we like least, those we find hardest to forgive, are more important than things. When human beings try to limit themselves to a world of things they can buy and have, they lose, as Dr. Ott points out, their awareness of the wholeness of being human, and they lose their stories.

People who try to sell us cheap grace equate integrity with self-indulgence, freedom with anarchy, liberation with chaos. It doesn't work. Only discipline and obedience to the strict law of love allow us to be free. It is only the daily discipline of work at my desk which frees a book to be born. It is only the discipline of daily prayer which allows the freedom of meditation and contemplation. A river isn't a river when it overflows its banks. The stars would be raging, flaming destruction if they had not been set in their beautiful courses. So with grief; each day of our lives is preparation for grief, preparation for living in Jesus so he may live in us.

I structure my life in the daily reading of Morning and Evening Prayer, and in the Eucharist. Then, when tragedy strikes unexpectedly, as it so often does, the framework for grief is already there.

When I was in the hospital I.C.U., and later, when I was moved to a private room, I was hungry for the Eucharist; indeed, I was desperately lonely without it. A nurse had read an admission form to me, taking down my answers, and when she said, "Religion?" I replied "Episcopalian." It wouldn't have mattered if I had said Baptist or Lutheran; the churches can no longer afford chaplaincy services. At least they could not in the University of California San Diego Hospital Center. When Luci returned home to San Francisco and called me, I told her that I was not happy with my church's lack of response to human needs, and she immediately got on the phone, and a kind priest from a neighboring town came to me. But I felt grief that my church was not there for me or for anybody else in that hospital.

Sometimes I cause my own grief when I discover that, unwittingly, I have made a human being into an idol, and when that person behaves like a human being and not an idol, I feel that my trust has been betrayed. No. It is I who have been the betrayer by refusing to allow for the normal fallibility of flesh and blood. The grief is genuine, but the result must be my farewell to the idol and my discovery of a human being who, on occasion, can be a Christ-bearer for me, as we are all meant to bear Christ for each other.

Another deception of cheap grace is the confusion of integrity with self-fulfillment. It is sad that integrity, as I have mentioned earlier, has become for me a questionable word. Integrity has little to do with self-fulfillment; but it may mean holding to a position that is not popular, but which you believe, after deep prayer, is where Jesus would want you to be. It may mean refusing to make needed money by means which are not quite honest. It is not pandering to self. To love another is an act of self-abandonment. To weep with another is an act of self-abandonment.

In my church, the Episcopal church, less and less is demanded of us. Where no demands are made on us, the human psyche withers, and when a cause for grief comes we aren't able to cope with it. I have been deeply grieved at the number of church leaders who have left their wives and children for a younger woman, and particularly grieved when someone says tolerantly, "Oh, he's just going through a mid-life crisis." Does a mid-life crisis give us permission to fulfill ourselves at the expense of others? Wouldn't it be worth it to work through the crisis to the place where we could accept ourselves as no longer young and, instead, rejoice at our maturity? It's often more complex than this, and the only response is loving prayer.

Unthinking tolerance and permissiveness lead us to shallow lives, and emptying pews, and nowhere to go in time of grief. When I was in college I had a friend who was a brilliant young man. I remember walking across campus with him while he intoned, "I grow old, I grow old, I shall wear the bottoms of my trousers rolled," which was my introduction to T.S. Eliot. First he told me that there was one infallible test of whether or not you're in love with someone: can you use the same toothbrush? Then he went on to give me the one infallible test that shows you whether or not you trust your priest: would you want him or her at your deathbed?

How many of us, laymen as well as clergy, are willing to be at a deathbed, to go through death with someone? I believe that this, too, is required of us, all of us, not just those ordained. It was a special grace that I was allowed to share the death of my husband. It helped prepare me for the other deaths I have subsequently shared and which are costly grace, but grace indeed. Sharing death is part of the road to the Resurrection.

There was no joy in that jolly clergyman who came to see me in the I.C.U. and told me to call him any time. He was so embarrassed at simply seeing me full of tubes that I don't think he could have coped with a deathbed. And that is grief—especially for him.

When Jesus needed to mourn—when he learned that his cousin John had been beheaded, even his disciples were insensitive to his needs, and people kept crowding in, demanding miracles, refusing to leave him alone.

After several major miracles he managed to get away, to be alone with his Abba, and this is a message for us. When Jesus needed to be alone with the Father, to pray, to grieve, to be refilled (not fulfilled), ultimately he left, walked out, whether his friends and disciples liked it or not. When he walked out, were there a number of the lame, the halt, the blind, who felt he had failed them? He walked out, anyhow.

To find himself by losing himself in the Creator. God's demands are always more important than the demands made on us by people. God's demands are to be heeded. There is no permissiveness whatsoever about this.

The search for grace, costly grace, involves the acceptance of pain and the creative grief which accompanies growth into maturity. Don't be afraid the pain will destroy the wholeness. It leads, instead, to the kind of wholeness that rejoices in Resurrection.

No one dares to grieve who does not dare to love, and love is always part of costly grace. It has been said that before we can give love we must first have received love, and indeed love is a response to love. To be a Christian and not to be a lover is impossible. We cannot grieve in any healthy way in total isolation—solitude, yes, but not isolation. Grief, like Christianity, is shared by the entire body. Nothing that affects one part of the body does not affect it all.

But in thinking about love and grief we must be careful not to confuse either with that sentimentality which is part of cheap grace. The kind of loving grief I'm talking about involves acceptance of the precariousness of life and that we will all die, but our wholeness is found in the quality rather than the quantity of our living. Real love, between man and woman, friend and friend, parent and child, is exemplified for us in the life, death and resurrection of Jesus Christ who offered us and still offers us the wholeness of that costly grace which gives us the courage for healthy grief.

We live in a time where costly grace is what makes life bearable; more than bearable—joyful and creative, so that even our grief is part of our partnership in co-creation with God.

The world around us is full of racial tension; the problems of starvation across the globe grow greater with each year; the planet is still torn apart by war; the result of our technocratic affluence is an earth depleted, an air polluted, and a population suffering from more mental illness, suicide, and despair than our country has ever known. So perhaps we finally have to accept that the great do-it-yourself dream hasn't worked, and we've been dreaming wrong, dreaming nightmares. The original dream had to do with a wholeness which touched every part of our lives, including grief, and it had to do with grace, costly grace.

The extraordinary thing is that it is not we who pay the price of costly grace, but the all-loving God who set the stars in their courses, who created us, and dwelt among us. For love of us, God is the one who pays. What a story!

◆ ◆ ◆

I was grateful at Christmastide to have time for these thoughts, away from the busy schedule which never seems to let up in the city. Here, at night, I can listen to the silence which is broken not by sirens and taxi horns but by the creaking of a house that is about two hundred and fifty years old. It was built by hardy folk. They didn't have the machinery we have to make things easier. Men and mules did the work. The wood for our house didn't come from a lumberyard, but from the great forest that surrounded the original village; it must have taken incredible strength to have felled the tree that is our roof beam.

And those who built had to be hardy spiritually as well as physically. The doors at Crosswicks are Cross-and-Bible doors. The hardware is H L—Help Lord—and they needed help. The weak survived neither the long, cold winters nor the heat of summer. Women and infants died in childbirth; grief was a daily companion, but it was also part of their spiritual life, their pattern of creation.

Every time there is a major death in a family the patterns change. I knew such changes after the death of my father, my mother, my husband. One of these changes is that Crosswicks now belongs to my son and daughter-in-law, and this is right and proper. There is no way I could have kept the old house myself; I would have had to sell it.

But the pattern is different. There are things I know that no one else knows. There are four pine trees now three stories high that I planted as baby pines one year with a friend, who was dead a year later. Another smaller pine came from an actor friend who was my mentor. These pines mean people to me. They are part of my story that I don't need to force on anybody else. There is more than enough memory for us all to share, and it is part of growing older that some of the memory that is pertinent for me is not for the younger generation, and that is simply the way of life. It is a gentle grief.

Some memories we share. The big salad bowl at Crosswicks, made from the bole of a tree, came from Tallis, who was Bion's godfather as well as my friend. The portrait of Bion's great-grandfather, after whom he is named, hangs on the wall over the piano. Bion and Laurie are gathering their own Crosswicks memories, special to them. My children have asked me to write down as many stories as I can ("Who is the man in this portrait?" "Romulus Saunders, the first Madeleine L'Engle's father."), and I'm trying to do so, setting down the stories that I think will be vital for them. It is not easy, because the world we live in and the life we live has changed so radically during my lifetime that some things that were normal for me are unrecognizable to them.

I think of the people who built this house, and of their vocabulary, much of which has gone out of daily usage—words such as *mortification*, which nowadays bring to mind sour-faced people who think of any kind of fun as sinful. If they have a choice of two things to do, the unpleasant one has to be the right choice, because whom God loveth he chastiseth, and the pleasanter choice has to be wrong. Ouch. If God loves us he punishes us? He's so angry at our sin and depravity that he punishes us anyhow?

The word *mortification* also conjures up visions of medieval monks or nuns in their cells, mortifying themselves by flagellation with lead-tipped whips. When Hugh and I were first making Crosswicks our home, we found in the cluttered garage just such a whip, called a cat-o'-nine-tails. Hugh went white with anger at the thought of how that whip must have been used, and disposed of it promptly.

Such things are a distortion, a perversion of what mortification really means. True mortification is to die to that within us which is selfish and self-willed, that which keeps us from each other and from God.

In one of my etymological dictionaries *mortify*, from the Latin, means "to make dead." But the dictionary goes on to explain this further, by quoting the Bible, from the Book of Kings (KJV): *The Lord mortifieth, and quickeneth.* The Lord makes us dead and then brings us to life. Any mortification that does not quicken us to new life in the Lord is not true mortification. Baptism is an icon of mortification.

The times I have been closest to God I have been least conscious of my own self, yet these are the times I have been most fully myself. Some have been times of grief. I remember one time when I was a child, visiting my grandmother in the South, and we had been to a funeral. That evening we sat out on the porch and listened to the ocean rolling in to shore, and I sat in my grandmother's lap, and she sang to me "Jesus, Tender Shepherd," and I knew that despite the nearness of death I was loved and that love was stronger than death. I wasn't old enough to articulate this, but children know intuitively more than many of us are capable of accepting as adults.

And mortification includes joy. In *The Summer of the Great-Grandmother*, at my mother's death at ninety, in her grandson's arms, I grieved deeply because she was a remarkable mother and I loved her, and I was also full of joy because her life had been full and rich, and we had been able to keep her at home to die, surrounded by those she loved. There were many, many cousins to phone. Some of them shared the joy and grief. A few were appalled that I sounded joyful. "How can you?" they asked. I replied, "She was ninety and it was time. There was nothing ahead for her but further sliding downhill. I am grateful beyond words to God for taking her." And that gratitude and grief and joy mortified me, got me out of the way.

♦ ♦ ♦

We are told to mortify our bodies. What does that mean?

Not to abuse our bodies, either by over-deprivation or over-indulgence. Paul, in his letter to the people of Corinth, is very specific on the subject: *Don't you know that you yourselves are God's temple and that God's Spirit lives in you? If anyone destroys God's temple, God will destroy him; for God's temple is sacred, and you are that temple.*

An awesome responsibility—we are to care for our bodies. Because they are temples of God's Holy Spirit, we are to honor them, to enjoy them. Right now part of honoring my body is to exercise it. I must walk at least half an hour a day, walk briskly. After the accident it still isn't always easy, but the more I walk, the easier it gets. When I can, I swim, exercising my whole body without putting stress on any part of it. I am trying to eat healthily, a high-fiber, low-fat, low-sodium diet. That part is fairly easy, because I've been trying to eat that way for years. I am trying to keep off the weight I lost at the time of the accident when I could not eat; my present weight is better than the weight I carried before the accident. This is mortifying the body that it may be quickened to new life.

In that new life I am newly aware of the total interconnection of all of me, body, mind, and spirit. I remember that I could not return to my beloved discipline of Morning and Evening Prayer until my body was able to accept food. I am still not completely healed from the accident of more than six months ago. My energy level is still low. And so, sometimes, are my spirits. And again I feel the Holy Spirit cautioning me to be patient. If my body is still bruised, so is my psyche, and *psyche* and *soma* are interrelated. Be gentle, the Spirit says. Be patient.

I try. And I think of James Clement (in *The Love Letters* and *Certain Women*) telling about the making of cider in the winter, when it is put outdoors to freeze. In the center of the frozen apple juice is a tiny core of pure flame that does not freeze. My faith (which I enjoy) is like that tiny flame. Even in the worst of moments it has been there, surrounded by ice, perhaps, but alive.

A friend told me about a clergyman who warned her that when someone is ill their faith must be clear and strong, otherwise it is inadequate. First, I wonder how much severe illness that clergyman has endured. Secondly, I think he misses the point of our interrelatedness. There *are* times when we are too ill to pray for ourselves, but we know the comfort and wonder of the prayers of others. Even when my prayer is at its strongest, I am still in need of the prayers of my family and friends as they, I believe, are in need of mine. Thomas More said, "Pray for me as I pray for thee, that we may merrily meet in heaven." If I thought my prayer had to be pure and perfect at all times there wouldn't be much merriment in my heart. But God lovingly takes whatever prayers I can give, even if all I can do is hold on to the name of Jesus. It is God's love that is adequate, not mine, and that love cannot be completely buried.

I remember a story about an event in Red Square in Moscow that took place not long after the terrible days of the Russian Revolution and the establishment of the atheist Union of Soviet Socialist Republics. The people of Moscow were called to a gathering in Red Square. There they were addressed by one of the new leaders, who spent well over half an hour proving to the populace that there is no God. His factual arguments about the nonexistence of God were incontrovertible, and the mob of people standing in Red Square was silent and subdued.

Then a priest who was standing with the people asked permission to say three words. Permission was granted, and he stood in front of the packed square, raised his arms, and cried out:

"CHRIST IS RISEN!"

And the entire mob responded joyfully, "He is risen indeed!"

The truth of faith was far greater than the rational arguments of atheism, and we have seen the truth of that faith resurrecting itself again in Moscow in recent months. *Christ is risen!* That joyful news cannot be suppressed. In Russia, in the USSR, it was forced underground, but it did not die. Those who know the truth that Christ is risen are forever changed by it. That is our story, and with it we live.

Exactly a year before the failed coup in August 1991, I was in Russia, going to St. Isaac's Cathedral, rejoicing in the harrowing of hell, feeling the excitement of the church once again becoming visible and audible and thoroughly alive. One of the great evenings was in Odessa, at the Cathedral of the Dormition, for the Feast of the Dormition. Dormition means falling asleep, the word so often used for death in the Acts of the Apostles, and here it refers to the falling asleep of the *Theotokos*, the Mother of God.

The story is a charming one. Mary, in her old age, is in Ephesus with John. When it becomes apparent that her mortal end is near, all of the disciples, with the exception of Thomas, are miraculously translated to Ephesus, where they bid farewell to Mary. She dies and is buried. Three days later Thomas finally arrives and is desolate at not having been on time. He begs to be allowed to see the body of the Mother of his Lord, and the tomb is opened. She is not there.

End of story. No explanations. Just great rejoicing.

The liturgy for this feast is extraordinarily beautiful. The cathedral, which holds three thousand, was jammed. We Americans were given places of honor near the *iconostasis*, the great screen of icons that separates the sanctuary from the nave. We were also given some chairs, because the kindly Ukrainian priests knew that many Americans (I'm one of them) can't stand for four hours. There was a choir of about two hundred fifty people, but every once in a while one of the priests, beautifully vested in pale blue, would conduct the entire congregation, and then three thousand voices rose in magnificent harmony, music which had not been forgotten during seventy years of repression. The truth was still there, shining and glorious.

The next morning the Divine Liturgy was celebrated, and we returned to the cathedral. The Orthodox Church does not yet practise open communion, so we knew that we would not be receiving the bread and the wine, but the liturgy is so rich that we felt in no way deprived. In any case, in the Orthodox Church it is not the custom for worshipers to receive at every Eucharist; one does not take the bread and the wine unless one has just made one's confession. But being there in the presence of the elements is joy enough. The priests have long spoons that they dip into the wine and then put into the mouths of those who are prepared to receive. The holy bread is passed among the people, and we were deeply moved because the *babushkas* who surrounded us saw to it that each one of us was given some, breaking off pieces of bread to hand to us. Although the emphasis is very different from that in the Episcopal Church, or, indeed, most Western denominations, the reality was universal; there was no division; we were one. Christ is risen, and we belong to that risen life.

It was also our privilege to witness to this truth in the hotels where we stayed and to have it joyfully received. We had brought Bibles, Russian Bibles, and our only problem was to make sure they were given to people who were hungry and thirsty for the truth of Scripture and not to people who wanted to sell Bibles for gain.

One of the loveliest of many lovely experiences came to me in our hotel in Moscow. In Odessa we had been put by Intourist into a marvelous old nineteenth-century hotel that had once been a bordello for officers! My room still had ancient flowered wallpaper on the walls and a balcony that looked very unsafe. I went out on it only after the power went off while I was reading my evening Scripture, and I wanted to make sure the power failure was just in the hotel and not all of Odessa. It seemed that in our hotel there was the equivalent of a disco with strobe lights, and whenever the strobe lights went on, the power went off.

In Moscow, where we went from Odessa, we were put up in one of these enormous cinder-block modern Soviet hotels, convenient, reasonably comfortable, but lacking the glamour of the old hotels. On each floor near the elevator was a desk with a key lady. When you needed to go to your room she would give you your key. When you left, you would turn your key in to her.

The first night we were there I left my key at the desk. I was wearing a Swedish silver cross that Luci Shaw had given me at the time my nine-year-old granddaughter had been hit by a truck and we did not know what the outcome was going to be. (Lena is now one of the wonderful college-age young women who has been sharing my apartment, so the story had a happy ending, and Luci's cross is very precious to me.)

The key lady saw the cross and pointed to it. I held it out to her so she could see it. She followed me out to the elevator so she could touch it. Had it not been that very special cross I would have taken it off my neck and given it to her. But I couldn't. However, I was determined that I would get a cross for her, and at St. Danilov's monastery I found one I could afford.

Our last night in Moscow when I went up to bed and put the key down on her desk, I said, "Sprakoine noiche"—peaceful night—and placed the cross, wrapped in paper, beside it, and went on to my room. A moment later there was a knock on the door and she stood there, laughing, crying, pointing to her neck and showing me where she would wear the cross. I embraced her and it was a wonderful affirmation of our mutual faith, a faith that she was just beginning to be allowed to express publicly.

After such experiences, the failed coup and all that has happened since have not surprised me as much as they would have otherwise. You cannot force people to be atheists.

Neither can you force people to be Christians. Story does not force. Facts are the merest beginning of my understanding of the Christian story. That there was indeed a man named Jesus who lived around two thousand years ago and who was crucified is about the only fact that we are assured of. That fact is far less important than the story, and that fact will be of little importance unless I have love in my heart and take that love into the world with me wherever I go.

Truth, love, and joy, go together, as do faith, hope, and charity. Faith is for the love deep in our hearts that can cause us to cry out, "He is risen indeed!" in an atheist country. Faith is behind my understanding that this marvelous universe was created by a God of love, a God who is not going to fail with Creation, no matter how much we falter, fail, sin.

When Jesus came to the disciples after the Resurrection, he did not say, "Why did you all abandon me? Why weren't you with me when I needed you most?" No. He said, *"Peace be with you."* Not one word of recrimination, but words of peace, comfort, and joy.

What do you suppose would happen to Paul if he came before a calling committee for a church looking for a new minister? He probably wouldn't make it through the first interview. Maybe we should look more carefully—look for the people God chooses rather than the people we would choose. What this tells me is that I must heed Jesus' warning: *Judge not, that you be not judged.* It's far too easy to see people's faults, to see their lack of qualifications, rather than to understand that these may be people particularly called by God. Sometimes we are called to make judgments—which is different from judging, from being judgmental—but it's a deep responsibility and must never be done from fear, but with awe and humility. If we are people of the Resurrection—and as Christians that is what we are called to be—we are people who know that God is perfect love, and Jesus promises us that perfect love casts out fear. When I am afraid, I am failing in my calling as a child of God and of the Resurrection.

One of the hardest lessons I have to learn is how not to be judgmental about people who are judgmental. When I see how wrong somebody is—how shallow it is to look at the Resurrection as a mere, explainable fact—when I see only the mistakenness of others, then I am blinded to their being children of God, who are just as valued and treasured as are those who more nearly agree with me. James warns us in his Epistle,

> Everyone should be quick to listen, slow to speak and slow to become angry, for man's anger does not bring about the righteous life that God desires. Therefore, get rid of all moral filth and the evil that is so prevalent and humbly accept the word planted in you, which can save you.

I try to receive that word each morning and evening as I begin and end the day with Scripture, and this is a saving grace. It helps me to stay close to the God of love who leads us into all truth, and to shun Satan, the imitator, who is very clever at selling us lies, and who often wins us over by flattery. God never flatters, never tells us what good Christians we are and how bad others are. God did not make it easy for Jesus, and el will not make it easy for us, but the joy of the Resurrection transcends all the pain.

Is it too much to ask that we pray for each other even when we disagree with each other? Perhaps God uses different means with each one of us to further the coming of the kingdom. So let us leave the judgment to God.

God made us all unique, each one different, no two alike, just as there are no two maple leaves exactly alike, and no two snowflakes exactly alike. We need to learn to glory in both our similarities and our differences. A maple leaf is a maple leaf and not a snowflake, and we are human creatures, each one sharing in our humanness, but each one also uniquely different. As Christians we are alike in being people of the Resurrection, but we are also different in our ways of glorifying God. I grew up in the Episcopal Church with its liturgy and stained-glass windows and formal, beautiful language, and my husband grew up in the Southern Baptist Church with its gospel singing and spontaneous praying, and we both learned from each other's treasures. By God's grace it did not separate us, but forged a deeper bond between us, and that is for me a wonderful example, an affirmation that we can be one despite our differences.

I have learned a great deal about prayer, praying for other people when the need arises, spontaneously and immediately, from my evangelical friends, and this is a lesson I treasure. Some of my friends have learned something about symbols as open windows to God from me and other sacramentalists. We can share with each other without being threatened by each other's differences because we know that we are united by Christ and that this union is a union of love and not of fear.

Love makes no false promises. I have known for a long time that God does not interfere with the free will given us human creatures, does not stop a driver from running through a red light.

One night last spring I had one of my unusual dreams. In it I was one of two small fish in a very large ocean. We were being instructed in life, law, faith, everything, by a very large and wise old shark. When he had finished instructing us, he ate us. When I protested, the shark said, "Not being eaten was never part of the promise."

I woke up and lay there thinking that the dream had deep theological import. It was not an unpleasant dream. In fact, I lay there thinking about it quite happily. Indeed, not being eaten never was part of the promise. (It was the first time I have dreamed that I was a fish!)

But the story that is part of the promise is revealed to me in the story of Jesus, a story that can be abused and distorted but not destroyed. I think of the faith in Russia that could not be quenched and of the priest in Red Square responding to the atheist speaker with three words only, CHRIST IS RISEN, and the thousands of people responding with deep joy,

"HE IS RISEN INDEED."

That is the promise that sustains us.

When that truck went through the red light on July 28, I was well aware that not being eaten is not part of the promise.

When I went under anesthesia I willingly said good-bye to this life of seventy-two years full of love and laughter, grief and joy.

But now I am seventy-three, and I am still here.

"Did you have a life-after-death experience?" I have been asked.

No. Not then. I've had what seems to me to be the equivalent of those transcendent experiences at other times when I was nowhere near death, as far as I know. The opening out of God's Creation into something wonderful beyond description has come, for instance, in the back seat of a car at night, holding a sleeping grand-baby as we drove across England. It has come while I was walking home from church on a warm July after-noon in the country, picking wildflowers and simply taking time to be, when suddenly that be-ing became something richer and deeper and more marvelous than can even be remembered once it has faded.

I am a little disappointed that I'm still the same old me. Have I learned anything?

I have to believe that I am wiser, that no experience is wasted. And if I haven't become a saint, at any rate I'm a little more aware of my failings, those things God still wants me to work on and has given me a chance to do so. Evidently there are still a few chapters to write of my story.

It is still winter. Today has seen a quick flurry of snow followed by blue skies and sunshine. We are moving towards Lent and then the glory of Easter, that most mar-velous holy day that radiantly bursts through the limita-tions of fact. This affirmation shines through the slogging along with the city routine, meetings at church as we try to hold a congregation together while we wait and search for a new rector. After dark I no longer walk the twenty-five blocks home. There are no safe places left on the planet, at least none available to me, but the cities are the most difficult.

But even at Crosswicks we lock up, mostly against teenagers who don't have enough to do. Now that the small dairy farms are giving up, one by one, teenagers no longer have chores to keep them busy, and so the opportunities for mischief multiply. It is, however, less frightening than the problems of the city, and on the rare occasions when I can get to Crosswicks for a winter weekend I am free to walk where I like as long as I watch for ice. In New York City I have to watch for muggers as well as ice.

My apartment faces west, and when I go to bed at night and turn out the lights I can see across the great Hudson River to the lights of New Jersey. I can often see the planes coming in, en route to La Guardia Airport, looking like moving stars, though even when the sky is clear there are few real stars visible because of the city lights that burn all night. I think of the nearest star, Proxima Centauri, about four light years away—about twenty-three million million miles. The rare stars I see may be three hundred light years away, and three thousand light light years away, and three million. When we human creatures look up at the night sky we are able to see into the furthest reaches of time.

Not only time, but space—vast distances. Galaxies trillions of light years across. Suns so enormous that they make our own sun a mere pinprick.

Time runs more slowly when it is near a massive body like the earth than it does when it is further away. The theory of relativity tells us that there is no unique, absolute time, but instead each one of us has a personal measure of time that depends on where we are and whether or not we are moving.

As one grows older, why does everything slow down except one's conception of the passage of time? And even

292

this, as I found out last August in the hospital, can alter. Time, instead of racing, slowed to a crawl. I was told of one procedure that would have to be done before noon, and when I remarked to a nurse that the clock on the wall read eleven-thirty, she said, gently, "Eleven-thirty at night." I was convinced that so much time had passed it had to be twelve hours later. This stretching out of time like an old rubber band continued until well after I was recuperating at Crosswicks. Now time is back to its usual gallop.

I continue my reading in the area of particle physics. Many sentences seem to be in the language of fairy tale. "A proton or neutron is made up of three quarks, one of each color. A proton contains two up quarks and one down quark; a neutron contains two down and one up." The words up and down do not mean what we mean by *up* and *down*. Quarks also have color, but their color isn't what we mean by *color*. This strange world of particle physics is as much tinier than each of us single human beings as galaxies are larger than we are.

I lie in bed and my heart turns again to the prophecy of Isaiah. *"See,"* God promises in this great book, *"I have engraved you on the palms of my hands."*

God is a great storyteller, and the Bible is the greatest of all storybooks. The early protagonists of the biblical stories had a directness in their encounters with God that was, perhaps, simpler in their simpler world than it is for us in our far more complex universe. Abraham dared to correct God: "Shall not the Master of the Universe do right?" he demanded. Moses talked with the God of light so intimately that it was contagious—his face shone. And Moses, like many of us, wanted to know what God looks like and was bold enough to ask to see God. God informed Moses that no one can look at the Lord of the

Universe and live, and in one of the most extraordinary passages in Scripture, he put Moses in the cleft of a rock and protected him with his hand, and out of the corner of his eye Moses glimpsed God's "hindquarters" as he passed by.

I do not believe that we're meant to take this passage literally. It does emphasize the fact that we human beings with our human limitations cannot see, with our finite eyes, what the infinite Creator looks like. The God whom Moses ultimately saw with Resurrection eyes was different from the God whose hindquarters he saw as God passed by.

When I sit quietly in my room to read Evening Prayer and Compline I can see pictures of my husband, my parents, my grandparents, my great-grandmother, Madeleine L'Engle, after whom I am named. They are now part of the Resurrection life. When I see them again I will know them, though perhaps not by sight, as the risen Christ was not known by sight. Their stories are part of my story, and part of the great story that God started in the beginning when God made our universe and called it good.

God's story is true. We know that God's story is true because God gave us his Word—that Word who came to us, as one of us, and died for us, and descended into hell for us, and rose again from the dead for us, and ascended into heaven for us. The Word became the living truth for us, the only truth that can make us free. Part of that freedom is mortification. Part of that freedom is the Cross, for without the Cross there can be no Resurrection.

When was the last time anybody asked you, "Do I have your word?" Or when was the last time anybody said to you, "I give you my word," and you knew that you could trust that word, absolutely? How many times in the last few decades have we watched and listened to a political figure on television and heard him say, "I give you my word . . ." and shortly thereafter that word has been proven false. In the past year alone, how many people have perjured themselves publicly? Sworn on the Bible, given their word, and that word has been a lie? Words of honor are broken casually today, as though they don't matter.

Small wonder that when God tells us, "I give you my Word," few people take him seriously.

"I give you my Word," said God, and the Word became flesh, and dwelt among us, full of grace and truth.

God did not break his Word, we did. Caiaphas thought he was doing the right thing. This man Jesus was breaking the law; the Roman overlords were getting uneasy, and if Jesus wasn't stopped the Romans would set their soldiers against decent, law-abiding Jews. "Certainly," said Caiaphas (with all the good will in the world), "it is expedient that one man die for the good of the nation."

And so Caiaphas, not Jesus, was the one who broke the law, one of those mysterious laws we grope to understand and which govern the stars in their courses.

I will turn my ear to a proverb; said the psalmist, *with the harp I will expound my riddle.*

Balaam, when confronted with two opposing commands ("Curse the children of Israel," said King Balak. "Bless them," said the Lord.), according to the King James translation, "took up his parable." A parable can be a heavy thing, a burden. I wonder what Simon of Cyrene thought as he picked up Jesus' cross and bore it? Like Balaam, he took up his parable, and like many of the dark parables it became clear only in the light of the empty cross, the opened tomb.

I give you my Word, God said, and I believe it. That is what enables me to cry out, in the darkness as well as in the light, *He is risen indeed!*